# Last Days of Glory

# Last Days of Glory

## *The Death of Queen Victoria*

TONY RENNELL

St. Martin's Press
New York

www.stmartins.com

Photo section credits
1, 2, 16, 18, 19: Hulton Getty; 5: Mansell Collection;
8, 9, 15, 17: Private collection; 13: The Royal Collection
© HM Queen Elizabeth II; 14: Bridgeman Art Library

ISBN 0-312-27672-9

First published in Great Britain by Viking, Penguin Books, Ltd.

First U.S. Edition: September 2001

10 9 8 7 6 5 4 3 2 1

For Tony Bambridge

# Contents

# Acknowledgements

My deepest thanks go:

To Mark Lucas, my agent and friend, who took me on, sat me down, and talked me through a period when it all looked hopeless. He has never once allowed me to doubt myself; I hope I have not let him down. To Juliet Annan at Viking Penguin, who caught the idea in an instant and then, with her breathless and breathtaking enthusiasm, made it happen. To Stuart Profitt, who provided inspiration at a crucial time.

To my daughter, Becky, for taking time off from the archaeological studies she loves to do a different sort of digging – into memoirs and diaries for contemporary accounts – and to my son, Tom, for all his encouragement. To Laura Sandys for helping get the idea off the ground. To Amanda Platell for the strength of real friendship when I most needed it. To Susan Clark and Declan O'Mahoney for giving me a home from home. To Sarah Foot for being all that she is and, not least, for her invaluable help and advice in checking sources and the revising of the manuscript.

To Barry Turner, Brian MacArthur and Maureen Waller for reading the manuscript and helping me make it better. To Mickey and Sandy Reid, two of the most gracious people I have ever met, for sharing their knowledge and their thoughts. To Kate Barker at Penguin for her meticulous care and attention and thoughtful advice.

To friends for their encouragement and moral support, among them Anthony Barnett, Georgina Capel, Simon Freeman, Barbara Hadley, Peter Hennessy, Jane Mays, John

Nichol, Cristina Odone, Audrey Pasternak, Harry Ritchie, William Shawcross, Christine Walker, Rosie Waterhouse and Lesley White.

To Her Majesty the Queen for permission to quote from the letters and journals of Queen Victoria and other members of the royal family. To Sir Alexander Reid for permission to quote from the diaries and papers of his grandfather, Sir James Reid, and to reproduce photographs and memorabilia from Sir James's scrapbooks. To his wife, Michaela Reid for permission to quote from her book *Ask Sir James*. To Lord Esher for permission to quote from his grandfather's correspondence. To Philip Mallet for permission to quote from the letters of his grandmother, Marie Mallet. To the family of Lord Sysonby for permission to quote from the memoirs of Frederick Ponsonby. To Lady Longford for permission to quote from her unsurpassed biography of Queen Victoria. To the newspapers of a century ago, endlessly fascinating in ther detail and diligence. To their reporters, anonymous and long dead but whose words have come to life again.

None of this book could have been written without access to the British Library in St Pancras and its newspaper section at Colindale, the London Library and Lambeth Palace library. Most of all, I owe a huge debt to Lady de Bellaigue and the staff at the Royal Archives in Windsor.

# Preface

The supreme woman of the world, best of the highest, greatest of the good . . .

The *Daily Telegraph* on Queen Victoria

To be born British was to win first prize in the lottery of life, according to that African adventurer of the nineteenth century Cecil Rhodes. And never did that seem more obvious than in the summer of 1897, when the sun shone brightly on the centre of the Empire for the celebrations in London of Queen Victoria's Diamond Jubilee. She waved and smiled from her carriage, and wept with thanks at her people's loyal tributes, shouted from streets overflowing with patriotic well-wishers. Sixty years a queen – but what an empire she now ruled, what a swath of red, white and blue across the globe! 'Happy and glorious,' they sang. 'Long to reign over us.' Rhodes was right. Under Victoria, Britain had spread and prospered. Sitting beside her, the Princess of Wales, her daughter-in-law, read out the messages hung from buildings, strung across her path. 'Our Hearts Thy Throne!' declared the biggest, 'The Queen of Earthly Queens'.

But the society she reigned over was one where change seethed beneath the surface. A new world was waiting to emerge – an uncertain world, in which old values, accepted ways, would no longer count. The government was still run by aristocrats, old land, old money, but socialism was the new fashion for intellectuals and the two million working men who were members of trade unions. The streets were clogged with horses, but the motor car was accelerating into the lives of the rich. Britain's industrial and commercial might, forged in the middle years of the nineteenth century, was losing its competitive edge to Germany and the United States. The first warnings were issued that Britain's education system was failing to deliver the right skills – 'this country will have to apply itself more assiduously to the work of true elementary education if we do not wish to take a back seat in trade, commerce and prosperity,' barked an anti-Tory newspaper in industrial South Wales.[1] Control of the seas was being challenged by an aggressive and expansionist Germany. The New Woman was making her presence felt in smart society. She smoked, she argued, she might even want the right to vote one day.

As the century neared its end, none of this troubled the popular imagination. The passage from the 1800s to the 1900s was welcomed on a wave of optimism and patriotism: Britannia was mighty and surely destined to be mightier yet. As one newspaper triumphantly announced in January 1900, 'The Empire, stretching round the globe, has one heart, one head, one language, one policy.'[2]

For more thoughtful minds, however, *fin de siècle* felt more like *fin du monde*. 'The times are strange and evil,' declared the classical scholar J. W. Mackail in a famous lecture in 1900:

To those who hope for human progress, the outward aspect of the time is full of profound discouragement. Compared with 50 years ago, there is a general loss of high spirits, of laughter and the enjoyment of life. We see all around us how vainly people try to drown in increasing luxury and excitement the sense that joy and beauty are dwindling out of life; with what pitiful eagerness they dress themselves up in pretended enthusiasms which seem to bring little joy to the maker or the user. The uneasy feeling is abroad that the nineteenth century, which has done such wonderful things, and from which things so much more wonderful were hoped, has been on the whole a failure. Fifty years ago, men's minds were full of ideals. Now cinder heaps smoulder where there once were beacon fires . . .[3]

In all this uncertainty, the Queen was the symbol, the embodiment, the guarantee, of stability and continuity. While *she* sat on the throne, the future held no fears. Family and Empire, duty and decorum – the widow of Windsor knew what was right. Victoria had become a living legend. No monarch, before or since, has surpassed the mass affection, verging on love, that she inspired in her old age. She had not always been popular, however, but she had survived the criticisms and come through her self-inflicted semi-exile in the years after the death of her husband Prince Albert – times when she was so little seen by her subjects that they almost forgot her and allowed republican feelings to become common chatter. In the last two decades of her life, all such talk had disappeared, replaced by veneration.

When her death came with little warning in January 1901, it was an immense shock, unsettling Britain and the Empire to a degree that now seems inconceivable. She was an old woman, in her eighties, and yet it seems that no one could contemplate the end of her reign. It had lasted so long that the very stability of everyday life seemed to depend on it.

Her death was instant news virtually everywhere, thanks to the information revolution that had taken place in her lifetime. Newspapers, aided by the telegraph system, had turned the nation into a village. She was the first monarch whose death was known and mourned in the same instant the length and breadth of the land. In the village of New Pitsligo in a remote part of north-east Scotland, they heard the news, via a telegram from the local paper, at the same time as it was being announced to the crowds outside the Mansion House in London. 'New Pitsligo joins the national mourning,' the village's correspondent wrote in a note published the next day in the *Aberdeen Journal*. The nation was united in its grief in a way that had never been possible before.

Everywhere, people wept openly in the streets. The sense of loss was immense – but even greater was fear for the future. Things could never be the same again. 'God have mercy on us all,' wrote Princess Augusta, the late Queen's cousin. 'God help us all,' echoed Princess May. 'The thought of England without the Queen is dreadful.'

The *Daily Telegraph* asked its readers, 'Who can think of the nation and the race without her?' It went on to beat its breast with unashamed hyperbole. 'How can our minds compass the meaning of what has happened? The golden reign is closed. The supreme woman of the world, best of the highest, greatest of the good, is gone. Never, never, loss like this. All that we have known is different now. All is altered . . .'

The glory days were over.

Today we are cooler about monarchy, though the death of Diana, Princess of Wales, unleashed a sentimentality and a stampede of emotion that ran in the face of all the supposed indifference and closet republicanism. It astonished us all. There are surface similarities between 1901 and 1997. For a while, as with Queen Victoria, dissenting words about Diana were not heard, were not allowed to be spoken in the immediate aftermath of her death. For her funeral, as for Queen Victoria's, a million people or more packed the streets of London and, as with Victoria, it was the sad, almost eerie, silence that stuck in the mind. The expressions of love were also similar. 'Empress of Hearts' was one popular description of the Queen; nearly a century later it was echoed in the 'Queen of Hearts' for whom thousands laid down a vast carpet of flowers at the gates of Kensington Palace. But there the comparisons must surely end.

Except for this. It is not what these events, separated by ninety-six years, tell us about the politics of monarchy that is important, or what they say about the relative merits of the individuals. It is the insight they provide into society then and now, people then and now. What connects the death of Victoria and the death of Diana is that, though these two women were as different in their natures and their lives as it is possible to imagine, they were both symbols of their times. One was a revered woman who died of old age after a lifetime of devoted duty – austere, awesome. In her people's minds she stood for family and faith, pride and patriotism. The other was a reckless, confused, unhappy girl who died young – self-indulgent and petulant, but loving and loved. She was adored by those who saw her as a symbol of angst-ridden self-expression and that relentless pursuit of individual happiness, whatever the cost, that characterizes modern life. If it is true that we measure ourselves by those whose loss we hold dearest, then Victoria and Diana were the two contrasting ends of the twentieth century.

Now, in a new century and a new millennium, we are as conscious of change and yet as nervous about it as the Victorians were. The electronic information economy is as challenging and unsettling as industrialization, electricity, the motor car and all the other technological inventions were to our great-grandfathers. It is doubtful, however, that, as people today contemplate the uncertainty of the times, they will look to the monarchy as a source of stability and reassurance as they did in Queen Victoria's day. Nonetheless, consider the similarities between then and now. We too have an ageing queen who has been on the throne for the lifetime of most of her subjects, who is seen as wiser and more experienced than many of her ministers (she has already been served by as many prime ministers as Victoria) and whose death will undoubtedly be felt as a watershed. As in 1901, there is also the problem of a middle-aged Prince of Wales whose succession is a source of nervousness (and, irony of ironies, whose mistress is a direct descendant of Alice Keppel, the mistress of that earlier Prince of Wales).

The passing of Queen Elizabeth II must come, though if she has inherited her mother's longevity it may well not be for another twenty or even thirty years, by which time she will easily have surpassed Victoria's record reign of nearly sixty-four years. Who knows how this nation, always fickle in its attitude to its royal family, will react then? Perhaps it will be with the same sense of reverence and instant nostalgia that saw Queen Victoria to her grave a century ago. For a fortnight, the nation — and the entire world — stopped in its tracks, mesmerized by the mortality of a little old lady, all eyes drawn to Osborne, London and Windsor.

# 1. The Eyes Grow Dim

I cannot help feeling uneasy . . .

Marie Mallet, lady-in-waiting,
on the Queen's failing health

Captain Frederick Ponsonby took off his frock coat and threw it over the back of a chair, ready to be put on in an instant should he be called back into the Queen's presence. He sat at his desk and considered the problem. His handwriting for the eighty-year-old Victoria would just have to become clearer, bigger and, above all, blacker. For much of his working day in the royal palace, be it Windsor Castle on the banks of the Thames, Balmoral in the Scottish Highlands or Osborne House on the Isle of Wight, he wrote letters for his sovereign. But ordinary ink was no longer good enough for the job, and he had already had to buy in some special concoction from the stationer's – thick and syrupy and resembling blacking for boots.

But even this she could no longer see properly, and, as she squinted at the fuzzy words on the pages, the irritated demand came for him to 'write larger and blacker'. Her eyes were growing dimmer. It was a sign of old age, and a hint, though no one chose to admit it, that a long and magnificent life could not go on for ever.

She knew it, though, even if those she ruled over did not. At Osborne on 1 January 1900 she sat in the oval-shaped room at the heart of the house, unable now to take in the sweeping view across the fields and trees and down the hill to the grey waters of the Solent, but focusing as best she could on the gold-framed portraits of her children and grandchildren on her desk. On a tall pedestal by the fireplace stood a white marble bust of her long-dead husband, Prince Albert, a wreath of fresh flowers round his neck. In her journal she scrawled her gloomy thoughts: 'I begin today a new year and a new century, full of anxiety, and fear of what may be before us! May all near and dear ones be protected. I pray that God may spare me yet a short while to my children, friends and dear country, leaving me all my faculties and to a certain extent my eyesight!'[1]

But her faculties were failing faster than she hoped, and it was Ponsonby, her assistant private secretary, who had to deal at first hand with the practicalities of her diminishing physical powers. Victoria was a prolific letter-writer – she wrote constantly and at great length, to her children, to her prime ministers and archbishops, to the members of her Household. With family she mingled gossip with imperious advice; to politicians she expressed her views, whether they liked them or not. With the staff she involved herself in the minutiae of their lives and hers.

And such minutiae for a queen and empress – as when Duncan Brown (brother of John Brown, her Highland servant who died in 1883) was being troublesome and she wrote a memorandum with elaborate instructions on how he was to be dealt with: given a post as gatekeeper at Windsor, 'where the duties are very light', but warned that he was in danger of dismissal, 'which, for the sake of his brother, I should regret, but he must promise in writing to do what are his duties; if he refuses to do so he must be pensioned'.

She wrote at her brass-edged desk in her sitting room,

squeezing space among the clutter of photographs and trinkets, her dead husband Prince Albert's writing table next to hers, his empty chair a constant reminder of the empty space in her life since his sudden death in 1861; she wrote at a field table under a canopy in the garden, her Indian servant standing guard; she wrote after dinner, often for two hours or more before going to bed. Always she sat bolt upright, telling her newly married eldest daughter, 'Don't stoop . . . Remember how straight I always sit, which enables me to write without fatigue at all times.' Ream after ream of notes poured from her, memoranda, letters – all marked V.R.I. and edged in black for her years of widowhood – plus her journal, scribbled out daily in a hand that was increasingly spidery and faint and difficult to decipher. And poor Fritz, as Ponsonby was known to everyone, including the Queen, had to cope with much of the torrent.

He was, however, no mere clerk. Eton-educated, an officer in the Grenadier Guards, he was a courtier from the patrician class that still held sway in the Britain of the turn of the century. His father, Sir Henry Ponsonby, had been the Queen's private secretary for twenty-five years and much admired for the subtle way he handled his difficult and demanding employer, acting as an intermediary with her ministers in political matters, organizing her life and her Household, while never letting the inevitable irritations of his job show through, remaining unfailingly courteous to everyone, high and low. Thinking to please Sir Henry, the Queen had personally summoned his son from Bombay, where the young subaltern was aide-de-camp to the Viceroy, Lord Elgin. Fritz, as he noted whimsically in his memoirs, had hoped for active service on the North-West Frontier, fighting at the very edge of the Queen's empire. Instead he was drawn back reluctantly to its very centre, first as an equerry, then, not long after Sir Henry's death in 1895, as assistant to her new private secretary, Sir Arthur Bigge.

It was a position of trust. One task was to copy her letters, even those to her family. He found it odd seeing personal notes with remarks such as 'William is quite wrong', referring to the German Kaiser, Victoria's eldest grandson, or 'Bertie and Alix must not do this', an instruction about the Prince and Princess of Wales, all in his handwriting. But his greatest difficulty was with the telegrams in code that came flooding in from Downing Street, from family and friends, and from British envoys all over the world, encrypted so that telegraph clerks at either end of the cable could not pry into royal business.

Deciphering them was easy enough, but then they had to be copied out for Her Majesty to read, and some of them were immensely long. Ponsonby's problem was that the ink he was now having to use was so thick that it defeated all attempts to blot it. Bigge came to the rescue, inventing a special drying device – each page was placed on a small copper tray heated from beneath by a spirit lamp – but, as the royal eyes grew weaker and the ink got blacker, even this failed to do the trick. Worse still, the ink was now seeping through to the other side of each sheet. Fritz's solution was to write on one side of the paper only. This worked for a while, until the pernickety Queen complained that some of the messages she was receiving were on so many pieces of paper that she was put off reading them. It was 'very inconvenient', she said, and Captain Ponsonby would please return to writing on both sides.

Fritz tried a new tack: thicker paper, which he went to the trouble of having made specially by the Stationery Office and stamped and headed to look exactly like the normal writing paper. The subterfuge worked for a while – until she noticed and complained again. The Queen kept all her decoded telegrams in a case, which was rapidly filling up because of the bulkier paper. A message arrived with Her Majesty's insistence on a return to the ordinary paper.

Ponsonby grasped then that

it was hopeless and I consulted Sir James Reid [the Queen's doctor] as to whether it would not be possible to explain all the difficulties to her. But he said he feared her sight was going and that any explanation would therefore be useless. So I went back to the ordinary paper and ordinary ink, and of course received a message to say would I write blacker, but as it was hopeless I didn't attempt to alter anything.

None of this came as a surprise to Sir James. He had been the resident doctor at Victoria's court since 1881, first as a subordinate to the eminent Sir William Jenner, her physician-in-ordinary, who made a weekly call on his patient, leaving the younger man to minister to the Queen on other days, if necessary. To begin with she preferred to wait for Jenner's visit, but gradually her confidence grew and, when Jenner retired on health grounds in 1889, Reid stepped up to be her principal medical adviser.

He was her doctor and, increasingly, her friend and confidant. It had not always been such a close relationship. Reid, a Scot from near Aberdeen, was the son of a country doctor and part-time farmer. When he came to court he found himself in a social no man's land, lodged uneasily between the servants below stairs and the aristocratic elite – eight ladies of the bedchamber, eight women of the bedchamber, eight maids of honour, eight lords-in-waiting, eight grooms-in-waiting and eight equerries – who made up Her Majesty's Household. His memorandum of appointment made clear his position – or, rather, made clear its ambiguity. He would not, it was spelt out for him, be an official member of the Household, though he would have breakfast and lunch with its members. But emphatically not dinner. Unless, that is, the Queen herself specifically invited him to do so. Which, the note pointed out without explanation, would always be the case when they were at Balmoral.

Reid's good humour, tact and natural charm eased him through this social obstacle course. He was no country cousin but a hugely intelligent man who had started at Aberdeen University at the age of sixteen and spent three years reading arts subjects before he was old enough to begin medicine. He had also travelled in Europe, completing his medical studies in Vienna and educating himself in other ways with a job tutoring an eight-year-old Austrian aristocrat, the Count de Lodron. In the summer of 1875 he supervised his young charge on a trip round the Tyrol visiting relations in their castles. Though he did not know it, this was a foretaste, an appetizer for his future life.

How intimate a friend and adviser Reid was to be is worth considering. He kept copious notes of his years with the Queen, leaving vast scrapbooks, two hundred letters and notes he had received from her, and forty pocket diaries which he had filled to overflowing with his observations in neat, tiny writing. In these accounts, Sir James was a pivotal figure in royal events, almost a successor to the dead John Brown in winning her trust if not her affection, another Scot who spoke his mind and refused to be browbeaten by Her Majesty. He became embroiled in matters far beyond (or possibly beneath) medicine. He was called on to settle squabbles between members of the Household. He was the recipient of confidences in letters from the Queen, as when she expressed to him her peevishness about Sir Henry Ponsonby who 'has no backbone, is always placid, . . . [who] agrees with me and then is talked over by others and agrees with them'. (This was a harsh judgement on a man who was only doing his job and trying to smooth out another difficulty between the constitutional sovereign and Mr Gladstone, the Liberal Prime Minister she utterly detested.)

On Sir Henry's death, Reid was the sounding board for everyone on who should succeed, consulted by the Queen, her daughters Princess Helena and Princess Louise, and particularly those who thought to gain by having his ear. One conspirator sent a suggestion of how the positions in the private office should be carved up, putting himself down for a promotion and a handsome £1,000 a year salary, and ending his note with the ridiculously melodramatic suggestion that Reid should 'burn it at once if you think best'. Reid's biographer, his granddaughter-in-law, Michaela Reid, wrote that 'Reid had become indispensable now, not only to the Queen but to her Household too, as being the only male member who had a ready approach to her. His importance as a liaison between the Queen and the outside world was inestimable.'

But was the small, dapper doctor – so theatrical in appearance with his balding head, bushy handlebar moustache and pince-nez glasses – really such a leading light in the drama of palace politics? We have his word for it, and from the letters of Princess Louise confirmation that she at least sought and valued his opinion. Perhaps he played up his own importance a little. But there can be no doubt that, as the Queen's doctor, he saw more and more of the monarch as her strength sapped and her health declined. And in the undoubted drama of her final days, if not before, he had a crucial role.

By then, having tended her for close on twenty years, he knew his patient's medical history well. He was less familiar with the actual body he was ministering to. Extraordinarily, he had never examined her unclothed, and never would while she was alive. But the nature of her ailments was such that he probably did not need to. For her age, she was remarkably healthy, given that she had been through childbirth nine times by the age of thirty-eight, was struck by a debilitating grief bordering on depression on being widowed at forty-two, and had thereafter eaten excessively. She was prone to indigestion and troubled by wind. She worked hard and worried a lot too – about her ever-expanding family and her ever-expanding empire. Today we would call it stress, but a hundred years ago it was dismissed as 'fits of nervousness'.

However it was described, it took its toll. Politics, which she could not and would not leave alone, shredded her nerves almost as much as those of the ministers who came into her presence nervously to flatter and cajole, or to say their piece and face her peremptory disapproval. Lesser events troubled her too, and gave her headaches – saying goodbye to a favourite aide at court, posted to the fighting in Egypt, brought on neuralgia; the death of a general she barely knew led to tears. And it took only a slight roughness in the throat for her to send urgently for her doctor to deal with another outbreak of regal hypochondria. She complained a lot, and demanded the one thing her position guaranteed – instant attention.

Once when Reid dared to take a holiday (he was allowed six weeks a year – 'at Her Majesty's convenience', of course) she interrupted it with a letter recalling him to Balmoral because 'I have this tiresome huskiness which every now and then causes me to cough, and then almost immediately after you left I got this pain between my shoulders again and again which generally leaves me after a day or two but which returns again and again and which I feel right through me.'

The doctor's guess was that his sovereign was gripped by another bout of flatulence, but nonetheless he rushed off to see her. When he arrived it was her heart that she was now worrying about. He examined her as best he could, given that he was not allowed to listen to it through his stethoscope – she hated the instrument, and its use alarmed her – found nothing wrong, and prescribed soda water and ginger to settle her stomach after meals. But that was not the last interruption to his holiday. He was pursued by more letters, complaining of eye strain and a twinge of 'pain in my hip, just the sciatic nerve' when she got out of bed in the morning.

Reading the correspondence between the Queen and her doctor in all its detail, it is a surprise to realize how much of the supposedly prudish Victoria's time was apparently spent pondering the state of her stomach and her bowels. 'The bowels are right, upon the whole, but there is an inclination to griping,' she wrote to him during one of his absences from court. If that is what she confided to him in writing when he was away, one can only imagine how long and involved must have been the discussions of the subject when he was there in person for his daily doctor's call on her. And she never seems to have taken the point of his advice. She talked of 'oppression after meals' and 'a rising' and 'acidity', but chose to carry on bloating herself with her favourite food.

Eating was a royal obsession, and often carried out on the grandest of scales. In 1891, when the Prince of Naples was a guest at Windsor, the banquet began with cock-a-leekie soup, followed by whitebait and fillets of sole. Then came three different roasts – venison, beef and quail – and two puddings, one of them a vanilla meringue. And, for anyone still peckish, there was a buffet of cold chicken, tongue and beef left at a side table to top up from.

This, of course, was a state occasion. Day-to-day royal meals were not so elaborate, but they were far from frugal. There would be thick brown Windsor soup laced with wine, then boiled chicken, mutton, and haggis too at Balmoral. They were invariably eaten fast – the Queen expected to get a family dinner over in thirty minutes. She bolted her food (and, as soon as she had put down her knife and fork, the footmen leaned over and instantly removed her plate – and, to the consternation of those who had not yet finished, everyone else's as well). Reid had to deal with the after-effects. He once stayed up all night nursing her through a bad attack of indigestion until she finally managed to fall asleep at 5.30 in the morning. And all because of a heavy pudding she had had at dinner. What could he do?

He put her on a diet of Benger's Food, a concoction of cereal and milk intended as a gentle stomach-filler and a substitute for the real thing. She took the Benger's but tucked into her normal meals as well. The doctor must have despaired, as did Marie Mallet, one of her ladies-in-waiting. 'If she would follow a diet and live on Benger's Food and chicken, all would be well,' she told her husband. 'But she clings to roast beef and ices! And what can you expect then?'

But not everything the doctor had to deal with was self-inflicted or the whining of an elderly woman who liked attention. The Queen had good reason to complain of the rheumatism which stiffened her joints and made movement slow and painful. Its cause, though, might have taken the edge off some of the sympathy for her condition, particularly from those in her entourage who had shivered through unremittingly icy stays at dank Balmoral and draughty Windsor. Osborne at least had a system of background heating, but the Queen was reluctant to have fires lit as well and, as Marie Mallet discovered when she sat there with her, the drawing room could be 'Siberian'.

She had a passion for the cold – consuming it (she adored chocolate ice, washed down with ice water), sitting in it, driving out in it in her carriage, insisting that her guests should share in its virtues. The result was crippling. In 1893 one rheumatic attack was so bad that she had to be carried up and down the stairs at Balmoral, and, though it eased, within a year she needed a stick wherever she went. At Osborne, where she spent the summer and Christmas, a hand-operated lift was installed to take her from the drawing room up to her sitting room and bedroom. She would perch on a red leather seat as an equally red-faced footman in the basement below put all his strength into cranking the wood-panelled and carpeted compartment up twenty-five feet to the first floor. A venerable actress, Mrs Keeley, was presented to her, struggled to make the expected curtsy, but could only bob a little and ask her sovereign's indulgence, 'owing to rheumatic pains in my knees'. The Queen knew exactly what she meant. 'I cannot either, for the same reason,' she confided sympathetically, one infirm old lady to another.

Now the limbs were getting even wearier. The stick was not enough and she would have to lean on the arm of one of her Indian servants for even the shortest walk from room to room or on to the terrace or to the front door to be lifted into her carriage. Not that anyone was permitted to know this. An illustrated newspaper dared to print a drawing of the Queen on her servant's arm. Outrage. A sharp official reprimand was winged off to the editor, telling him that the Queen could only ever take the arm of another sovereign or of her son, the Prince of Wales – of a servant, never. The editor apologized, though he must have known he was in the right. The issue became irrelevant, however: soon she was in a wheelchair wherever she went.

As for the deterioration in her eyes, which the ingenious Fritz Ponsonby was now having to find ways to work around, Reid had been aware of this worsening problem for a good

few years. As early as 1892 the Queen had complained that
she could not find a pair of glasses that suited her – the ones
she had were 'wrongly focused', she moaned – and insisted
she could see better without them. But the real problem was
cataracts, the slow clouding of the lens of the eye that comes
with old age and which in the 1890s, unlike today, could not
easily be treated. Specialists came and went, their diagnosis
unchanging. Even a noted German professor, Hermann Pagenstecher, whose apparently 'miraculous' cures for near-
blindness the Queen had heard of, could not find the answer
– largely because, as even he admitted, his healing powers had
been much exaggerated and his real skill was in making his
patients feel happier. He visited Osborne, he examined her,
he was soothing, reassuring. As he looked into her eyes he
muttered, 'Good', 'Very good' and 'Quite healthy', all in
German, which was doubly comforting for her. But that was
the limit of his eye-opening. Herr Professor Pagenstecher
departed, leaving the Queen, in Reid's words, 'much relieved
and satisfied with his visit though in reality we are exactly
where we were'.

The eyes were dimmer, they were also increasingly filled with
tears. To live into old age with your family around you was a
blessing – as the Queen had once observed, 'the older your
children grow, the more our feelings will be in harmony'. But
it was a curse too, as those children entered middle age and
beyond.

She had lost one daughter, the thirty-five-year-old Princess
Alice, her third child, a victim of diphtheria, in 1878 – and,
with horrible coincidence, on 14 December, the anniversary
of Albert's death. Six years on and her youngest son, Prince
Leopold, the Duke of Albany, the faintly rebellious one in the
family despite his constant ill health (he was haemophiliac), was

dead too at the age of thirty-one, killed by a brain haemorrhage while on holiday in Cannes.

The generation after was in mortal danger too. In 1892 Prince Albert Victor, known as Eddy, the eldest son of the Prince of Wales, a young man born to be King one day, died from influenza. It was a personal tragedy, though not a dynastic one. His younger brother, George, was a much better bet in the kingly stakes. Lazy and dissolute, the twenty-eight-year-old Eddy was singularly unsteady, and strange enough in his habits to attract theories later on that he had been the Whitechapel serial killer Jack the Ripper. Almost as great a crime, as second in line to the throne, was his insistence on engaging himself to a Roman Catholic. His grandmother, though, spoke of Eddy's death as this 'overwhelming misfortune' and in a message to the nation she wrote, 'My bereavement during the last 30 years of my reign has indeed been heavy.'

She would be weighed down again soon enough. In 1896 the family was in mourning once more when the Queen's newest son-in-law, Prince Henry of Battenberg, died from fever on a military expedition in South Africa, leaving the Queen's youngest child, Princess Beatrice (always known to the family as Baby), a widow with four small children. The Queen had been reluctant to let the shy and browbeaten Beatrice marry at all, preferring the last of her daughters to trail after her, a spinster companion in her old age. Now she had Baby back at her side, and in mourning weeds like her own. (The Princess would live on until 1944, her forty-eight-year widowhood exceeding even her mother's epic of devotion.)

The Prince of Wales had had his scrapes with death too, almost succumbing in 1871 to typhoid like his father and seemingly getting as close to death's door as possible without actually crossing the threshold. Surprisingly, he turned out to have more fight in him than the Prince Consort, who, exhausted and hysterical, had given in to his illness. Bertie battled against the fever, and his recovery was marked with national rejoicing.

But there would be no such relief for the Queen's oldest child, Vicky, with whom her mother had a relationship marked by all the special love and affinity that attaches to a first-born. Vicky, the Dowager Empress of Germany, having married into the Prussian royal family, lost her husband, the Crown Prince, to a dreadful cancer of the throat only ninety-nine days after his accession to the imperial throne, and had seen her impetuous, vainglorious son become Kaiser William II in 1888. She exchanged letters with her mother all her adult life, eventually as Empress to Empress.

Towards the end of 1898, on a prolonged visit home to Britain, she was seen by her mother's doctors, including Sir James Reid. The diagnosis was breast cancer, and, according to the surgeons who had examined her, it was inoperable. To begin with, mother and daughter kept the information to themselves, the Queen advising Vicky not to mention it in their correspondence, which others might see – 'you had better write about your precious health on a separate sheet'. Vicky responded with generalities – 'pain comes and goes' – and euphemisms – 'the evil . . . which cannot be cured' – and carried on her public life as if nothing was wrong. Then in October 1899 references began to 'my lumbago', which 'is worse than ever and defies all remedies'.

She was now in almost constant pain, for which 'lumbago', a term that describes the symptoms rather than pinpoints the cause, was hardly adequate. But her German doctors continued with massage and electrical treatments and reassured her that it would go away. It would not. Whether they knew the truth and were keeping it from her or simply did not get the diagnosis right, the fact was that the cancer had spread from her breast to her spine. As the century ended, she entered the new one in excruciating pain. No position of her body — lying, sitting, walking — could give her relief. Bouncing along in a carriage was agony — she gave up the rides. Turning in bed was torture — she had to haul herself over with the help of a rope tied to the post. She wrote in despair to her mother, 'It is so trying and so wearing to suffer so much for such a long time! They say it will get right and go away etc. and only wants patience, but I own I fear sometimes I shall never be rid of it any more, as no remedy seems of any use!'

All this cast a melancholy shadow over the Queen. There was so much to trouble her as the old century petered out, a *fin-de-siècle* weariness that took no joy in the future. Her family apart, at the top of her list of woes was the war in South Africa.

Since hostilities had begun in October, the Boers had been demonstrating the inadequacies of the Empire's military machine and in particular the tactics adopted in the field. In guerrilla raids and sieges, men dismissed contemptuously as uneducated farmers baffled Britain's pith-helmeted and parade-ground-trained armies. More and more British soldiers were hurried across the seven thousand miles of sea to the Cape, to fight and to die. The Queen did her bit, leading her ladies-in-waiting in knitting socks and scarves for the troops.

One of those ladies, Marie Mallet, was alarmed when she returned to court in February 1900. Like other members of the rotating royal household, Mrs Mallet (a Maid of Honour until marriage and the niceties of royal protocol transformed her into a Woman of the Bedchamber) spent just four months of the year at her sovereign's side. In the summer of 1899 she had been amazed by how well the Queen was — 'a picture of health and in excellent spirits' she told her husband, Bernard, a civil servant at the Treasury — even if she was a little forgetful and her memory was not quite what it used to be. It was two

months after the Queen's eightieth birthday, and Sir James
Reid had confided to Mrs Mallet his opinion that anyone who
reached eighty without serious illness had every chance of
going on for years and years.

But now, eight months later, she was alarmed at the deterioration. 'She has changed since I was last here and looks so
much older and feebler.' It wasn't the Queen's cough that
concerned Mrs Mallet, though that was bad enough; it was
that she was forever dozing off and then getting cross with her
ladies-in-waiting and her daughters if they failed to wake her
up. But it would not have been seemly to prod the Queen of
England awake, so there was much rustling of papers and
dropping of fans. When they were out driving, the women
would noisily rearrange her dress and petticoats to keep her
from drifting off. She did not always respond. One afternoon
she was so deeply asleep in her chair that when her maids
came in and found her they thought she was dead and were
very scared.

But, as so often with the elderly, if the Queen snoozed in
the day, she found sleep impossible at night, and Sir James was
under pressure to give her drops that would knock her out.
He had been doing this on occasion for years – a little Dover's
Powder, which was 10 per cent opium, or, if he was worried
that she might be getting hooked on this, some natural remedy
such as henbane.

The Queen dismissed any suggestion that she was unwell,
but Mrs Mallet was not reassured. 'I cannot help feeling
uneasy. I wish warmer days would come.' The Queen's health
was a dangerous subject to discuss, however. Had there been
an instruction to be silent, or was there just an unspoken
conspiracy by those close to her to make no mention of what
they all could clearly see? Whichever it was, Mrs Mallet told
her husband emphatically, 'Never broach this to a soul!'

But others noticed the change in the Queen and drew their conclusions. The Revd Cosmo Lang was vicar of Portsea, a parish on the mainland, opposite the Isle of Wight. He often preached at Osborne and was a dinner guest of Her Majesty. He adored her – 'her soft kind voice and simple manner, her grace and simplicity, her charming smile, her laugh a sort of gurgle of pleasure'. He last saw her in the autumn of 1900 and 'I could see a very marked change. At dinner she was very silent and at times seemed to have some difficulty in keeping awake. When I talked with her after dinner, she was less bright than usual and was plainly soon tired. Though we did not then realize it, the shadow of the approaching end was drawing nigh.'

As autumn turned to winter in 1900, Balmoral was a gloomy place to be. Marie Mallet sat writing letters of gratitude and condolence on behalf of her mistress to wounded soldiers in hospitals and orphaned children at home, the silent evenings broken only when telegrams arrived. She brooded on her mistress's fate, and her own. 'She has grown so thin and there is a distressing look of pain and weariness on her face. It makes me very sad . . . The dear little Queen makes heroic efforts to be cheerful but her face in repose is terribly sad. I do not want to be very old; the penalties are too great!'

The mood seemed to catch the whole Household, as if everyone sensed the decline. By now the Queen had gone from eating too much to taking very little sustenance at all, at teatime just some arrowroot and milk instead of the scones and cakes she had once loved to wolf down. Her loss of appetite and interest was quickly picked up by the servants. Mrs Mallet smelt whisky on the footmen's breath and complained that they were slow to respond when she rang for them. Discipline was breaking down. 'Although they do not speak rudely, they stare in such a supercilious way. As for the

Queen's dinner, it is more like a badly arranged picnic.' At Windsor a few days later the small dish of noodles the Queen had requested did not even arrive, so she had nothing to eat at all. Mrs Mallet left the court midway through November, convinced that the Queen was fading away. She told all this to her husband, who wrote in his diary, 'Marie says the change in her state since August is alarming: loss of weight, size, appetite etc.' His conclusion was a dramatic one: 'One feels it must be the beginning of the end.'

The significance of this did not escape him, nor the effect that any news of the Queen's decline would have if it became general knowledge, though the secret was safe with him. He added, 'Not a hint of all this appears to have reached the outside world.' But it is safe to assume that, as private secretary to Arthur Balfour, the First Lord of the Treasury, the nephew of the Prime Minister, Lord Salisbury, and the leader of the Government in the House of Commons, he passed on to those who needed to know his sense, gathered from one near to the Queen, that a great event was coming closer and that a mighty upheaval in the history of Britain and the Empire was about to take place.

How great a change would it be, how cataclysmic did the imminent death of Queen Victoria seem to those few in the know? To say it would be the end of everything familiar sounds hyperbolic to the point of hysteria. But that was the truth. She was a fixture in the lives of almost the entire population of the British Isles.

As the century turned and they rang out the old year and welcomed in 1900, she had been on the throne for 62 years, 6 months and 12 days. To have known a time before she was Queen, a man or woman would have to be nearing his or her seventieth birthday and even then the memory would be a hazy one. It was a thought that caught the imagination of her grandson the German Kaiser, William II. 'Just think of it,' he was to say:

she remembers George III, and now we are in the Twentieth Century. And all that time what a life she has led. I have never been with her without feeling that she was in every sense my Grandmama and made me love her as such. And yet the minute we began to talk about political things she made me feel we were equals and could speak as Sovereigns. Nobody had such power as she.[2]

In strict constitutional terms, the power she had was an illusion – something that the young Kaiser always failed to understand about his English relations. His hands were not tied in the way that a British monarch was roped in, ruling but not governing, subject always to Parliament. The Queen could disapprove – and she often did – but she could not disobey. So Mr Gladstone, whom she loathed for both his person and his politics ('he talks to me as if I were a public meeting', she complained), came and went and came again, and she had to steel herself for their meetings and be good, if not gracious.

What she had, though, and what she exercised, was influence. It came with age and experience, and it saved the British monarchy from the ridicule it had fallen into under the sons of George III – her uncles, the gouty and ridiculous George IV, with his painted face and pampered mistresses, and William IV, old and silly and reluctant even to have a proper coronation. As her eminent biographer Elizabeth Longford put it, 'it was from this low ebb, both physical and moral, that [Victoria] rescued the royal line'.[3] A teenager when she succeeded to the throne, she hardly seemed capable of such a rescue. As she was driven home from her coronation, Thomas Carlyle caught sight of the slight, white figure in her gold coach and thought,

'Poor little Queen, she is at an age at which a girl can hardly be trusted to choose a bonnet for herself; yet a task is laid upon her from which an archangel might shrink.'[4]

Her achievement was to stabilize the monarchy at a time when the country was going through radical social and economic change. The path to success in this was not by any means smooth. She clashed with prime ministers, took sides in party disputes, and saw the man she revered, admired and later canonized, her husband, Prince Albert, become a focus for dissent by press and politicians. She went into hiding after his death, neglected her subjects and her duties as she drowned in her sorrows, and was ridiculed by high society for her close friendship with a kilted servant, John Brown, and later a turbaned one, the Munshi. But age and endurance got the better of the critics. The jubilees in 1887 and 1897 had sealed it. She had become an icon of the age. She managed to be the embodiment both of family values and of political might. She was Britannia and she was Mother.[5]

Victoria's personality and life were characterized by contradictions. She was alone but always surrounded by people; she was autocratic and humble at the same time; she was charitable in her thoughts and yet egocentric and rude when dealing with those close to her; she was hard-working and also self-indulgent. She was intensely private, but wrote two best-selling books about her life at Balmoral. She was a widow who shut herself away from her subjects, but her image as Queen in statues and pictures was everywhere. She was remote from the people she ruled, but inspired devotion from millions of her subjects, most of whom never saw her in person or heard her speak.

The vast majority of them, however, were happy to take the word of someone who often saw her and had many times heard her silvery voice, the Poet Laureate, Alfred Tennyson.

He was a neighbour on the Isle of Wight, and she was fond enough of him to accord him an honour not normally allowed to anyone outside the family, taking him in person to see the mausoleum at Frogmore, on the Windsor estate, where Albert was buried. She was glad of his approval of its sepulchral whiteness. For the Golden Jubilee in 1887, he wrote a celebratory ode:

> Her court was pure; her life serene;
> God gave her peace; her land reposed;
> A thousand claims to reverence closed
> In her as Mother, Wife and Queen.

Ten years later, Sir Arthur Sullivan marked the Diamond Jubilee festivities in similar vein with a special hymn:

> Oh royal heart with wide embrace
> For all her children yearning!
> Oh happy realm, such mother-grace
> With loyal love returning!
>
> Where England's flag flies wide unfurl'd
> All tyrant wrongs repelling;
> God make the world a better place
> For man's brief earthly dwelling.

However unreal, almost ridiculous, such flowery devotion and over-lavish praise now seems, it was undoubtedly the authentic voice of the time. It is no exaggeration to say that the Queen was not just admired and respected but loved by the people. The worldly-wise and well-travelled William Makepeace Thackeray, author of *Vanity Fair*, knew how widespread was her popularity. He reported in 1857:

Whenever I had to mention the name of Her Majesty the Queen, whether it was upon the banks of the Clyde or those of the Mississippi, whether it was in New England or in Old England, whether it was in some great hall in London to the artisans of the suburbs of the metropolis or to the politer audiences of the West End – whenever I had to mention her name, it was received with shouts of applause and with the most hearty cheers.

She had come to be the embodiment of England – which was curious for someone so German at heart. But, as the *Pall Mall Gazette* put it, 'the lump in the throat that arises whenever the Queen is seen is a silent tribute that enables each one of us to realize that secret thing, the depth of an Englishman's inmost feelings'.

Victoria was the first royal superstar with mass appeal. Partly this was because there were for the first time during her reign newspapers with big enough circulations to create something approaching a mass market.[6] Readers were agog for royal news, and the Queen herself was one of the first to feed that new demand. She fuelled the curiosity with her own books. *Leaves from the Journal of Our Life in the Highlands*, essentially extracts from her personal diary, was published in 1868, sold 20,000 copies instantly, and was reprinted several times. It outsold *The Moonstone* and *Little Women*, both published in the same year.

Its fascination was that it told readers what the life of their reclusive Queen, who had distanced herself from her subjects since the death of Albert seven years earlier, was really like. She may have hoped it would satisfy people's curiosity and dampen the demands for her to be seen more in public. If so, she was wrong. She had misunderstood the public appetite, just as many of her successors were to do. A century later, in 1969, Elizabeth II, Victoria's great-great-granddaughter, granted television cameras access to the royal family and opened the floodgates to an insatiable press and public. But it was Victoria who had been the first to invite her subjects in and to make the royal family part of the lives of everyday people. *Harper's*, the American magazine, saw the dangers and asked whether the Queen's personal revelations about her domestic life, showing her subjects that she was flesh and blood like them, were not the beginning of the end of the British monarchy.

It was a warning that went unnoticed, because there were to be *More Leaves from the Journal of Our Life in the Highlands* in 1884. Her excuse to those, mainly within her own family, who criticized her for this new book was that it would drive out the false biographies of her, of which, she said, 'endless ones have been published'. She was wrong again. There would be many more books about her, and newspapers would publish lengthy day-in-the-life reports, often under intriguing bylines – no name but a description that suggested inside information, such as 'By a lady of breeding who knows Her Majesty well'. The tenor of most of this growing coverage was respectful and respectable (though in 1897 a book called *The Private Life of the Queen* by 'One of Her Majesty's Servants' was deemed too intrusive and Arthur Pearson, its publisher, was forced to withdraw it; it was published instead in the United States).

Through the press, through books, through the celebrations for her jubilees, Queen Victoria became a familiar, a friend, a member of the family. She gave the monarchy a human side it had never had before. Lady Frances Balfour, who knew her, thought 'she was the first to make the throne a vibrant living centre'. Before her, monarchs had been aloof from their people. 'Respect was neither asked for, nor received, affection was neither sought, nor was it rendered.' Somehow Victoria had come to understand that a monarchy could work in modern times if it took its meaning and its legitimacy from the people's love and will. 'Out of her own womanliness, she made it a living force in the hearts of her people.'[7]

Equally important, her face was known to everyone through paintings, posters and the new technology of photography. Her picture was on the walls of countless homes. For the first time, the people knew for sure what their monarch looked like – a little old lady, stern, generally unsmiling, dressed in black with a white cap. They would have seen – or thought they saw – the look that inspired one of her contemporary biographers to proclaim:

She has the air of command natural to her lofty station, with the refinement of bearing that comes from high culture . . . Deep furrows, traced by affliction, experience and meditation, mark the thoughtful face. One who saw the Queen without knowing who she was would look at her again and again, as at a woman of strong character, of high position and accustomed to great responsibilities.[8]

Such responsibilities, all agreed, she carried out to perfection, and with a wisdom that put her politicians in the shade, whatever the niceties of the constitution. Ten prime ministers had served under her, and by the turn of the century she had outlived all but two of them. Five archbishops of Canterbury and ten Lord Chancellors had come and gone, and still she went on. The Countess of Antrim, one of the Queen's ladies-in-waiting, watched her mistress in action and was filled with admiration. 'Her experience was phenomenal. She knew exactly what should be done about every problem, and what would "never do".'[9]

The Countess's view was shared by millions who never had her direct access to the Queen. The *St James's Gazette* summed up their feelings when it wrote, 'Shallow publicists and hasty politicians have said from time to time that the Queen's power was not real. Millions of her subjects thought otherwise, and they were right.' The Queen would have agreed with them. She knew the constitutional imperatives that kept her in check, but whether she ever truly believed in them was another matter. The writer Sir Edmund Gosse, relying on inside information from her closest courtiers, thought that her private views about monarchy owed more to her Stuart predecessors than to Walter Bagehot. 'She hypnotized the public imagination so that, in defiance of the theories of historic philosophy, the nation accepted the Queen's view of her own function and tacitly concluded with her that she ruled by Right Divine.'[10]

The world was changing constantly, or so it seemed in 1900: science, technology, politics, international relations, business – everything was in flux. It was exciting but, more than that, it was frightening. There had to be something fixed and steady to hang on to. 'The Queen! God bless her!' was the unashamed toast in many a crowded, raucous, smoke-filled public house and at genteel private dinner tables too. 'Long may she reign!'

The twentieth century was dawning, but the death of this woman, born just thirty years after the outbreak of the French Revolution and now old, infirm, half-blind and forgetful, was simply unthinkable.

# 2. Trials and Anxieties

A horrible year, nothing but sadness and horrors . . .

The Queen's description of 1900

Of all the days in the year, 14 December was the one when members of the royal family had an appointment that could not be broken. It was the anniversary of the death of the late, constantly lamented but still very much present Prince Albert – dead since 1861, but at the turn of the century as much as ever the paterfamilias. When he died, the Queen simply could not believe it. And when finally she believed, she decided to keep him alive. Everything they had done together would be remembered; everything that happened to her would be a reminder of him.

Typhoid had done for Albert, a common enough illness in those insanitary times, and often fatal. It had reached epidemic proportions in Britain's bursting cities, overcrowded with the rush of population from the countryside to industry and urban life and ill-equipped to deal with the sewage they generated. But it was not just the poor who suffered, nor was the problem confined to Britain. Only a month before Albert fell ill, typhoid had killed the twenty-five-year-old King Pedro of Portugal, a cousin and protégé of the Prince Consort, who took the young man's death very hard as he morbidly contemplated his own. He was sick, he fretted, he would not rest; his doctors were reluctant to face facts, to take charge, to order him to bed and nurse him through the crisis. A bad situation was allowed to get worse. Albert convinced himself he would die – and he did, calling out for his '*liebes Frauchen*', his '*gutes Frauchen*'.

In her journal, scrawled in notes at the time but not properly written until she could bear to do so more than ten years later, Victoria described the end:

Two or three long but perfectly gentle breaths were drawn, the hand clasping mine, and (oh! it turns me sick to write it) *all, all* was over . . . I stood up, kissing his dear heavenly forehead and called out in a bitter agonizing cry: 'Oh! my dear Darling!' and then dropped on my knees in mute, distracted despair, unable to utter a word or shed a tear.

She blamed his excessive zeal. He was so young, just forty-two, but hard work and devotion to duty had aged him before his time and tired him to the point of exhaustion. He took the title of Consort seriously: this was no mere honorific, it was his job, his mission in life. He saw himself as the Queen's personal guide, trying to discipline her mind and her impatient temperament – to overcome 'your fidgety nature', as he put it. It was a severe task that he did with love, which made it acceptable, because he was, after all, the 'most perfect of human beings, my adored husband'. He was also her political guide, leading the way through her constitutional duties, acting as an intermediary with her ministers (though 'interfering' was more the word, some would say). There were so many problems to take on, he had once compared himself to the donkey on the treadmill at Carisbrooke Castle near Osborne.

Not least of his worries was their eldest son, Albert Edward, the Prince of Wales – such a disappointment. Bertie lacked his father's drive and purpose. 'Blasé' was the Queen's contemptuous word for his attitude to life, despite all the efforts to concentrate his mind with rigorous studies and demanding tutors. Let off the leash for once, he had been allowed to join the Guards for a ten-week stint of military training and had allowed himself to be led astray. An actress (a weakness for the rest of his life) by the name of Nellie Clifton. A liaison. In November 1861 word got back to Prince Albert, whose debilitating dismay at his son's behaviour coincided with the start of his illness.

How much did the Queen blame Bertie for the greatest tragedy in her life? A little, certainly; perhaps a lot. Vicky, her eldest daughter, wrote to her mother from Germany begging her not to take it out on Bertie. But her son's misdemeanour remained one of the many 'what ifs' that were to make up the widow's mighty mythology about her dead husband.

The Queen was changed by his death. Necessity made her reinvent herself in his image; she had to find within herself all his best qualities – his focus, resolution and strength of mind. When in doubt, she would ask herself what Albert would have done. He always knew. Moreover, he was always there. In her bedroom at Osborne, she had three portraits of him. One showed him in the bloom of young manhood when they had first been married, romantic in medieval armour, a broadsword at his side, his helmet beside him, her good knight. A miniature of him lying peacefully in death was fixed to the bedhead, next to a pocket containing his repeater watch, which through the night chimed out the hours of her widow-hood. From the day he died, nothing was moved in his study or his dressing room. Fresh hot water and towels were put out for him every day and left to get cold, unlike his memory.

Such morbidity now appears shocking and ghoulish. A century on, in a society that recoils from the idea of death and treats it as a taboo subject, to surround oneself with the dead as Queen Victoria did would be deemed unhealthy, a sign of insanity. Was she, in this sense, mad? Certainly her grief was extreme, and during her lifetime eyebrows, if not outright questions, were raised about her obsessive behaviour. There were even rumours that she took part in seances to try to get in touch with Albert, and that John Brown's hold over her was that he was her spiritualist channel to the other side.[1]

But there is no convincing evidence of the occult, and her closest spiritual adviser for the last twenty years of her life – Randall Davidson, Dean of Windsor, then Bishop of Winchester and eventually (after her death) Archbishop of Canterbury – was firmly conventional in his theology. He knew all about her behaviour, how she would often use Albert's dressing room as a place to sit and talk with close friends. 'I have again and again had talks to her there before dinner with the hot water actually steaming,' he recalled. He thought her attitude to the physical effects of the dead a little odd, but no more than that. There was no question of her communing with ghosts.

As for morbidity, he rejected that too, in favour of a more earth-bound explanation. When Albert died, she had, in her immediate grief, ordered that the daily routine should carry on as usual and nothing should be changed. The servants took her command literally – his room was cleaned and dusted, his shaving water was duly delivered. Davidson's point was that the Queen had simply never got round to countermanding the instruction, and the habit became so ingrained that eventually no one had the temerity to suggest to her, even decades later, that it was time to stop.

This explanation is a little too pat, particularly since it comes from a prelate who was also a courtier and who prided himself perhaps a little too much that he was one of her inner circle. He was not one to be critical. On the other hand, Davidson did discuss religion with her, preached to her often in church, and had a strong sense of what she did and did not believe. Her faith, he recorded, was very down-to-earth – commonsense, straightforward and simply held. She had confided to him occasional 'waves or flashes' of doubt about whether there really was a hereafter, but she had come to the conclusion that it was 'simply impossible' that all those loved ones who had died 'can really have come then to an utter end or that we shall not see and know them hereafter'.

Four months after Albert's death, she spelt out in a letter to a family just recently bereaved like her the beliefs that kept her going. Writing of herself in the third person, as she always did when addressing one of her subjects, she told them in April 1862:

That our beloved ones are not really separated from us but merely visibly and perceptibly, is what the Queen most strongly feels, and indeed, without which she would be unable to struggle on. The certain belief that her adored one is near her, watching over her, praying for her and guiding her is, next to the blessed hope of eternal reunion, her only comfort in her overwhelming affliction.[2]

It was a conviction that stayed with her for the rest of her life and which each year on 14 December brought her and her family without fail to the mausoleum at Frogmore in the Great Park at Windsor, where Albert's body lay. On the morning of that day in 1900, she went into the Prince Consort's bedroom and placed fresh palm branches on the bed – an emblem, as she saw it, of his Christian faith. Then the procession of carriages moved out of the castle at 11.30 and down the Long Walk before turning off, crossing the bridge over a stream, and stopping at the porch. The Queen was helped out and, on the arm of the Prince of Wales, made her way through the door, passing beneath a bronze tablet with the Latin inscription she had chosen: 'Here at last I shall rest with thee; with thee in Christ shall I rise again.'

Long before his death, she and Albert had talked about being buried together in a place like this. There had been a mausoleum at Claremont, where she was brought up, and the Coburgs, his side of the family, had had one too. Within four days of his death, she had chosen the site and busied herself, a solace for her grief, to find architects and builders. The foundation stone was laid just three months and one day after he died. The centrepiece of the octagonal building was the vast white marble sarcophagus on which rested an effigy of the sleeping Prince. Around this in 1900 the Queen, her eldest son, his son the Duke of York, and a dozen other royals grouped themselves while the choir of St George's Chapel, Windsor Castle, began to sing. There was a new hymn this year, composed specially by Arthur Benson, a housemaster at nearby Eton College, its mawkish verses and insistent rhymes sinking the small congregation deep in sentimentality:

> They who loved and left us,
> Of their love bereft us,
> Are their hearts still turning
> Home in restless yearning?
>
> Nay, the loved ones yonder
> Gaze in loving wonder,
> Smile upon us sighing
> As they smiled in dying.
>
> Yes, they want us smiling,
> Strong in hope, beguiling,
> Severance swiftly fleeting
> With the thought of meeting.

★

Where precisely the Queen's thoughts now were, whether in this world or the next, it is hard to say, but she was weighed down by them. She was ill and exhausted, but the work never seemed to stop despite her age. The day before going to the mausoleum she had talked at length to a New Zealand colonel seriously wounded in South Africa and now an invalid, welcomed the new ambassador from Brazil, accepted back various wands of office from retiring officials and handed them over to their successors, and received a loyal address from the House of Commons. More disturbing was her presentation of Victoria Crosses to five of her soldiers – a proud occasion, in spite of the underlying message it conveyed.

As the citation for Private C. Ward of the 2nd Battalion, Yorkshire Light Infantry, was read out, it can only have brought home to Windsor the horror of the distant war that had distracted and depressed the Queen for the whole of the past year. Ward's troop had been attacked by five hundred Boers; two officers had been badly wounded and all but six of the men were dead or out of action. 'Through a storm of shots from each flank', Ward ran through the enemy lines to a signalling station 150 yards away, called for reinforcements, and then headed back 'from a place of absolute safety' to tell his commanding officer that the message had been delivered. On the return trip he was shot down. So many of her soldiers were killed or wounded in just this one incident. How much grimmer must the total picture be.

A quarter of a million British soldiers were now in South Africa, spurred on by the year's most popular music-hall song, the call to arms of 'Goodbye, Dolly Gray'. 'Goodbye, Dolly, I must leave you, though it breaks my heart to go,' the soldiers sang as more and more of them boarded the troop ships heading south. But it was not just their love lives that were to be broken; it was their bodies too. By December 1900 the death toll had reached 11,000 and, as much as the military command and a largely compliant press tried to spin defeats into victories, the casualty lists told a different story.

The war had been a popular one among the public when it began, a chance to hammer down the two independent Boer republics, the Transvaal and the Orange Free State, which threatened British supremacy in South Africa. In reality it was the imperialist scheming of Joseph Chamberlain, Britain's Colonial Secretary, eager to expand into the Dutch areas and plant the Union Flag over them, that had made war inevitable. Cleverly, though, he had lured the Boers into making the first belligerent move. As far as the British public was concerned, this was an honourable cause to defend British interests against an untrustworthy invader – and it would be quickly fought and won. The dying came as a shock. Defeats at Spion Kop and Colenso and the sieges at Mafeking and Ladysmith were not what the jingoists had prophesied.

A change of commander brought a change in military tactics and a change in fortune in the field. The popular Lord Roberts – known familiarly as Bobs – took charge, reversed the reverses, and chased the Boers back into their own states, but there he and his men were harried by a hit-and-hide guerrilla army. As 1900 came to its end, victory seemed tantalizingly near, but the fighting dragged on (and would do so for another eighteen months) and the casualties mounted. So too did the hostility towards Britain. This was not a popular war elsewhere. The French opposed it, and so did Germany. 'There is hardly a nation that loves England,' wrote a contemporary commentator. 'We are held to be a pirate nation, a state that abuses its power to trample on the weak and helpless. Indeed, in many countries the one point on which the nation agrees is hatred of Great Britain. The people in Russia, in Germany, in Holland, in Belgium, in France and in Spain are all anti-British.'[3]

The Queen had followed the course of the fighting in great detail and in high anxiety. 'I am horrified at the terrible list of casualties, 22 officers killed and 21 wounded,' she telegraphed the Marquis of Lansdowne at the War Office, and followed up with precise advice. 'It is quite imperative that Lord Roberts should not move till he has plenty of troops. Pray impress this on him.' When she heard a rumour that Prussian officers were fighting on the side of the Boers, she wrote an angry letter to her grandson, the Kaiser, asking him to investigate. She also hoped the newspapers in his country would 'cease abusing and reviling us and telling lies about our army'.

She feared Boers under the bed – 'the country is full of spies' – and worried that Balfour was not dealing firmly enough with 'unpatriotic' critics of the war. 'If the government are firm and courageous, the country will support them,' she told him. 'If not, the number of Boer spies will telegraph back to South Africa and great harm will be done. You must all show a firm front and not let it be for a moment supposed that we vacillate in the least.'

Be firm. If boys like bugler James Dunn could, so should the men. Fourteen-year-old Dunn came to Osborne to tell her in person how he had been shot in the arm and chest at Colenso and, despite his wounds, had swum a river to get back to the ranks. He had lost his bugle; she gave him a new one. He was 'a nice-looking, modest boy'.

Good news made her deliriously happy. When Ladysmith, under siege for four months, was relieved on the last day of February 1900 'my joy was unbounded and I let everyone in the Castle know'. She spread her joy, making a rare visit to London and driving the streets through (in her own words) 'enormous crowds and incessant demonstrations of enthusiasm'. Then, after dinner, she stood in a window at the front of Buckingham Palace with a light shining behind her so that the cheering crowd outside could get a glimpse of her. Lord Rosebery – her Foreign Secretary under Gladstone and her Prime Minister for a year until 1895 – was moved to write to her in admiration:

It was as if a great wave of sympathy and devotion had passed over the capital . . . I saw your Majesty three times in the streets and in the Park; and my overpowering feeling was 'What a glorious privilege to be able to make millions so happy!' No one who saw London then will ever forget it, or will cease to pray for the prolongation of your Majesty's life, and of your Majesty's priceless and unceasing exertions for your Empire.[4]

It was the same when she went to Woolwich – first to the Arsenal, 'where 20,000 workmen were assembled, who are working day and night on munitions', and then to a hospital to visit the wounded. She was in her wheelchair; they were in theirs. Tears flowed.[5]

She did her bit in other ways too. Private James Humphreys was convinced he owed his life to her generosity. A Boer bullet that hit him in the stomach should have destroyed his spleen, but it was stopped by the tin of chocolate he carried in his haversack, a Christmas present to all the troops from the Queen. He had his life; he wanted her to have the tin and the bullet.

But it all wearied her. In May she had celebrated her birthday at Balmoral, her eighty-first and last as it would be. There were 'many pretty' presents laid out on a table in her sitting room – the 'lovely' chain from the Prince and Princess of Wales was conventional; the bronze replica of the Duke of Wellington's hands that they also gave her was bizarre but even more welcome. Six extra telegraphists had to be called in to help deal with the messages of congratulation from every part of the world. Answering them was 'an interminable task'.

So, it seemed to her, was her life. She wrote in her journal, 'God has been very merciful and supported me, but my trials and anxieties have been manifold, and I feel tired and upset by all I have gone through this winter and spring.' She was feeling her age – too many aches and pains; too many nights when she could not sleep, despite going to bed earlier. As Marie Mallet noted, however, it was 'not early enough'.

Life at court was increasingly sombre, and not just in mood. The women around the Queen had always had to dress down. They were permitted white, grey, purple and mauve – though not the bright mauve that had so excited the entourage on their last visit to Nice. Out of the question. Then, in the summer of 1900, it was back to black. 'I am sending for my mourning trappings,' Mrs Mallet told her husband. 'We never escape jet for long.'

The deaths began at a distance, among the family of monarchs rather than the immediate loved ones. The King of Italy was murdered at the end of July 1900, gunned down in his carriage by an anarchist while distributing the sports prizes at a school near his summer home in Monza. The Queen was horrified. It confirmed her growing belief that the Continent was a dangerous place to be, which is why she had cancelled her usual holiday in Nice that summer. 'It was a fear of something happening on the road which made me give up going,' she confided to her daughter Vicky.

The unpopularity of the war made her a target, just as four months earlier the Prince of Wales had been targeted by a man with a gun in Belgium. He was on his way to Denmark with his wife, Alix, to visit her parents, having decided against a trip to Paris, where anti-British feeling was running high. Dodging the insults put him in greater danger. At Brussels railway station an Italian anarchist pointed his revolver through the window of the train and fired at point-blank range. Somehow he missed and was dragged away by the stationmaster before he could fire off his other five bullets.

The Prince remained cool – it was all so quick, there was no time for any other reaction – but his mother was 'greatly shocked and upset'. She wrote to Vicky:

What a merciful escape dear Bertie has had from a very real danger. The indignation felt everywhere is very great, but it shows the harm such atrocious vilifications of us, including even me, have [done] and the totally mistaken idea of the war which affects the minds of weak, ignorant and ill-disposed people. I am thankful I did not attempt to go abroad.

Bertie was spared; the family was not. Alfred, her second son, the Duke of Saxe-Coburg, a dangerously heavy drinker and heavy smoker, was seeing specialists in Vienna about a persistent pain in his throat and tongue. The diagnosis for 'Affie' was not good but an attempt was made to keep the news from the Queen, to spare her any more grief. She was 'much distressed' when she found out. 'The physicians think most seriously of poor dear Affie's state of health. The malady it appears is incurable, and alas! one can only too well guess at its nature!' Cancer. It was killing Vicky; now it had its stranglehold on her son's throat.

The first news she had of his illness was on 25 July. He was dead within the week. The Queen was just finishing dressing in her room at Osborne when her daughters Princess Helena and Princess Beatrice knocked at the door. Helena broke it to her. 'Bad news, very bad news.' It was too much to bear. She wrote in her journal:

Oh God! My poor darling Affie gone too! We shall never see him
again or hear his voice and merry laugh. My third grown–up child,
besides three very dear sons–in–law. It is hard at 81! One sorrow,
one trial, one anxiety following another. It is a horrible year, nothing
but sadness and horrors . . . Felt terribly shaken and broken, and
could not realize the dreadful fact.

As it sank in, she was annoyed at having had the seriousness
of his illness kept from her. She had had no time to prepare,
which made the sudden shock of his death that much harder
to bear. Now she could only seek the solace of her memories
of him as a little boy. Marie Mallet sat with her:

The Queen cried so gently and seemed so patient and resigned in
her great sorrow, but she did not sob. She recalled his early days
here [at Osborne], his birthdays had always been spent here (he
would have been 56 next Monday), and his childish likes and
dislikes. To her he was once more the happy boy, and I could see
that.

After tea the Queen and her daughters drove down by the
sea, but it did no good. The next morning she woke refreshed
for just a second, until the realization of Affie's death dawned
on her again. A visit from the Prince of Wales was not soothing
– he was too upset at the loss of his brother. Only listening to
Beatrice reading from 'some of my favourite religious books'
gave her comfort.

She would not even see her son buried. His funeral was in
Germany, and there was no question of her travelling. A
simultaneous service was held at Osborne, with her prayers
for her son punctuated by a salute of guns from HMS *Australia*
out in the bay. But the Prince of Wales had made the journey
to Germany, and the Queen was worried for him. The fear of

assassination gripped her, and it infected Mrs Mallet, who noted, 'These crimes are as catching as measles and there seems to be a deep-seated anarchical plot which is to involve all the sovereigns of Europe.' Gloom was breeding paranoia. It would get worse.

Marie Mallet kept one piece of information to herself: Affie had been ill and in pain for at least *two years*. For the last two months of his life he had been fed by a tube, he was so sick. But all this had been kept from his mother until the very end. It seems to have been the way with the royal family. Nobody ever owned up to sad truths or faced the facts, often for fear of upsetting Mama. When it came to Mama's turn, as we shall see, they did the same thing, for fear of upsetting themselves.

But it was not just Mama who had been unaware of Affie's long illness. His oldest sister, Vicky, had also been kept in the dark about her brother's health. Only three days before his death she wrote to the Queen from Germany, 'What can be the matter with him? Is it gout? Or eczema? Or are the kidneys not right?' Even after his death she seemed unaware that it was cancer that had killed him – 'What can have been the matter with him?' she quizzed her mother. She was all too aware, however, of the awful blow it was for the Queen. She wrote to her:

The thought of your grief is an agony to me. That this blow should fall on you in the midst of the trials and anxieties of our war is too cruel. To think of our darling beloved Affie being taken at this time – at his age – is too dreadful. It is too heartrending, three of your nine have gone home and followed beloved Papa.

How could it possibly get worse?

The Queen was so weary, and longed for some rest. Others took it. Why couldn't she? Sir George Goschen, a minister she had been friendly with for years, wrote from the Admiralty with news of his retirement. He was in his seventieth year; he had been in politics for thirty-seven years. It was time for 'relief from its engrossing duties'. Reluctantly – he would be 'a most serious public loss' – she gave him her blessing to go. He was, she wrote, quite right in wishing for rest. 'The Queen wishes she could have the same,' she added plaintively, 'even for the shortest period. For she does need it, and feels the constant want of it; at 81 – very trying and fatiguing.'

Her exhaustion was showing. Marie Mallet knew how quickly the Queen had aged and had warned her husband, Balfour's private secretary. Other members of the Government were getting the message too. Lord James, the Chancellor of the Duchy of Lancaster, saw the Queen in October after an absence of five months and was horrified. She was fading away. 'The greatest change had taken place. The Queen had lost much flesh and had shrunk so as to appear about one half of the person she had been.' Her spark had gone. In May she had been very cheerful, eager to talk about the war in South Africa, 'enjoying any anecdote or smart conversation according to her nature'. By October 'her spirits had apparently left her'.[6] Dispirited, she would soon be crushed.

Her favourite grandson was Prince Christian Victor, a handsome soldier in his early thirties, everything the Queen admired. 'Christle', the eldest son of Helena (Princess Christian as she had become on her marriage to Prince Christian of Schleswig-Holstein), had fought with Kitchener against the dervishes at the battle of Omdurman in the Sudan and been in one of the very first detachments to head out to South Africa when the war began. She had frequent reports of how well 'the beloved boy' was doing, and was delighted. But she worried. 'I hope and pray dear Christle may be spared,' she wrote in her journal.

It was hardly a glorious death. He was playing cricket one day; the next he was down with malaria. A week later he had typhoid too. He struggled on for another fortnight, getting weaker as his lungs congested, and on 29 October he died. His sister Thora (Princess Helena Victoria) was calm as she broke the news to the Queen on a rainy day at Balmoral. She was inconsolable. 'This dear, excellent, gallant boy, beloved by all, such a good as well as a brave and capable officer, gone!' He had survived so many scrapes in his military career without so much as a scratch, only 'to fall victim to this horrid fever'. It was unfair, 'really too piteous'.

As they buried him with full military honours six thousand miles away, she mourned him at church in Scotland, moved to floods of tears. The gloom would not lift. She felt 'very poorly and wretched. My appetite is completely gone and I have great difficulty in eating anything.' She told Sir James Reid she was 'quite crushed'. He noted that she was often in tears. Marie Mallet was now very worried and, pushing royal protocol aside, held out the hand of friendship. It was eagerly seized. 'When she breaks down and draws me close to her and lets me stroke her hand, I quite forget she is far above me and only realize she is a sorrowing woman who clings to human sympathy and hungers for all that can be given on such occasions.'

Back at Windsor, on 10 November the Prime Minister, Lord Salisbury, came to discuss changes in the Government and to ponder why the war was 'dragging on', and she handled the day well enough. But the nights were awful and not even the opium in Dover's Powder could help. Food still disgusted her and she no longer bothered to go to the dining room for dinner. Reid, who was by her side as she tried to sleep, noted she had 'foul tongue, no appetite, digestion very bad, much emaciated'. He was deeply worried, and his fears did not go away even when she rallied after several days. Mrs Mallet, though, was optimistic, taking heart when the Queen had coffee and an egg for breakfast. 'There is no reason why she should not be herself again if she could be made to take more nourishment.'

Feeling better, the Queen managed a large lunch party, but she exhausted herself by having to shout at her daughter-in-law, the Princess of Wales, who had been deaf from rheumatic fever for more than thirty years. It made Mrs Mallet cross. 'She resents being treated as an invalid and as soon as she feels a tiny bit better she over-tires herself and collapses. Sir James has never been so anxious before in all these years.' He was so worried he went to see the Prince of Wales in his room to voice his fears. It was a long discussion, but the doctor clearly had difficulty in making the Prince appreciate his mother's real condition. There is no record of what Bertie thought – he was not one for published journals – but his son the Duke of York gave an indication of the family's understanding of her state of health. He told the Queen's private secretary he was firmly convinced Her Majesty, who had been 'quite seedy', was getting better.

But 'seedy' was hardly an adequate description for the Queen by now. In pain, insomnia, no appetite. Her journal was a litany of her woes – 'wretched night', 'miserable day', 'went to neither luncheon nor dinner'. Her daughters must have known how she was feeling – since her eyes were not up to the job, they had to write down the words for her. They were also with her for much of the time and could hardly fail to notice how she was ailing. But the Prince of Wales, whose visits were occasional, appears to have been blind to the obvious. Reid decided to spell it out for him.

His report to the heir to the throne began by acknowledging that the Queen had seemed to be getting better in the past few days and her eating and sleeping had improved. But he quickly warned that this should not be misinterpreted as meaning everything was fine. 'She is not what she was before, and I begin to fear that her health may remain permanently on a lower plane than hitherto.' How could the Prince not see it? Age was getting the better of his mother. 'She is feebler generally than she used to be, her voice is weaker, and her nervous system is a good deal shaken. I am very doubtful whether, at her age, they may regain their former level.'

Reid had sought a second opinion, bringing in Sir Thomas Barlow to examine the Queen just two days earlier. The eminent Dr Barlow had come to the same conclusion. 'Although, like myself, he sees no evidence of organic disease,' wrote Reid, 'he thinks the Queen has gone downhill since he last saw her over a year ago.' And her condition was bound to worsen – 'in the course of nature this must be progressive' – though it could be a slow process if she had constant care and attention. On the other hand, 'there is always present the risk of some sudden illness which would be very serious at the Queen's age and in her enfeebled state'. One thing he knew for sure: it would be unwise to make plans for her to travel abroad on holiday. Far too risky.

The Prince's reply was contradictory. He told Reid he fully understood, but then showed he didn't by adding, 'The Queen has much extraordinary vitality and pluck and I hope that the present shock and the indisposition from which she has suffered may keep away.' The optimism – wishful thinking more like – was groundless. Reid knew it was precisely her 'vitality and pluck' that the Queen had lost. Nor was her condition an 'indisposition': it was the inexorable state of ageing, and could have only one outcome, sooner or later. But the Prince would not be told. This was to remain his attitude throughout the weeks ahead, though why he was so reluctant to face up to her rapidly failing health is something we can only speculate on.

It may have been a simple thing: a devoted son's love for his mother blinding him to her frailty. That would be understandable. Or it may have been that his own life had once been written off. When in 1871 he had gone down with typhoid, out of his mind with fever as his temperature soared to 104, his doctor had declared him 'on the very *verge* of the grave', according to the Queen. The country had prayed for his recovery; there had been discussions about issuing a bulletin to prepare everyone for the end. But he had pulled through, sitting up in bed and asking for a glass of Bass. He had defeated the disease with sheer determination – 'vitality and pluck', you might say. If he could do it, how much more would he expect from his iron-willed mother?

But perhaps too there was fear of facing the future. It would not be surprising. He had waited all his adult life to be King, and had spent much of that life being told he was unworthy of the position. His mother had deliberately excluded him from the business of government. He had settled into a comfortable life of family and mistresses, dinner parties, shooting parties and horse racing. Now nearing sixty, why should he want all that to change?

If he feared his own accession, there is evidence that, weary as she undoubtedly was, his mother still had serious misgivings about whether he had it in him to be a king. As Marie Mallet sat with her, she was surprised by how determined the Queen was to go on living. 'After the Prince Consort's death,' Victoria confided to her lady-in-waiting, 'I wished to die. But now I wish to live and do what I can for my country and those I love.' It may have been no more than the usual expression of duty that came often from the Queen's lips, but Mrs Mallet thought it curious. She wrote to her husband, 'Do not repeat this but it is a very remarkable utterance for a woman of 82 [*sic*] and this is not the first time she has made the same remark. I wonder if she dreads the influence of the Prince of Wales?'

Determined that his mother would be well again and unwilling to accept Reid's gloomy prognostication, the Prince now urged Reid to let his own doctor, Sir Francis Laking, examine her – a demand he would scarcely have made if he was satisfied with Reid's assessment. Reid was not an admirer of Laking, but he felt he had been given a command and could not refuse. Laking was sent for. Brimming with confidence for the Queen, he told her she would soon get over her 'squeamishness' and 'discomfort' and recover her appetite. He recommended regular doses of milk and whisky.

The medicine failed to lift her spirits for Mausoleum Day. The prayers and the music were beautiful, and she loved having her family around her as they remembered the hard-to-forget Prince Albert, but the afternoon was 'dull and dark' and she felt unwell again and could hardly bring herself to go to dinner. Two days later she was feeling so bad that Reid was summoned from his bed to see her at 5 a.m. and gave her a drug to make her sleep. That night he buttonholed Lord Salisbury in the corridor after dinner and told the Prime Minister of his anxieties. But Salisbury, a sick man himself and anguished by grief over his wife, dead for a year, refused to be alarmed. He did not want to contemplate another death of a woman he loved and respected. His suggestion was that the Queen just needed to get away for a holiday in the sun.

Unable to persuade the heir to the throne or the country's political leader that the monarch was seriously unwell, Reid prepared himself for a difficult Christmas with an elderly patient who was now virtually an invalid.

★

From Windsor Castle to Osborne House is a distance of around sixty miles. Wrapped up in a tartan rug, the Queen was taken down the hill in an open carriage to the station to board her own train direct to Gosport, on the other side of the harbour from Portsmouth on the south coast. She was smiling as she left the castle through a line of her servants, but some of them realized that this might well be the last time they would see her alive. Though the sea was choppy, the royal yacht *Alberta*, an elegant paddle steamer, was only a little late as it ploughed its way across the Solent to the Isle of Wight. At Trinity Dock a carriage was waiting for the climb up the steep hill out of East Cowes, through the ceremonial gate and along the drive to the house that Victoria and Albert had built for each other. The Queen had dozed for an hour on the train and taken some soup, but there had been railway officials and civic dignitaries to meet and greet at every juncture and by the end of the four-hour journey on 18 December she was exhausted.

The carriage pulled up under the portico of the house, barely fifty years old but designed to look like a classic Italian palazzo with an elegant campanile and ornamental gardens. It was a frugal building and fraudulent, constructed on the cheap but made to look good. The stone of the exterior was in reality bricks covered in cement rendering. Inside, the marble walls were painted plaster. The Queen loved it.

In a state of 'nerve restlessness and depression', according to Reid, she was carried into the hallway, into her lift and up to her bedroom. That night Beatrice read to her to try to help her sleep, but it only made her more restless. Next day she managed a carriage ride with her granddaughter Thora but nothing more, not even dinner downstairs. It would be the pattern for what little remained of her life. She was cantankerous too – cranky when she couldn't sleep, cranky when she did. 'I was very annoyed,' she noted after being left to lie in until just before noon one morning. Her drives out became irregular, depending on when she was awake.

The Prince of Wales continued to believe all was well with his mother. She just needed taking out of herself. Back in the summer he had told Reid it was her meagre diet he was worried about. His own appetite was gargantuan – breakfast alone was fish, chicken, bacon and at least three eggs – and had given him a forty-eight-inch waistline and the nickname of Tum Tum (though anyone foolhardy enough to use it to his face risked exile from his presence). His mother's problem was that she was 'not taking sufficient food and wine to keep herself up'. Now he felt a good bit of Christmas cheer would do the trick for her, just as it had done a year ago. Then there had been a lively tea party for the wives and children of soldiers on active service in South Africa, the Queen rolling up and down the lines of tables in her wheelchair before handing out presents. From Germany, Vicky had sent her a lovely inkstand, which the Queen had put on the desk in Albert's study. As he left Osborne for Sandringham to celebrate his own Christmas, the Prince must have hoped for a repeat. It would not be so.

There was little festive about Osborne that Christmas. Prince and Princess Christian arrived but were still deeply shocked about the loss of Christle, and even the Queen noticed how much the ordeal of his son's death had aged her son-in-law. Meanwhile Arthur, the Duke of Connaught, the Queen's third son, was worrying about how his mother had aged. He thought 'Mama very feeble and unable to do anything; she comes to no meals and goes out at odd hours'.[7]

There was another source of melancholy for the family – the suffering of Vicky. The cancer was now rendering her totally helpless and she had been virtually bedridden for months. Her joints were so swollen that, to her great distress,

her wedding ring had to be cut off. For her sisters back in
England there was a terrible dilemma: should they be censors?
As they read aloud Vicky's letters to their mother, or accounts
from others of her suffering, how much anguish and detail
should they gloss over to save the Queen from knowledge
that could only hurt her? The Duke of Connaught had no
doubt that she should be spared anything that might upset her.

On Christmas Eve, presents were laid out in the Durbar
Room, the banqueting hall built just ten years earlier and fitted
out with magnificent mouldings of peacocks and elephant gods
to look like the throne room of an Indian raja. The family
gathered around the Christmas tree, which was hung with
lights and French and German bonbons, their gifts for each
other laid out on tables. Much to everyone's surprise, the
Queen joined them. The Duke of Connaught had not really
expected her to come down. He had just written to his sister
Louise (who was staying at Sandringham), 'I very much doubt
her being able to come to the Christmas tree – this throws
quite a gloom over our already sad Xmas.' But she made the
effort, though she could hardly see her presents – perhaps not
even the most appropriate one, a magnifying glass that Vicky
had sent. Princess Beatrice thought her mother 'very depressed
and generally weak'.

Down in the dining room on the 25th the Household
assembled for Her Majesty's Dinner. On the sideboard sat a
200 lb baron of cold beef, which had been cut according to
tradition from a Devon ox on the farm at Windsor, ceremonially
roasted, and adorned with the letters VRI in shredded
horseradish. The magnificent menu card – prettily embellished
with a colour drawing of Osborne, the royal coat of arms and a
frieze of flowers and Union Flags – promised a feast: as well as
the beef, there was turtle soup, turbot, roast turkey, boar's head,
game pie, plum pudding, mince pies and chocolate eclairs. They

ate it without her. In her room, directly above the dining room laid out with a meal worthy of a monarch, the Queen dined on Benger's Food and broth. And sad memories.

She was distraught. Another death – that very day. Jane Churchill was a lady-in-waiting but, more than that, a close friend for half a century, and a link back through the years to Albert. There had been the fun of a summer excursion in Scotland forty-one years ago. Under assumed names, Victoria, Albert and friends had travelled from Balmoral for two days of hiking and sightseeing, staying at a common inn and trying not to be noticed (though the crown emblazoned on the side of the carriages was a clue not to be missed). Jane Churchill and her husband had been in the party for what the Queen christened 'The First Great Expedition'. They had tumbled down Craig Nordie and all laughed so much.

A co-conspirator in those good times when Albert was alive, Lady Churchill had remained a companion through the bad. Now widowed herself, she was a guest at Osborne, though, because her heart was not strong and she had a history of illness, the Queen had worried about her coming at this time of the year. It was barely light on Christmas morning when Reid was woken up and summoned to Lady Churchill's room in the Household wing of the house. A maid had brought early-morning tea and had been unable to wake her. She was dead, killed by a heart attack in her sleep. The Queen had to be told – but gently, otherwise the death of one old lady might lead instantly to another. It was a time for subterfuge.

The Queen had had another bad night, trying to sleep, failing, then dropping off in the morning just when she wanted to get up. In a grumpy mood, she went out in the carriage at one o'clock, and Princess Helena, having been briefed by Reid, told her that Jane Churchill was ill again, a bad heart attack. Back in her room, the Queen sent for Reid and quizzed him. 'She is very ill,' Reid said solemnly, and left it at that. Thoughts of 'dear Jane' preoccupied her during her afternoon drive, and on her return she sent for Reid again. This time he came clean. 'I was just coming to tell your Majesty all was over,' he said.

Distressed by the news — 'she was one of my most faithful and intimate friends' — the Queen managed to get through a small service in the drawing room. Princess Beatrice played the harmonium for the three hymns, and the vicar of Windsor, who was staying at Osborne, said some words. Afterwards the Queen went upstairs to rest, and to record her thoughts. 'This has been a terribly sad Christmas for us all,' she concluded. And she had discovered the truth about the kind deception her doctor and daughters had played on her. 'They had not dared to tell me for fear of giving me a shock, so had prepared me gradually for the terrible news.' But, though they may have blunted the blade, she was still cut to the quick. The next day she wrote in her journal, 'The loss to me is not to be told.' And when Lady Churchill's son came to take his mother's body home she was so affected 'I could hardly speak.'

Jane Churchill's coffin lay in the chapel at Osborne, beside it a wreath of lilies of the valley that the Queen had knotted and twisted into shape with her own hands. The wind howled through the woods and fields that day, forcing her to cut short her carriage drive. The next day, as her old friend's remains were being ferried back across the Solent, it was worse, and as the storm raged she worried frantically in case there might be a shipwreck and more deaths. To take her mind off these fears, she did her duty, signing some papers, 'though I could hardly see a word I wrote'. She told Vicky in a letter that it had been one of the saddest Christmases she remembered since the one immediately after Albert's death.

The old year, so full of loss, blew itself out with a vengeance. Not only the Isle of Wight suffered. In the Shetlands, twenty-two fishermen from one village were drowned when their boats foundered. In the Bristol Channel, the SS *Brunswick* from Liverpool went down with the loss of seven lives. A four-masted sailing ship, the *Primrose Hill*, tried to ride out the storm off Holyhead but her anchors would not hold and the crew of thirty-four died as she split in two and sank in minutes. To her Prime Minister, Lord Salisbury, the Queen sent a card with an unseasonal greeting for the new year, its message devoid of earthly hope. 'The Old Year dies,' it said. 'God beckons those we love.'

As the rain and wind lashed the outside of Osborne on New Year's Eve, there was an atmosphere of deep gloom inside — a bleak, beleaguered mood, as if they were all under siege by dark and hostile forces. By nine o'clock the Queen was in bed. The next day she sat at her desk and dictated her thoughts for her granddaughter Thora to write down in the journal: 'Osborne, 1st Jan, 1901. — Another year begun, and I am feeling so weak and unwell that I enter upon it sadly.'

# 3. Whispers and Denials

No one outside knew anything, and we all hoped it would
pass off . . .

Fritz Ponsonby

The new year began with torrents of rain. In Gloucestershire,
the river Severn burst its banks and spread out over mile after
mile of farmland. Hundreds of sheep and cattle floated away
on the flood. Then came the bitter cold. After just one week
of 1901, London, a city now of more than four million people,
bursting with energy and ideas, the centre of a worldwide
empire if not of the world itself, was deadened under several
inches of snow.

It was fun for some. The young, the sporty and the healthy
hurried off in their thousands to Tufnell Park and Hackney
Marshes to skate on the frozen ponds. For others the sub-zero
temperatures were unwelcome. 'Many deaths from exposure,'
reported one newspaper, though this winter cull of the old
and the infirm was not thought important enough to merit
more than a single-column story towards the bottom of the
page. What was so newsworthy about elderly people dying?
It happened all the time.

The snow and ice snarled up London's horse-filled streets.
Hooves skidded and slipped on the frozen wooden blocks, flat
stone and occasional stretches of asphalt that made up the road
surfaces, and the thousands of buses and cabs, private carriages

and tradesmen's delivery vans slowed and stopped. The fetid
steam from the horses' nostrils filled the icy air, mingling with
the sharp smell of oats and manure that was the lingering
aroma of this pre-petrol age. The crash of horseshoes, the
clanking of carts and cabs, the crack of whips, the shouting and
hollering, all deafened the ears. On the pavements, hobnailed
boots crunched into slush as men (and, increasingly, women)
hurried to work using the commonest form of transport –
their legs. The walkers felt far safer than the cyclists, who
found it hard to keep their grip, though the new-fangled
pneumatic tyres helped. Chain-driven bicycles, replacing the
unwieldy and expensive penny-farthings, were growing in
popularity and in numbers, and with the cheapest on sale for
a little over four pounds they were now just within the reach
of many working men.[1] Until then private transport had been
prohibitively expensive – a new carriage, a brougham or a
landau, would set a man back a hundred guineas or more, and
as much again for the horse to draw it. The bicycle was such
a democratic form of transport, so liberating in every sense.
The masses were on the move.

There were horseless carriages caught up in the traffic chaos
too, mainly steam-driven but with a few motor cars among
them. The very first, a two-seater Benz, had arrived in the
country from Germany just six years ago. In a characteristically
British reaction to innovation, its driver, Henry Hewetson,
was stopped by the police as he drove it away from the docks
and warned that he should have been preceded by a man with
a red flag. It was not the law, however, but the prohibitive
cost of the new machines that led some to doubt they would
ever catch on. It was true that the Prince of Wales had bought
himself three Daimlers, but that only advanced the argument
that this was a rich man's toy and never likely to be a common
mode of transport for the hoi polloi.

In this world and this society, distinctions of class and money mattered so much. They defined every aspect of life. On the surface, they were as unyielding as the weather that new year. As the temperature dropped even lower, the middle-class wives in the hilltop suburbs of Hampstead in the north or Sydenham in the south ordered the live-in maid to haul up some more coal from the cellar and fling it on the fire. Down in the mean and miserable streets of the East End, a different sort of warmth was on tap in the public houses, gin palaces and beer houses on virtually every street corner – to the horror of the temperance movement, London had a staggering seven thousand of them. A recent health scare after traces of arsenic were found in some beers had done little to reduce consumption.

Meanwhile, in smart Mayfair and its newly fashionable annexe, Belgravia, the well-off and the well-bred had their own way of dealing with the cold. They would escape it altogether. The Dowager Lady Albemarle had rounded up her daughters and was taking them off to Rome, where she was almost certain to run into the Dowager Duchess of Newcastle, who was visiting her daughter, the Princess Doria, there. The more adventurous could take a steamer trip down the Nile to Luxor to see the miracles of ancient Egypt, or go even further afield for a winter cruise in the West Indies – sixty-five days on a Royal Mail steam packet-boat for an all-in price of sixty-five pounds. There were short breaks too. Moneyed young people with a fortnight and ten guineas to spare were away skating, skiing and tobogganing in Chamonix.

But it was the South of France that was the popular destination for the international set. The King of the Belgians was due to arrive in Cannes, though he had had to leave his wife behind. Bronchitis, apparently. Her illness was nothing to worry about, even in Brussels. *Particularly* in Brussels, if the

*Daily Express* was correct in its conclusion that she was 'not very popular with the genial Belgians', who, it was said, mistook her shyness for hauteur and despised her accordingly. Which, as the paper's readers would have been quick to agree, was no way to treat a queen.

Victoria received no such disrespect. The court circular from Osborne was reassuringly terse as it reported that Her Majesty 'drove out yesterday', taking to her carriage for a trip through the grounds 'accompanied by their Royal Highnesses Princess Christian of Schleswig-Holstein and Princess Henry of Battenberg', which the royal-watchers – and who was not one? – would know to be her much loved daughters Helena and Beatrice. The *Express* felt for her in her old age, and it spoke on behalf of every strand of society when it fervently hoped she would be up to the journey she was shortly to make to Nice for a well-deserved holiday. 'She has been severely tried in the past few months by domestic bereavements,' it ventured, but beyond that it carried no hint of anything serious to worry about. On the contrary, the Prince of Wales was off to Chatsworth for some shooting with the Devonshires on their Derbyshire acres. Business as normal, then.

Reassured by what they read in their newspapers about the Queen, Londoners could feel relaxed about the prospects for 1901 too. They could take comfort, for example, in the news that the Circle Line, open now for fifteen years, was at last going over from noisy, smelly steam to electrical power, following the example set by the Metropolitan Line. The days of nearly choking to death in the smoke-filled tunnels on the way to work in the City were over.

There was plenty of entertainment to take their minds off the cold, some of it faintly exotic. Queues formed, as ever, outside Madame Tussaud's, where there were new waxworks of the Chinese emperor and his court. At the Crystal Palace –

the huge glasshouse built for the Great Exhibition in 1851 (can it really have been half a century ago?) to show off the wealth of Victorian industrial enterprise – the Russians were in residence. The Imperial Circus boasted five acrobatic bears, fifty horses and a particularly intelligent elephant which won the hearts of the audience. And, best of all, it was the panto-mime season. At the London Hippodrome, Miss Amy Farrell was starring in *Cinderella* ('seats from one shilling'), while music-hall legend Dan Leno was on stage at the Theatre Royal Drury Lane in a strange seasonal concoction called *Sleeping Beauty and the Beast*. There was more demanding fare at His Majesty's Theatre, where the ever dramatic H. Beerbohm Tree (so famous that he was billed simply as 'Mr Tree' – it was enough) was a heroic Herod, though to see Henry Irving and Ellen Terry would mean taking a trip out of town – they had decamped to Brighton and were doing *The Merchant of Venice* by the sea.

For those happy to stay at home for their culture, there was a new book in the shops from Count Tolstoy to be snapped up (*Resurrection*) but a disappointment for fans of Sherlock Holmes awaiting another adventure. His creator, Arthur Conan Doyle, was so busy chronicling the facts of the Boer War that he had put his fiction-writing on hold. Shortly before Christmas he had put an advertisement in the personal column on the front page of *The Times* asking officers fighting in the war to send him letters and papers about their experiences. That would keep him busy.

The war was still the prevailing topic of discussion – was the War Office's military strategy too reliant on infantry? why were they underusing the cavalry? Details of skirmishes and troop movements filled the newspapers. Lord Roberts, a tiny man of immense stature in the land, was returning from South Africa, his journey by ship monitored port by port by enthusiastic readers of the newspapers as if he was on a royal progress. The Boers had been pressed back; he had left Kitchener to complete the job and was coming home to assume the exalted position of Commander-in-Chief of the British Army. A triumphal procession through the streets of the capital was planned, and seats on balconies or in windows with a good view were already selling out along the route. But the casualty lists were still alarmingly long, and 1 January began with a report of a marauding band of five hundred Boers derailing a British supply train and making off with five wagonloads of provisions. If this was victory, it was still remarkably similar to the disasters that had gone before.

But, that aside, there was plenty of reason to feel confident and content. True, the Bishop of London was in extremely bad health and not expected to last long, and over in America President McKinley had a cold – perhaps the same one that was making the nose of the Kaiser run in Berlin. But the Queen was taking her daily carriage rides. The court circular said so. All must be well with the world.

*The Times*, counting 1900 as the last year of the nineteenth century, welcomed in 1901 as the true start of the twentieth. It glowed with grandiloquence and confidence. If there was to be a new wave out there, Britannia would surely rule it.

The twentieth century has dawned upon us, and as we float past this great landmark on the shores of time, feelings of awe and wonder creep over us. What will be the history of mankind in the hundred years whose first hours are even now gliding by? What will be the changes the new century will witness? Will the last generation of the twentieth century differ very much from the first? We have a reasonable trust that England and her sons will emerge triumphant at the end of the twentieth century as at the end of the nineteenth, and that then and for ages to come they will live and prosper one united and Imperial people, to be a bulwark for the 'cause of men'.

It ended with a tribute to 'the august and venerable Lady who from the very first day of her reign has made herself one with the joys and sorrows of all, and to the very last day of her life will reign revered, beloved and supreme in all our hearts'.

The 'august and venerable Lady' herself was putting on a brave face. When his ship arrived back in British waters and anchored off Cowes, Lord Roberts's first call was on his sovereign at Osborne on the second day of the new year. But she was so late getting up and so behind for the rest of the day that she was almost late for him, getting back from her afternoon drive only just in time to receive him in her drawing room. It was a heartfelt moment. She shook his hand, and he trembled with emotion when she conferred on him the Order of the Garter. He was so thrilled with the honour that he forgot himself and slapped the Duke of Connaught, a prince of the blood royal, on the back. Roberts and the Queen talked of Christle and how his death had taken them both by surprise. 'We deeply deplored the loss of so many valuable lives,' she noted in her journal after Roberts had gone.

Death was on her mind, and became a topic of conversation. How had Christle faced it? She wanted to know. His sister Princess Thora had discovered details of his last days in hospital in Pretoria and how he had asked for and received the comforts of the Church as he lay dying. The Queen, a religious believer but with a less than charitable view of the ecclesiastical hier-archy, was sceptical. 'I wonder whether he really wanted to receive the holy communion,' she asked, 'or whether they got him to have the service.' Knowing her brother, the Prin-cess had no doubt that his wish would have been to take

Communion. But the Queen, always alert for what she called 'over-churchiness', was not satisfied. The idea of anyone's last moments being hijacked by the clergy with wine and wafers obviously needled her. 'Well, I don't feel at all sure that I should wish for it just then,' she told her granddaughter. But she did not want to rule out all spiritual assistance into the next world, for she added, 'But I should certainly like to have prayers.' She had taken to finding comfort in religious books. 'I did so hate them when I was young,' she confessed. 'Now it is different. I feel I want and like something of the kind.'[2]

She took her spiritual nourishment, but could not stomach other forms of sustenance. Food was a constant problem for her now, so that even a small snack was important enough to be mentioned in her diary. She had grown fond of the Benger's: it was 'very soothing and nourishing'. But little else seemed to relax her or lift the gloomy moods she sank into – when she wasn't asleep, that is. She wanted her doctor beside her much of the time, which made Sir James's wife, Susan, more than a little peeved. As a former lady-in-waiting, she was no stranger to the Queen's demanding nature, but she confided to her sister-in-law Mary how tiresome it was that she barely saw her husband. He was supposed to be having a week off from work, taking his ease at their cottage in the grounds at Osborne, but he had managed to be home for dinner only twice. He spent most of his nights in his room in Osborne House, close at hand and constantly on call. As Susan explained, 'She can hardly bear Jamie out of her sight! . . . She does depend on him entirely.'

What vexed Sir James, however, was not the hours he had to spend with his patient but that too many of those around her seemed sure that all the Queen needed to buck her up was a holiday. It had been the Prince of Wales's view and the Prime Minister's. The family felt the same. So did Harriet

Phipps, the Queen's influential lady secretary and, apart from her daughters, her closest companion. Get her away from cold and foggy England, they all argued; park her in the sun on the Riviera and let her recover her strength.

Reid was in two minds about his patient's condition. Sometimes he thought she was getting better, and he wrote to Marie Mallet in optimistic mood. 'Just a line to tell you that the Queen is now much better. She has continued to improve ever since she consented to be treated as an invalid, and she now causes me no present anxiety.' That was on 4 January. A little over a week later he was describing her as 'rather childish and apathetic'. But on one thing his opinion never changed: it was useless to talk about taking her abroad. The strain of the journey alone would kill her. Why couldn't those who loved her so much see this? And why would they not leave her alone? He wanted complete rest for the Queen, but family and courtiers continued to wait on her, vying with each other to attract her attention and 'overtiring her by too much talking', as his wife put it. None of it was going to make her better.

But the business of the court and the Government had to go on. There was much discussion about what sort of honour should be given to officers who served with distinction against the Boers. The Queen was consulted about establishing a new 'African Order', but she felt there were far too many orders already. Or should they make a special extension to the Order of the Bath and St Michael and St George for the six thousand men who would be eligible? It was all so trying in her condition. On 10 January she received 'a good telegram' from Lord Kitchener, and thought well enough of it to mention it in her journal. It was the last entry she ever made about matters of monarchy – all those issues of state that had filled her thoughts and the pages of her journal for more than sixty years.

The few remaining entries would be about family affairs. On 12 January she woke after a good night and even managed some breakfast. In the afternoon, she went out in the carriage for an hour, despite the fog, and ate again on her return. 'Afterwards little Leopold played charmingly on the violin, Beatrice [his mother] accompanying him, and then she and Minnie Cochrane played some very nice duets. Took a *lait de poule*, then signed and dictated to Lenchen [the family's nickname for Princess Helena]. Harriet read to me after my supper, and Lenchen and Beatrice came up afterwards.'

The next day was a Sunday:

Had a fair night, but was a little wakeful. Got up earlier and had some milk. Lenchen came and read some papers. Out before one, in the garden chair, Lenchen and Beatrice going with me. Rested a little, had some food, and took a short drive with Lenchen and Beatrice. Rested when I came in, and at five-thirty went down to the drawing room, where a short service was held by Mr Clement Smith [vicar of Whippingham, the local parish for Osborne], who performed it so well, and it was a great comfort to me. Rested again afterwards, then did some signing, and dictated to Lenchen.

The book was closed. Her last word had been written.

For the second time in a fortnight, Lord Roberts came to see her, on 14 January. She sat in the bay window in the sumptuous drawing room to receive him, perched on her favourite chair – simple, straight-backed, its gold upholstered seat surprisingly faded. To her side were ranged stark white statues of her children when small, notably a life-sized Beatrice at the age of one, sitting serenely in a conch shell. Behind her sat the real Beatrice, forty-two years on and now a mother herself, her face full of concern that the Queen should not overexert herself. The Princess and her sister had dreaded the effect of Lord Roberts's visit on their mother, and had hatched a plot to cut it short. After fifteen minutes – twenty at the most – someone would come in and interrupt and bring it to an end. As the Field Marshal waited in the billiard room outside, Beatrice told her mother of the plan, only to be slapped down imperiously. 'You shall do nothing of the kind,' the Queen ordered. 'I have a great deal to say to Lord Roberts and a great deal to hear from him and I won't be interrupted.'[3]

It was a flash of the old Queen – the one who would not be crossed, who terrified their brother, the Prince of Wales, so much that, as a grown man, if he was late for dinner he would skulk behind a pillar, wiping the nervous sweat from his face while plucking up the courage to go in and face her cold stare. She had had her way then, and she would have it now. A footman pushed aside the heavy curtain that cut off the billiard room from the drawing room and summoned in the Commander-in-Chief. He bowed before her; she acknowledged his greeting and motioned him to a chair. They talked until they had both had their say, and she was alert and animated to the end.

But those who saw Lord Roberts come and go were a little mystified by his behaviour. According to newspaper reports, he had travelled down from London almost incognito, in civilian clothes, not his field marshal's uniform, and there was a marked absence of the subalterns and staff officers who would normally buzz around a military mogul on the move. And when he left Osborne he was visibly shaken, almost moved to tears. On his return to the War Office he cancelled all his public engagements for the foreseeable future. Was the war going that badly? Or had he sensed something during his audience with the Queen that deeply disturbed him? As he sat opposite the obviously frail old lady, perhaps he realized the truth: that this was the last official engagement the woman who had been Queen of England for sixty-three years would ever perform.

The Queen's world was rapidly diminishing. She had sat in the drawing room and the council room of Osborne for the last time. Her life was now squeezed into her familiar, comfortable bedroom. It was not a grand chamber, as her millions of subjects around the world might have supposed. Her empire was so large that its furthest part took many months to reach, but here, at its heart, barely a dozen paces would take you from door to windows and the space between was further limited by an obstacle course of chairs and occasional tables. The chaises longues – there were two of them – were covered in a pretty floral design, the same as the curtains and the heavy tasselled canopy that towered over the bed. The carpet was brown and rustically patterned. A set of shining mahogany wardrobes cleverly disguised the way to the unmentionable terrain of her private bathroom. To Victoria, this bedroom had always felt snug and cosy – *gemütlich* was the word – as it should be in any good German home. Just as Albert had wanted it.

It was as if she was shutting down, but so slowly that those who were with her all the time could hardly notice the difference. To occasional visitors, however, the change in her when they saw her was a shock. A fortnight between visits had been enough for Lord Roberts to tell. Dr Pagenstecher, the German eye specialist, came after a much longer interval and spotted a little deterioration in her sight but a much greater collapse in her overall health. He told Reid, who took it as confirmation of the fear he had kept to himself for weeks: that her mind was going. 'Cerebral degeneration' he called it, and it resulted in apathy and lack of concentration. She wandered; she didn't care. Many things that once irritated her now went unremarked. Her dressers, the maids who were her most intimate servants, noticed that when she woke from sleep it took a while before she realized where she was, perhaps even who she was.

Reid could now judge this for himself, because for the first time he was allowed to see his sovereign in her bed. Previously such an intrusion had been expressly forbidden, and he had always examined her, bolt upright, in her sitting room. But on the morning of 16 January she would not, could not, wake up properly and, anxious about her, he insisted on being taken into her bedroom. The dressers must have been shocked, but they agreed. She was so drowsy, anyway, that there was little chance of her noticing that an unbreakable rule had been broken. He stared at the large mahogany bed. Seven foot long and six foot wide, it dwarfed its tiny occupant, who 'was lying on her right side huddled up. I was struck by how small she appeared.'

She looked well enough, and her breathing was quiet and normal, he thought, but she could not be roused out of her sleep. He left her lying there while he sought out her assistant private secretary, Fritz Ponsonby, in his study. He told him the Queen was now too ill to be troubled with telegrams, even those addressed directly to her. Would Ponsonby intercept them, please? This was easier said than done. The telegraph clerks had been personally commanded to take all communications directly to her and to no one else. They would have to be told to ignore that command and pass everything through him. Ponsonby agreed, though reluctantly. He had had a similar request from Reid when the Queen was ill once before. It had landed him in a difficult conversation with the chief telegraph clerk, who was unhappy at having a specific royal order countermanded by anyone other than the Queen herself. Ponsonby had got the man's cooperation only by giving him the instruction in writing. And then the Queen had recovered the next day, so the whole exercise had been pointless and embarrassing. Was this another false alarm? Ponsonby wearily went through the procedure all over again with the telegraph clerks, but 'I did not think it serious.'

It was well into the evening before the Queen was awake enough to be eased out of bed, into her wheelchair, and taken through to her sitting room. For dignity's sake, a dress was loosely draped around her. There was some colour in her cheeks, which was a good sign, but she was dazed and confused, and her speech was indistinct. Reid sought a second opinion and asked Sir Francis Laking to examine her. Laking spent forty-five minutes with her and, to Reid's amazement, came away saying she was fine. She had chatted away to him about a great many topics 'and was quite herself'. Reid must have been annoyed. His diagnosis was being challenged yet again, and he found himself arguing with Laking. The Queen, he told the doctor he was increasingly viewing as a competitor rather than a colleague, always put on a special effort for those people she did not know very well. 'I told him it was only an instance of how wonderfully she could pull herself together when she saw anyone but her maids or me, and that I should not wonder if she were quite confused again after he had left.'

Reid was absolutely right. Ten minutes later he was called in to see the Queen again, and she was as exhausted and as confused as ever. But Laking had gone, missing the relapse, confident in his diagnosis. Being first and foremost the Prince of Wales's doctor, there could be little doubt that he would pass on the wrong message – the one the Prince wanted to hear: that the Queen was nowhere near as bad as Reid was making out. All Reid's efforts to press home the seriousness of her condition were being thwarted. He went back to his

room and wrote to the Prince of Wales to tell him directly
how ill his mother was. He also sent a telegram to the heart
specialist Sir Douglas Powell, warning him that he should
prepare to drop everything he was doing and come to Osborne
at a moment's notice.

The next morning, 17 January, Reid slipped into the
Queen's bedroom early, examined her briefly, and was more
concerned than ever. One side of her face was slightly flat-
tened, and she was more drowsy and more confused than the
day before. These were indications of a stroke. He concluded
that she was on the edge of slipping into a coma, and that
meant only one thing – the Queen was actually dying. 'I did
not at all like her condition and thought she might die within
a few days,' he noted with almost clinical understatement. It
was a momentous conclusion. He had always known the time
would come. Now it was upon him, and there was much to
do. As the Queen lay in bed, drifting in and out of conscious-
ness, Reid took his anxious news to Princess Beatrice and
Princess Helena and, with their permission, wired Powell to
come at once.

Reid realized the significance of the event that was about
to happen. He felt the weight of duty resting on him. She was
his patient and he had to think of her welfare, but she was the
Queen and Empress too. Her people had a right to know that
she was ill and would not survive for long. 'Being so anxious
to prepare the public for what I feared was coming, and also
thinking that her condition was too serious for it to be kept
longer from the public, I thought a statement ought to be
made in the Court Circular.'

The circular was the announcement of events at court that
was issued to the newspapers every day. For the sixty-three
years of her reign, it had been the official noticeboard through
which the Queen kept her subjects informed of what she was

doing. It recorded all the comings and goings – from the distinguished visitors such as Lord Salisbury, down even to which equerry had left and who had replaced him. She took a personal interest in the information that was published in her name, often scrawling out the details herself. One of Fritz Ponsonby's duties was to make a fair copy – in large script and as black as he could manage, of course – for her to see before it was telegraphed to London and on around the world. Since the beginning of January the circulars had generally been terse. The quick visit of the Right Hon. Joseph Chamberlain, Secretary of State for the Colonies, had been listed; he was in and out the same day. So had been the arrival of the Hon. Miss Phipps and the departure of the Hon. Sylvia Edwardes. And Lord Roberts's first visit had stretched out the circular to a dozen paragraphs or more. But on most days it was now limited to one sentence and one reassuring message: 'The Queen drove out yesterday accompanied by . . .' It was the truth, more or less, but it was not the whole truth. Her subjects were being led to think that all was normal at Osborne.

There was chatter in the social pages of the papers, but none of it had enough import to disturb the official line. On 14 January the 'Society Days' column in the *Daily Express* had mentioned in passing that the Queen's health was 'not entirely satisfactory', but this was contradicted four days later with an altogether sunnier outlook. 'So genial has been the weather in the Isle of Wight that the Queen has been seen driving through High Street, Newport in an open carriage,' the paper reported. 'So bright was the sunshine that her Majesty, who looked in excellent health, carried an open sunshade.'

The weather had indeed lifted briefly, the wind had dropped and the rain stopped. That was miraculous enough in January. But had there been another miracle too, bringing the ailing Queen back to rude health? The truth was that there had been a carriage ride to Newport, but it had been ten days earlier, and if those who glimpsed her thought she looked healthy then it can only have been because her daughters had animated her, leaning over to rustle her petticoats and coughing loudly to keep her awake. The court circulars continued to tell of carriage drives and nothing else. On 16 January the announcement was that 'The Queen drove out yesterday afternoon accompanied by Her Imperial and Royal Highness the Duchess of Saxe-Coburg and Gotha.' It was correct only in the sense that the Queen had been placed in her carriage alongside poor Affie's widow, Marie. They sat in the porch waiting for the rain to stop and the fog to clear, but when there was no break in the cloud the Queen was carried back to her bedroom, and never emerged again.

The fiction that she was perfectly healthy was welcomed by those who controlled the lines of communication in Osborne and in London. The well-connected Lady Frances Balfour, with relatives in the Cabinet and in the royal family, knew what was going on – 'a heavy cloud was darkening the sky – the Queen was failing'. But 'all the news published from her court was calculated to cheer her people'. In this climate, Reid's intention to let the cat out of the bag was not seen as helpful. With the Queen's private secretary, Sir Arthur Bigge, he drew up a bulletin detailing the seriousness of her condition, and Bigge telephoned the Prince of Wales at Marlborough House, his home off The Mall in London, for approval. The word came back: His Royal Highness wished no statement whatever to be made. The next day the circular carried news of a dinner attended by the Prince of Wales in honour of Lord Roberts at the Hotel Metropole. But there was no mention at all of the Queen. This did not go unnoticed. Lord Esher, for one, spotted the omission and noted that rumours about the Queen's health were 'very persistent'.

It is a puzzle precisely why the Prince of Wales dithered. He appears not to have trusted Reid's diagnosis, and his distrust would have been reinforced by talking to Laking, his own medical man on the spot. Perhaps he was just being cautious, not wanting to jump too quickly to Reid's conclusion. Perhaps too he was mindful of an overeager heir many centuries ago. Shakespeare portrayed Henry V trying on the crown for size before his father had expired. This Prince of Wales would not want to be seen as anticipating his mother's death. Or did he just find it impossible to make the decision? This was a matter of importance to the country, the Empire, the whole world. It was the sort of issue his mother always dealt with; but on this occasion she was the one person who could not be consulted. And what if he sounded the alarm and the fire did not happen? If she was not at death's door, he would have to face her wrath when she recovered.

In her lucid moments, the Queen was also worrying about who knew she was ill. She asked her daughters whether the fact that she had not been out for days was causing alarm among the Household and the servants – were people 'beginning to be frightened'? Princess Helena assured her that the weather was so awful that no one could possibly be surprised that she was confined indoors. The explanation did not satisfy her. She always went out in the rain, she retorted, and everyone knew it! To Mrs Tuck, her principal dresser, she confided her fears about Reid's health rather than her own. She was worried that he might be overworked. Mrs Tuck delivered the message that he was to look after himself and not become ill, because, as the Queen had told her, 'he is the only one that understands me'.

That night Sir Douglas Powell arrived and, having barely had time to find his room and put down his bags, was ushered in to see the Queen. There had been concern that his unexpected presence might alarm her, but she hardly seemed to notice. Nor did she make any effort to pull herself together, which is what she had always done before when someone she knew only slightly came into her presence. He asked her questions. Her replies were indistinct. Outside the room, Powell agreed with Reid's diagnosis of cerebral degeneration, though his prognosis was slightly more optimistic than his colleague's. He thought her condition was 'precarious but not hopeless'. By now, Fritz Ponsonby had concluded that this was no false alarm. Things were beginning to look bad. A true courtier, he took comfort in maintaining secrecy: 'Still, no one outside knew anything, and we all hoped it would pass off.'

Throughout the next day the Queen lay in bed. Reid noticed that the left side of her face was beginning to droop. She was very weak and showing no signs that she might rally. The doctor decided once again that he should not have to smother the news, that it was high time the truth found its way to the outside world. But the route he chose was an odd one, and would have an important bearing on the story that was about to unfold.

Some years ago, Reid had struck up a relationship with the Queen's grandson, the Kaiser. It had begun in 1889, when the young German King arrived for the Cowes Regatta, at the end of which Reid was presented with a diamond and pearl scarf pin to thank him for his friendliness and affability. They came to an agreement. The Kaiser was not always well loved by his English relations and he feared that he might be the last to be told if the grandmother he adored was ever dangerously ill. He asked Reid to be his informant. If the Queen died suddenly or was terminally ill, the doctor agreed he would quietly let him know.

On the afternoon of Friday 18 January, Reid cycled to the telegraph office in Cowes and sent his urgent message.

'Disquieting symptoms have developed which cause consider-able anxiety. This is private. Reid.' He did not seek permission, nor did he tell anyone. He knew that Princess Helena and Princess Beatrice did not want their bombastic and pompous nephew anywhere near the Isle of Wight – at this time or any other. They would not be pleased to know that he had been tipped off, and certainly not by the doctor, whom they all considered to be their confidant.

In fact Reid was not the first to break the news to the Kaiser. The German envoy in London, Baron Hermann von Eckardstein, had heard the gossip in the most English of places – his club. He was an expert snooper in high places, and had picked up rumours that the Queen was unwell from the very beginning of the year. He had even taken a few days' holiday in the Isle of Wight and had called in at Osborne to make discreet inquiries among his friends there. Reid, keeping his counsel to himself, had assured him there was no need for alarm. But the Baron was not deterred. He had been staying at Chatsworth, where Joseph Chamberlain, a recent visitor to Osborne, was another house guest, and on his return to London on the night of 17 January he ran into an old court official at his club. 'He told me in confidence that the end might be expected at any moment, and as I knew him to be a most reliable authority, I immediately telegraphed to Berlin so that the news reached the Kaiser the following morning.'[4]

The club where the Baron was given this inside information was the Marlborough, in Pall Mall – which was ironic, because the club's president was the Prince of Wales. (He had set up the Marlborough himself after being asked to put out his cigar at White's in St James's; he had taken offence and stalked out.) Fellow club members may have been facing up to the reality of the Queen's death, but the Prince was still clinging to his belief that his mother was not in danger. He was aided and abetted by Laking. The doctor, who had finally left Osborne, much to Reid's relief, and joined his master in London, sent a telegram to Reid: 'Everything considered quite satisfactory.' Reid confessed to being surprised, but he must have been furious at the lack of comprehension. It was Friday, and the Prince was so relaxed about his mother's condition that he was planning to go off to Sandringham for the weekend, in entirely the opposite direction from Osborne.

That night Reid sat beside the Queen in her sitting room as clean sheets were put on her bed next door. Was the Prince of Wales 'in the house', she asked. No, said Reid, but he could come if she wanted to see him. 'I do not advise it at present,' she replied. But the matter would soon be out of her hands.

# 4. The News Breaks

We all utter this morning the dear and familiar words, God Save The Queen!

The *Daily Telegraph*

Dr Reid had stopped the supply of telegrams to the Queen's sickbed, but he could do nothing to prevent them chattering into the telegraph office at Osborne, urgent and inquiring. They came from newspapers and from people who had heard rumours. How was Her Majesty? Were the stories of her ill health really true? Please advise. Please explain. An inquisitive world, a modern world, wanted to know, and it had a means of instant access.

The telegraph had been an early invention of Victoria's reign, and one of its most important. It brought the world and the Empire together in an instant. Even a traditionalist like the Prime Minister, Lord Salisbury, in every sense a deep conservative with a belief in what was increasingly being seen as an old-fashioned way of life, put aside his instincts when it came to the telegraph. He was fascinated: 'it has assembled all mankind upon one great plane, where they can see everything that is done and hear everything that is said, and judge of every policy that is pursued at the very moment these events take place'. Now the world was becoming aware of just one event.

Arthur Bigge, the Queen's secretary, bore the brunt. He picked up a more recent invention (and one still comparatively rare, particularly outside London) and telephoned Marl-borough House. The Prince of Wales should know that alarming reports were in circulation. He was overwhelmed with inquiries about the Queen's health. Surely it was time to make some sort of official statement? At last the Prince agreed, though the statement was not to be alarmist. Even a mention of Sir Douglas Powell being summoned to Osborne was considered inflammatory and therefore omitted. On the night of 18 January the first bulletin indicating that the Queen was not well issued from Osborne. It read:

The Queen has not lately been in her usual health and is unable for the present to take her customary drives. The Queen during the past year has had a great strain upon her powers, which has rather told upon her Majesty's nervous system. It has therefore been thought advisable by her Majesty's physicians that the Queen should be kept perfectly quiet in the house and should abstain for the present from transacting business.

The statement was bland in tone: the Queen was not going out; she was confined to the house and not doing any work for the time being. Nonetheless it was front-page news for one morning paper on Saturday 19 January – but only one. The *Daily Express* had been founded just nine months earlier, in April 1900, by the publisher Arthur Pearson deliberately to win a slice of the *Daily Mail*'s lower-middle-class readership, now on its way to a million. Its unique selling point was a front page of headlines and news stories instead of the lucrative columns of paid-for advertising that all other papers still preferred to have underneath the masthead.

The *Express* was cool about the news from the Isle of Wight. The fighting in South Africa was still the principal story of the day – 'British successes: Boers defeated: De Wet's new raid:

Gallant defence of a Cape force'. The casualties in Colonel Grey's advance at Ventersburg had been 'slight' – one man badly wounded – against four Boer dead, one prisoner taken, and rifles, bandoliers and saddles captured. Meanwhile Lord Methuen was driving off the enemy in the mountains near Taungs, though two of his men had been killed in the process. In Amsterdam the war was sliding into farce. In temperatures below zero, a local group of actors and skaters was presenting a colourful dramatic tableau on a frozen canal – Lord Roberts, President Kruger and Joseph Chamberlain on ice! Aghast British visitors were in the audience for this pantomime. Fortunately, a thaw was on the way.

There was other foreign news at the top of the page. Mascagni's new opera, *Le Maschere*, had opened in Italy and been hissed; the general opinion was that it was awful, his worst work ever. The German Kaiser had had a busy day in Berlin, where celebrations were in full swing to mark the two-hundredth anniversary of the kingdom of Prussia. He had led six hundred 'princes and notable personages' in a service of thanksgiving, entering the church 'to the sound of drums and trumpets, the Empress on his arm and holding by the right hand her little daughter, prettily dressed in pink'. Later there had been a banquet for twelve hundred guests and a gala performance at the opera. 'Tonight,' the *Express* told its readers, 'Berlin is illuminated, no window being without a light of some sort.'

The darkness at Osborne was confined to the last column – 'The Queen's Health: Official statement as to a nervous breakdown'. The news was 'unwelcome and disquieting', the paper said, but then it turned to a much more optimistic note. There had, it said, been improvement in her condition last night. On the Isle of Wight, those close to the royal family had been spinning a positive story to the pressmen who had rushed to Cowes and were beginning to mass at the gates of Osborne. The *Express* was reassuring: 'Happily we have it on the best authority from Osborne itself that there is no cause for alarm.' Certainly the Queen had shown signs of weakness and had been suffering from insomnia – 'but not to an alarming extent':

Her millions of loving subjects throughout the Empire will learn with heartfelt relief that there is nothing in her Majesty's condition to cause disquietude, or that a few days of complete rest cannot remedy. Perhaps the best evidence that the grave anxiety which was aroused by the reports of her Majesty's health yesterday is groundless, except so far as the natural solicitude of her people is concerned, lies in the fact that the Duke of York left London for Sandringham yesterday afternoon and that the Prince of Wales will follow him thither today, leaving St Pancras by the 2.35 train.

The *Daily Mail* also felt sure enough of its sources close to events at Osborne to carry a similar upbeat message. Indeed, it went a step further, taking its readers inside the mind of the Queen herself to reassure them that 'her Majesty is cheerful and feels no alarm'. The *Globe* was confident: 'there is nothing to occasion surprise and still less to call for apprehension. A lady who is over four score years may well begin to feel the weight of years. She is in skilful hands and we may fairly anticipate she will be restored to her usual health.' The *Daily Graphic* was sanguine too. 'Happily there does not seem to be any ground for serious anxiety. We do not doubt that under the advice of her physicians her wonderful physical powers will soon assert themselves again and that we shall be able to announce that she has resumed the transaction of state business to which she is so attached.'

But *The Times* found this matter of 'business' disturbing.

The Queen had a reputation for being the hardest-working woman in the world, and

rare indeed have been the occasions throughout her long reign when her Majesty has failed to transact the daily business which presses so heavily and inevitably upon the wearer of the imperial crown of Great Britain. We note that it is only since Tuesday that she has intermitted her drives, and that on Monday she gave an audience to Lord Roberts. We trust that her physicians have insisted betimes on perfect quiet, and we must find consolation in the words 'for the present' in their communication about the transaction of business.

But consolation fell short of outright confidence that everything would be fine.

The *St James's Gazette*, whose main constituency was the politicians and clubmen of central London, urged the Queen to be a good patient and 'to observe the spirit as well as the letter of the doctor's orders'. It suggested an acceleration of her holiday plans – she should be off to the 'sunny shores of the Mediterranean' as soon as possible. The sense that all would be well was overlaid with pride. Even in her illness, Victoria was the centre of the world:

As we try to convince ourselves there is no real ground for grave apprehension, it may be safely asserted that no illness of any individual human being has ever called forth such widespread sympathy and concern as will this indisposition of Queen Victoria. There has probably never before been a human being whose very name was known to so large a portion of the human race. There is not a corner of the habitable globe where the Queen of England has never been heard of, and among the countless millions to whom she is something more than a mere name, it is certain that she does not possess a single personal enemy.

The commanding influence which the Queen exercises throughout Europe is based on the profound respect which is felt for her
character, her unrivalled experience and her proved statesmanship.
It will be long before the public of Europe will realize the extent to
which Queen Victoria has swayed the destinies of the world, and
always in the direction of the maintenance of peace. There is not a
court or a chancellery in Europe that will not be profoundly moved
by the news that the Queen's health gives cause for disquietude. It
is needless to say what her life means to the subjects of her own
empire in every continent. However they may differ among themselves on every subject of human interest under the sun, they will
be firmly united in earnest prayer to Almighty God that our beloved
sovereign may quickly be restored to health and strength.

   This was echoed in the *Daily Telegraph*, but with the Empire
rather than Europe in mind:

From India and Australia and Canada and South Africa, as well as
from every town and village in our country, will come the earnest
prayer that the Queen may gain all benefit from her enforced rest,
and that with restored health she may be spared to reign for a further
span of fruitful years over the Empire which venerates her name.
Not with merely conventional heartiness but because it touches a
profound note in English hearts, shall we all utter this morning the
dear and familiar words, God Save The Queen!

Or, as the *Sun* (then a London evening newspaper, but one
which shouted its popular wares on its masthead, proclaiming
itself 'an independent, up-to-date newspaper for up-to-date
people') put it in a simple, bold, three-word headline, 'God
Bless Her.'
   Amid all this patriotic optimism, a few papers sensed the
reality. The *Star* thought it 'hardly possible to exaggerate the

gravity of the melancholy news'. There were enough straws
in the wind for alert royal-watchers to catch and build bricks.
It was the fact that she had not been out driving that led the
*Daily News* to fear the worst. 'As all her Majesty's subjects
know, her love of fresh air has taken her out of doors in the
most inclement weather. It cannot be doubted that the health
of her Majesty is precarious.' The paper found this difficult to
grasp. 'It seems almost impossible to believe that she should
be ill. No form of weakness has ever been associated with her.
She seems to be exempt from sickness and decay. The situation
is therefore strange to the present race of Englishmen. They
had almost come to regard the Queen as immortal and as
beyond the reach of disease.'

But mortal she was. That Saturday morning, as papers were
being read in homes and on street corners and the news passed
from mouth to mouth, the Queen's illness had already passed
from concern to crisis.

The nineteenth of January was a milestone. The Queen was
81 years and 240 days old, and that made her the oldest
monarch ever to sit on the throne of Britain. She had beaten
the record of her grandfather, George III, and had now not
only reigned longer but lived longer than any of her predecessors. But when she woke that morning she was insensible
to the fact, or to anything at all. She ate the food that was
spooned into her mouth, accepting it automatically, like a
child, apparently without realizing she was doing so. Sir James
Reid had seen her through a reasonable night, but he thought
her weak in the morning. Her mind was wandering, and he
was very worried about her.

Others saw things differently. Princess Helena considered
her mother much better – after all, she had slept well and
taken food. The Princess, who was doing her family duty and

keeping her brother the Prince of Wales informed, scrawled out a telegram saying she felt much happier about their mother's condition. Reid was appalled at this conclusion and how the Princess had ignored all the signs that he knew meant quite the opposite.

Reid hurried downstairs from the Queen's bedroom and went to see Sir Arthur Bigge, who was on the phone to Marlborough House again and updating the Prince of Wales's private secretary, Sir Francis Knollys, on the Queen's condition. Was it going to be all right for the Prince and his entourage to continue with their plan to go to Sandringham for a weekend of shooting? The train was waiting for them, and all they needed was the all-clear from Osborne. As Reid walked in, Bigge asked the doctor for his considered opinion. Reid was unambiguous. 'Tell the Prince of Wales that he ought not to go to Sandringham but to remain in London ready to come here at a moment's notice.' His examination of his monarch that morning had left him in no doubt: 'I consider the Queen's condition is a most serious one. I think it quite possible she might be dead within a few days.'

Bigge passed on the message, but then found himself bemused when Princess Helena's telegram to her brother dropped on his desk for him to put into cipher before it was sent. He could not possibly give the Prince of Wales both these opinions. They flatly contradicted each other. Marlborough House would be left in a state of total confusion. Bigge went to find the Princess to try to sort the matter out. She was furious and demanded to see Reid. What did he mean by taking a view on her mother's health and making a recommendation to her brother that was so different from hers?

The doctor stood his ground against this onslaught. He had been asked for his opinion, he insisted, and he had given it truthfully. Reid knew the Princess did not want the Prince of

Wales to come to Osborne; she had been telling him this for days. The meanest explanation for her attitude would be some family jealousy, but a more charitable reason is that she feared the presence of Bertie would cause her mother too much alarm and anguish. Probably, like Reid, she had been told by the Queen in a moment of lucidity that there was no need for the Prince to come. She may have been mindful too of an incident many years before, when the Queen had been ill with an abscess on her arm that would not respond to treatment. Her doctor was so alarmed he thought she might die, and it was suggested that her children should be sent for – until a wise courtier pointed out that the shock of their turning up unexpectedly at her bedside would certainly kill her.

She had been by her mother's bedside for days now, watching her weaken but desperate that she should not die. She had 'wilfully' shut her eyes to the truth, and opening them to reality was a shock. She was tired and fretful, and she directed all her anger and frustration at Reid. But in the end she calmed down and, recognizing that the doctor knew best, conceded the point. 'Then the Prince had better come,' she told Bigge, and that was the message he duly sent down the wire to Marlborough House.

The grand red-brick mansion with white stone facings, designed by Christopher Wren and tucked away between the gentlemen's clubs of Pall Mall on one side and the grand ceremonial avenue linking Trafalgar Square and Buckingham Palace on the other, had been the Prince of Wales's home for nearly forty years and the centre of his London social life. His louche friends flocked there for dinners, balls and garden parties. They tobogganed on trays down the stairs and played illicit games of baccarat in rooms filled with cigar smoke and an air of decadence. They were untroubled by the fact that the books on the shelves were just spines displayed for effect.

This was a place of 'roaring fun', according to one regular guest. The news from Osborne called a halt to the frivolity.

The Prince's entourage switched plans. Less than a mile away, at Victoria station, a train was ready and orders were given that it would leave at 1.30 p.m. for Gosport. Word was sent to the Princess of Wales, who was already at Sandringham, and she immediately set off for London, leaving behind her eldest son, the Duke of York, who was out shooting when the message arrived and could not be contacted before she left. He would have to make his own plans to come later. In London, the Prince took lunch – he was not a man to miss a meal – before stepping into his carriage with Sir Francis Knollys and his equerry Captain Holford to drive down The Mall.

As they passed Buckingham Palace, it was a chance to glance up and reflect on this gloomy edifice, bought by George III 140 years earlier but unloved by his granddaughter, the Queen, who seldom stayed there. The Prince felt differently about it. The stone at the front was crumbling and the whole façade was in desperate need of a facelift. He had dubbed it The Sepulchre, but perhaps the moment had come when it would become central to the life of the monarchy again.

The horses swung to the left past the gold-trimmed gates, trotted along Victoria Road, and then turned into the station forecourt and on to the platform. The Prince took his seat in the train, and then sat fuming as he waited for his sister Princess Louise, the Duchess of Argyll, who was coming from Kensington Palace. She was anxious to get to Osborne and had telegraphed ahead to Dr Reid to ask if she could be of any help to him when she got there. 'Ready for anything,' she told him. But now she was late – though it was hardly surprising, since it was only forty minutes ago that her brother had sent a message telling her she had to go with him. The fourth of the Queen's five daughters and the only one married to a commoner, albeit one with a grand title and a distinguished ancestry, she was often out of step with royal convention. She was the only childless one of the family, temperamental and capable of causing upset among them. Now she was not averse to trying the patience of the King-in-waiting. For twenty minutes he sat there, until she finally arrived and the train could get up steam and head off across the Thames, out through the London suburbs and down towards the Hampshire coast. It was to be a well-worn route during the next days and weeks.

At Gosport, where they arrived just under two hours later, there was an irritation. Some months before, an Isle of Wight ferry had smashed into a bridge that took the railway track from the town station directly to the harbour. The damage was still not repaired, and so the royal brother and sister were ushered into carriages to be driven down to the royal yacht *Alberta*. A guard of honour from HMS *Majestic*, the flagship of the Channel Squadron, had been drawn up alongside the yacht, but the Prince hurried past it. This was no time for formalities and inspections, not even a salute from the guns of the navy ships as the yacht nosed out into the Solent in the evening light and headed across the grey waters to the island home where his mother lay dying.

Around the Queen's bedroom, all was quiet. Only the few people involved in nursing her dared come near and, in the dark little corridor outside, conversations were hushed. But the rest of Osborne hummed with activity. There were long lists of people to be kept informed, complex arrangements to make. Fritz Ponsonby was busy telephoning and encoding messages for the men in the telegraph office to send. One went to Lord Esher, who had been expected at the house on Monday but was now told not to come, because there would no longer be room for him. Three of the ladies staying in the house had to pack their bags and leave to make room for members of the royal family who were expected to arrive shortly.

Osborne would soon be full to overflowing, and rooms had to be arranged for the various entourages in the other houses and cottages on the estate. The Master of the Queen's Household, sixty-four-year-old Lord Edward Clinton, a veteran of the Crimean War, also had to find food to feed all these unexpected guests. That night there would be a royal dinner for six and a Household meal for fourteen. Major-General Sir John McNeill had the job of making sure that carriages were available to meet the ferries from the mainland and, most important of all, any passengers coming over on the royal yachts. Traffic would flow virtually non-stop up and down the steep hill from the pier to the house. The intricate arrangements the General made were not helped by the constant rain and high winds that made any form of travelling tiresome. This royal death was going to be hard work. 'Busy,' Lord Edward wrote in his diary.

Seven hundred miles away, a man who was already a king was also on the move to the Queen's bedside. The Kaiser's decisiveness put his uncle the Prince of Wales to shame. He had made preparations to rush to his ailing grandmother as soon as he heard she was seriously ill. And it was not just a shooting weekend he had to cancel: it was his nation's birthday party. Berlin had been dressed in finery for a display of patriotic extravagance that bore no relation to reality. It was only thirty years since William I, the Kaiser's grandfather, had united the German principalities under one emperor, but three decades hardly added up to a long and ancient tradition. Deep roots were what bound a nation together, and if they did not exist they would have to be contrived. It was two centuries the

Kaiser and his people were celebrating – the two hundred years since the birth of Prussia. There had been processions and balls, glorious military pageants and services to offer up thanks to almighty God for all things German. There were more extravagances on the agenda. The Kaiser cut them short.

The seriousness of the Queen's illness demanded action, and action was his defining attribute. He liked to be in control. As if to prove the point, he even stood on the footplate for a while and took the controls of the royal train that now sped him across Europe, from Berlin to the North Sea coast to cross to England. It was a typical gesture – the more so since he did it to impress his Uncle Arthur, the Duke of Connaught, who had been in Berlin representing Queen Victoria at the festivities.

The Duke had been telegraphed frequently from Osborne about his mother's condition, and the latest message had urged him to return as soon as possible. He had hoped to catch the next express for Flushing on the Dutch coast. When he told his nephew of his plans, the Kaiser took it as confirmation of the news he had already had from Dr Reid and Baron von Eckardstein and he knew what he had to do. The imperial train was already in steam, and that evening the Kaiser put on the uniform of the Queen of England's Prussian regiment and, with his uncle in the uniform of the Ziethan Hussars, they drove to the Potsdamer station and boarded the train. The German newspapers applauded the Kaiser's 'filial piety'. The London *Times* had nothing but praise as well. His action demonstrated his 'intense personal devotion to his royal grandmother, the august ancestress of so many imperial and royal lines'.

There can be no doubt of the forty-one-year-old German monarch's love for his grandmother. She was 'unparalleled', he told the British ambassador in Berlin, Sir Frank Lascelles, before he set off. But beneath the sincerity of his dash to be at her side lay ambition – for himself and for his country. In his heart, the Kaiser must have seen himself as Victoria's real successor – not, of course, to the throne of England, but to the wider dominion she had created over the years. Through blood ties and marriages, she was the head of a dynasty that dominated Europe, its strands extending not only to Germany but to Russia, Greece, Sweden, Denmark, Norway. The family tree was growing all the time. After her, if there was any natural leadership in the family, surely it resided in him, not his uncle the Prince of Wales, for whom he had scant respect.

How much the Queen loved and admired him in return is a matter of conjecture. His birth had been difficult. His mother, the Queen's eldest daughter, Vicky, had endured a terrible labour before he came into the world upside down. The breech delivery and the deep forceps dislocated his left arm, and it remained withered for the rest of his life. The difficulty of his birth carried into his boyhood. He was self-centred, bad-tempered, demanding. There were tantrums. At the age of six he was staying at Osborne and Prince Albert's private secretary, General Sir Charles Grey, took him down to the beach one day to play with his little daughter, Louisa. She never forgot how spoilt he was when, thwarted in what he wanted to do, he snatched the General's walking stick, threw it into the sea, and then aimed a kick at the furious man. To the courtier's credit, he ignored the boy's royal status, grabbed his leg before it made contact, and toppled him into the sand. The humiliation only added to the boy's unpleasantness. Louisa, who later became the Countess of Antrim and was one of the Queen's ladies-in-waiting, was also convinced that, as a boy, he was intensely jealous of his Aunt Beatrice, the much loved 'Baby', who was only two years older.

He was brought up in a Germany that was growing to be a force in European politics. His grandfather, William I, with his visionary chancellor Otto von Bismarck as his guide, set about fashioning Germany along militaristic Prussian lines. The boy's own father, Crown Prince Frederick, rejected this 'blood and iron' autocracy, fell out with Bismarck, and aligned himself politically with liberal ideology. The family was split, and the young Willie had to choose his future. He decided to be the inheritor of his stern grandfather's legacy rather than be his father's son. He rejected his parents both politically and personally. An English diplomat at the court considered him 'a hot-tempered intolerant youth' and was shocked by his rudeness to his mother in front of strangers. Queen Victoria, who had welcomed him into the world as her 'darling grandchild', was shocked too, by his self-importance. She could not understand why he always signed himself 'William Prince of Prussia' at the end of his letters to her.

His character was flawed, but was it so surprising? Daisy Cornwallis-West married into minor German royalty and, as Princess of Pless, knew the Kaiser well enough to have some sympathy for him. She saw him as 'a high-spirited sensitive boy who has a ready brain and a quick but not profound intelligence'. The problem was that, as heir to 'one of the greatest positions in the world', he had been the object of flattery and intrigue all his life. It had made him obnoxious. He 'always thought he knew and no one dared to tell him he was sometimes wrong. He hated to be told the truth and seldom, perhaps never, forgave those who insisted on telling him. In his vanity he was not very different from the rest of us, but what is comparatively harmless in private life can be disastrous in great affairs.'[1]

Those 'great affairs' overtook him too soon. In March 1888 the old Emperor died and Frederick took the throne. He was already terminally ill with throat cancer, and ninety-nine days later he too died, leaving Germany to his arrogant twenty-nine-year-old son.

The conflict with his mother, Vicky, was instant. At the very moment that she was kneeling at her husband's bed and watching him close his eyes for the last time, convulse, and fall into a coma from which he never awoke, her son was ordering a regiment of hussars, rifles in their hands, to surround the palace. No one was allowed through the cordon, in or out. The telegraph office was sealed off. Even the weeping Empress was stopped as she tried to make her way into the garden to cut some roses to lay on her dead husband's body: an army officer stood in her way and forced her back inside. In the name of the new Emperor (but on the orders of Bismarck), desks were searched and rooms were ransacked for any documents that might suggest a plot, a conspiracy. Years later, the Kaiser would explain his actions as 'severe but necessary'. The intention was 'to prevent state or secret documents being conveyed to England by my mother, a possibility of which Bismarck had warned me'.[2] It was not the behaviour expected of him. Queen Victoria had urged him in a telegram to 'help and do all you can for your poor dear mother'. Locking her in and rifling through her personal papers was hardly what she had had in mind.

Mother and son had always been at odds; now they distrusted each other deeply, and the family in England could never forgive the new Kaiser for that. His behaviour as Emperor inspired them to even more loathing. In Vienna, he snubbed his uncle the Prince of Wales over some imagined slight. His arrogance was too much to bear. His grandmother confided to Lord Salisbury that he expected to be treated as 'his imperial majesty' in private with the family as well as in public. She dismissed such pretensions as 'perfect madness'. 'If he has such notions,' she declaimed, 'he better never come here.' He did, though, in 1889, donning the blue uniform and gold braid of an English admiral for the occasion. He was so proud – 'fancy wearing the same uniform as Nelson', he remarked, 'it is enough to make one quite giddy' – and the visit was a surprising pleasure for everyone. But then he came back for another regatta at Cowes in 1895 and offended everyone by his pomposity. The Prince of Wales remembered the occasion for 'the perpetual firing of salutes and other tiresome disturbances'. He objected to the way his nephew had made himself 'boss of Cowes'. In the hearing of English guests, the Kaiser dismissed his uncle as 'an old peacock'.[3]

It was four years before he was invited again, and then the motives were largely political. There was bad blood over South Africa, and the governments of Germany and Britain needed a public demonstration of their friendliness to each other. The Prince of Wales approved the invitation, 'whatever I may think personally about my nephew'. In the event, the Kaiser could not come that summer but he sent his yacht to join the racing – and wasted the goodwill by sending an abusive telegram to the race committee complaining about the way it ran things. Three months later he did come to England, bringing with him 'his odious wife', as Queen Victoria had once described the Empress Dona, staying with the Prince of Wales at Sandringham and seemingly healing the rifts between them. Baron von Eckardstein accompanied them and thought relations between the Kaiser and his uncle were 'of the friendliest character'. 'Not one single incident occurred to mar the complete harmony of the proceedings.'

The Kaiser could be charming, he could be self-effacing, and as he set out for England he promised to be so this time. He wrote to the British ambassador in Berlin that he had told the Prince of Wales he was coming, begging him at the same time that no notice is taken of me as Emperor and that I come as a grandson. I suppose 'the petticoats' who are fencing off poor grandmama from the world – and, I fear, often from me – will kick up a row when they hear of my coming; but I don't care, for what I do is my duty. I leave with Uncle Arthur. Am sorry, very sorry.[4]

He was right about 'the petticoats', the Queen's daughters, Princesses Helena and Beatrice. At Osborne, lunch was about to be served on Saturday when word arrived that the Kaiser was on his way. The princesses were beside themselves. He had to be stopped. They sent an urgent telegram to their brother the Duke of Connaught, in Berlin, urging him to do all he could to prevent the train from rolling.

They were doing their job as their mother's guardians, exactly as she had decreed. She would not have outsiders around her sickbed, and it was their duty to be vigilant on her behalf. A quarter of a century ago she had given her then physician, Sir William Jenner, precise instructions, which he had preserved in a memorandum:

In the case of serious illness, she should only be attended by her own doctors who always attend her, only calling in, after consultation with Princess Beatrice (supposing she was too ill to be herself consulted), any such doctor or surgeon whom her own professional physicians knew the Queen liked, or thought fit to consult, or who was not a total stranger to herself, and not to yield to the pressure of any one of her other children, or any of her ministers, for any one they might wish to name.

The Queen's daughters Princess Helena, Princess Louise and Princess Beatrice are fully aware of her wishes on the subject. She wishes to add (which they likewise know) that she absolutely forbids anyone but her four female attendants to nurse her and take care of her. Princess Beatrice, from living always with the Queen, is the one who is to be applied to for all that is to be done. If it is necessary to send for anyone of the rest of the family, it is on the express understanding that her wishes expressed in this memorandum should be strictly adhered to, and in no way departed from.

So her personal maids – the women who dressed her, not trained medical attendants – were nursing her, and the princesses, along with Lady Ampthill, the Lady of the Bed-chamber, and Harriet Phipps, were on watch constantly. They were anxious that she should not become anxious, and they were in no doubt that the arrival of the Kaiser would be unsettling for her. There were also personal animosities that gave them good reason to want to keep him away, particularly on the part of Princess Beatrice. He had insulted her late husband, Prince Henry of Battenberg, by refusing to acknow-ledge his royal status. Victoria had granted Liko (as he was known in the family) the right to be called His Royal Highness. But this cut no ice at the German court, where the Kaiser ordered that his place in the hierarchy was nothing more than a 'princely grace'. The Emperor even found chapter and verse in an international treaty to deny him his title. Such meanness was not easily forgotten, particularly now, almost five years to the day since Liko's tragic and untimely death from disease in Africa.

Dr Reid bumped into the princesses and felt acutely embar-rassed when they told him that the Kaiser was coming. They were 'most excited', and he was anxious in case they dis-covered that it was all because of him. He had been the spy, furtively contacting the Kaiser to tell him how ill the Queen was. The Kaiser was now rushing to her side. It had to be his fault. 'I had no doubt he was coming on account of my secret telegram to him, which they knew nothing about, and I

thought I might get into a pretty row if it came out.' Reid
kept his thoughts – and his secret – to himself, but what added
to his anxiety was that the Queen's condition had suddenly
seemed to improve.

At midday he and Powell had issued a second bulletin –
one which was to make the world realize that yesterday's
optimism had been misplaced. 'The Queen is suffering from
great physical prostration accompanied by symptoms that
cause anxiety,' it said. They had been at her bedside for most
of the morning, and this was their doom–laden conclusion. It
had a profound effect on the reporters waiting at the gates of
Osborne. The correspondent for *The Times* saw it as a sentence
of death. 'Medical men of this eminence, treating a patient as
illustrious as the Queen, are not wont to overlook things,' he
thought, and he felt 'grave apprehension'.

But then she brightened up in the afternoon. Reid went to
see her again, and she was thinking quite clearly and talking
lucidly. He worried that, if she heard that the Kaiser was
coming, there might be a relapse. It would undoubtedly alarm
her, 'give her the impression that we considered her dying
and help to turn the scale in the wrong direction'.

It occurred to Reid that he could stop the Kaiser in his
tracks. His destination was the Dutch seaport of Flushing.
The doctor would telegraph a message there, telling him not
to take ship to England but to wait for further developments.
Did he really have so much influence that the German
Emperor would halt in full flight on the say-so of a mere
medical man? Well, at the very least Reid could warn him
of the dangers – that, even if he did arrive, it might not be
a good idea for him to see the Queen, or rather for her
to see him. The various options buzzed through his head as
he sought out Sir Arthur Bigge for advice, but as soon as
he spoke to the private secretary he realized it was too late.

The Kaiser's train was on its way and a Royal Navy cruiser, the *Minerva*, had put to sea and was steaming through the Channel and into the North Sea to meet him and bring him to England. Reid 'gave up the idea' and let matters take their course.

Still the Queen seemed to improve. At six o'clock Reid sat with her and they talked. She had some difficulty with her speech, but otherwise she was clear and coherent. She thought she was on the mend. 'I have been very ill,' she told the doctor. 'Am I better?' He reassured her. 'Yes, your Majesty has been very ill but you are now better.' Before the doctor came in, her daughters had been reading her the latest telegrams from South Africa and she wanted to talk about the war. 'There is much better news today,' she said and it must have pleased her, though to Reid it indicated how much the battle with the Boers and the loss of life among her soldiers weighed on her mind. She could not forget it; it was a constant worry for her – as was the Prince of Wales, who, though she did not know it, had arrived at Osborne just an hour ago. She asked Reid if her son was aware that she was ill. 'I think he should be told I have been very ill as I am sure he would feel it,' she told the doctor. Reid confessed that he had kept the Prince informed. 'His Royal Highness does know as I have reported to him all that I think your Majesty would wish me to tell him. He is most concerned and is anxious to come as soon as your Majesty would like to see him. Would your Majesty like him to come now?' 'Certainly,' she replied, 'but he needn't stay.'

Reid left her bedside, firmly of the opinion that she was getting better. 'I became hopeful that she might still pull through after all.' The next day or two would be crucial, but he felt confident enough to issue an optimistic bulletin: 'Osborne, January 19th, 6 p.m. The Queen's strength has been fairly maintained throughout the day, and there are indications of slight improvement in the symptoms this evening.'

This did nothing to improve the humour of the Prince of Wales. He had come from London as a matter of urgency, and now found his mother not at death's door. He talked to his sisters with some annoyance, telling them he thought he had been brought down on false pretences. He even considered he had been made a fool of. The princesses were inclined to agree. They were still reluctant to accept that their mother was seriously ill and close to death. Beatrice in particular showed no signs of being upset and was being so matter-of-fact that those who saw her wondered if she had any idea what was happening. Reid was astonished by her behaviour. At one point in the day she was even out of the house when her mother called from her bed that she wanted to see her.

The Prince's anger was directed at Reid, though he contained himself when he saw the doctor face to face, merely expressing his surprise that Reid had been so adamant that the Queen's condition was serious. Sir Francis Laking and Princess Helena had given him a completely different impression. It cannot have been an easy interview for Reid, and as he stood in front of the Prince he must have felt deeply embarrassed. Not only was his professional advice continually being challenged, he was, in effect, being accused of panicking and wasting the time of the heir to the throne. But, as he had done with Princess Helena earlier that day, Reid stood his ground. He was not alone in the opinion he had expressed about the seriousness of the Queen's condition that morning. He took the Prince to see Sir Douglas Powell, who confirmed everything. The Prince's irritation may not have been totally assuaged, but at least he now knew that Reid had acted only after properly consulting his colleague.

They turned to what should happen next. The Prince agreed that it was better his mother should not be told he was there, and that he certainly should not go in to her bedside. Reid suggested he could, if he wished, at least see her without causing alarm. He could look in on her from the doorway without her knowing.

The discussion turned to the Kaiser. The Prince was totally in agreement with his sisters that their German nephew should be kept away from Osborne. He had a solution that fitted in with his own annoyance at having hurried down to Osborne apparently unnecessarily. He said he would go back to London in the morning to 'intercept' the visitor and make sure he stayed there. He would tell his nephew that nobody was seeing the Queen at the moment, not even the Prince himself. And, so that he could be totally truthful with his nephew, he decided he would not peep surreptitiously round her bedroom door after all.

The Prince had settled on a plan of action that would get him away from Osborne as soon as possible. It was a place he had always hated. It reminded him of lonely days he had spent there as a boy, separated from his friends and family, cooped up with the tutors he loathed, trying to learn, trying to live up to the expectations of his father, but finding both tasks beyond him. Why should he stay? His sister Beatrice, always the closest to their mother, seemed calm about her condition, though Helena was more tearful. Louise's presence was proving tiresome – with her usual tactlessness, she was upsetting her sisters, criticizing them, making mischief – but at least she was there, and the three of them had everything under control. His wife, the Princess of Wales, was also on her way by train from London, and the royal yacht *Alberta* had been sent to pick her up from Gosport. She would be at Osborne shortly after 10 p.m. He could depart in peace in the morning.

That night was stormy and bitterly cold. There would be a frost in the morning. Reid kept up his vigil, noting now that the Queen's condition had declined. She was 'not so well again and very weak'. He could reflect on a private conversation earlier in the day. He had gone in to see her and she had ordered everyone out of the room except him – even Mrs Tuck. Alone, she looked him in the eye and said, 'I should like to live a little longer as I have still a few things to settle. I have arranged most things but there are still some left, and I want to live a little longer.'

The doctor did not know what to say. His monarch seemed to be pleading with him for her life, as if he had the power to determine the outcome. 'She appealed to me in this pathetic way with great trust as if she thought I could make her live.' He knew he could not.

# 5. Clinging On

I should like to see Grandmama before she dies . . .

The Kaiser

The man the Queen had wanted to nurse her to the end could
not be at the royal sickbed. Years ago she had commanded
the presence of her Highland servant John Brown. He was
supposed to be there to comfort her as she died. The widowed
Queen had defied the gossips and the objections of her family
and let him be her protector after the death of Prince Albert.
Outspoken, strong-minded, he was always by her side, taking
control, helping her on to her horse, tucking her in a tartan
rug when she climbed into her carriage, and snapping at her
if she was difficult. 'Hoots, then, wumman. Can ye no hold
yerr head up?' he was once heard to say as he tried to adjust
her cape.[1] Her self-appointed bodyguard, he kept intruders
away, sometimes even members of her own family if he
thought they might upset her. And, though he had been dead
now for nearly eighteen years, he was there in the orders she
had written down about how she was to be treated in her final
illness.

In 1875 she had set down in writing her wish that when
she lay dying 'her faithful and devoted personal attendant (and
true friend) Brown should be in the room and near at hand
and that he should watch over her earthly remains and place
it in the coffin'. In Dr Jenner's memorandum, written on her

instructions in the same year, his role was further defined. Her daughters and her female attendants were the only ones allowed to nurse her, apart from

her faithful personal attendant John Brown, whose strength, care, handiness and gentleness make him invaluable at all times and most peculiarly so in illness, and who was of such use and comfort to her during her long illness in 1871, in lifting and carrying and leading her, and who knows how to suggest anything for her comfort and convenience. The Queen wishes no one therefore but J. Brown, whose faithfulness, tact and discretion are not to be exceeded, to help her female attendants in anything which may be required.

She anticipated opposition to this, and ruled decisively against interference:

If it is necessary to send for anyone of the rest of the family, it is on the express understanding that her wishes expressed in this memorandum should be strictly adhered to and in no way departed from. Her physicians should likewise inform the Prince and Princess of Wales, and any of her sons should they be there, of these her wishes.

These written instructions were now held by Reid. She had handed them over to him in February 1898, the content unaltered despite the fact that Brown had died from a chill, caught when out in the cold night air chasing imaginary Irish assassins, in 1883. Reid could not follow the letter of the law she had laid down, but he could maintain the spirit, with his own strong arms and understanding taking the place of Brown's.

That Sunday, 20 January, the nation was on its knees.

The hush of an invisible presence is over the land. Queen Victoria lies at Osborne in a critical condition, surrounded by her family and consoled by the love of her innumerable subjects. We trust that the personal vigour and power of endurance which have been displayed by her Majesty from her girlhood upwards will once more assert themselves and prolong still further her prosperous and memorable reign.

The hopes of the *Daily Chronicle* were echoed everywhere.

Thousands were at St Paul's Cathedral to hear Canon Holland 'beseech your earnest prayers for her who for so many years has been a mother to our nation. So long as we can remember anything, her name and her presence have been felt in every beat of our hearts. It is as if the nation lies stricken with her. Pray for her in body and soul. Pray that even yet she may be spared.' By the evening, though, the Bishop of Kensington was urging the same congregation to be disciplined in their sadness and to bear the bereavement, 'if the worst should happen', with resignation. In other churches the national anthem was sung softly at the end of each service – a mark, as Canon Fleming said at St Michael's in Chester Square, but a feeble mark, 'of our devotion and love'. Only the Archbishop of Canterbury, preaching at St Matthew's Church in Croydon, made no mention of the dying Queen in his sermon.

Those not praying were walking. From the East End of London, crowds in search of information headed for the Mansion House at the heart of the City to read the bulletins posted by the Lord Mayor. From the West End, a smarter and more affluent body of people congregated at Buckingham Palace and Marlborough House. Rumours flew that she was dead, and bells were mistakenly tolled in north London after Scotland Yard got its wires crossed. A message to the

Commissioner, Sir Edward Bradford, was misinterpreted by one of his staff and a report went out to all police stations in the capital that she had died on Saturday night. It was inexcusable, even in the atmosphere of anticipation that had overtaken the capital.

A short walk from Osborne, there was a bigger gathering than usual for the morning service in the little parish church at Whippingham. From the steps of the chancel, the vicar expressed his great anxiety and hope that 'in her hour of weakness, God will comfort the Queen and support her in His everlasting arms'. They sang 'O God, our help in ages past' and 'Art thou weary?', and many sank to their knees in prayer. As the congregation of villagers drifted away, they were replaced by a smaller group of worshippers, come to mourn. It was the anniversary of the death of Prince Henry of Battenberg, and the royal family, led by his widow, Princess Beatrice, had left the Queen's side to stand and remember in the church where he had been buried with full military honours five years ago. As the Princess placed a wreath of lilies on her husband's tomb, she was comforted by the words of an old friend, Randall Davidson, the Bishop of Winchester, the Queen's closest spiritual adviser.

The day before, the Bishop had been at Fulham Palace, paying his respects to the widow of the Bishop of London, Mandell Creighton, who had been buried earlier that week. Davidson had represented the Queen at the funeral. He was sitting with Mrs Creighton when a telegram arrived, sent on from his home in Farnham, from Sir Arthur Bigge with the news that the Queen was now seriously ill and the family had been called to her. It was not actually a summons to the Bishop, but he took it as such and set off for the Isle of Wight straight away. That night he arrived in Southampton, took a cab to the docks, and had to run through the pouring rain to catch the late boat to Cowes. He made the crossing in the company of journalists, telegraph clerks and a group of boisterous footballers, 'a strange companionship in an hour of such anxiety'. After a night spent at the rectory of St Mary's in the town, he went to Whippingham and after the service followed the royal family back to Osborne House.

There the Queen was in absolute seclusion, even her daughters under instructions from the doctors to let her rest. Reid had been up with her all night. Saturday's improvement had not lasted, and she was now very confused and restless. To help her breathing, a mask was put on her face and she took oxygen from a cylinder. It was not a good sign. By Sunday morning she was completely helpless, unable to move herself or in any way help those who were trying to help her. The double bed she was lying in was a problem: its size meant the dressers could not get near enough to nurse her. She needed to be moved to a smaller one – but delicately. However ill she was, she was still the Queen of England and her dignity must not be compromised. The operation was complicated, involving much pushing and shoving and a good deal of discretion.

Three workmen from the estate brought a screen to the bedroom door and Reid and the women fitted it round the bed so she could not be seen. The men were then allowed to come in and assemble a small divan in a corner. They then left the room and waited outside while the doctor removed the screen, pushed the small bed up to the big one, and lifted her, with some difficulty, from one to the other. This done, Reid wheeled the divan, with the barely conscious Queen in it, into the corner and put the screen back up, shielding her again from inquisitive eyes. The workmen came back in, heaved the heavy mahogany double bed out of the way, and left. Reid and the women pushed the small bed back into the middle of the room, relieved that they could now get to grips with their patient.

At 11 a.m. Reid and Powell issued a bulletin: 'The Queen has passed a somewhat restless night. There is no material change in her condition since the last report.' Outside the gates of Osborne, the waiting journalists stamped their feet in the cold, enjoying a crisp and clear winter morning. The early frost on the grass and trees had melted in the bright sun, and the mainland could plainly be seen across the Solent. The bulletin dampened their good spirits. It was 'disquieting' that there had been no improvement overnight. Or perhaps they were dismayed by the paucity of information they were getting. Servants coming from the house were pumped for details; the pubs in the town were full of gossips who knew what was really happening at Osborne. Invention was in the air.

It deeply disturbed the *Standard*, which railed against the 'purveyors of news who have invented gossip' – 'we hope that this solemn moment in the life of an empire will not be sullied by sensation-mongering'. James Vincent, the special correspondent from *The Times*, a 'colour' writer who had been sent from London to cover the occasion, felt there was 'a good deal of the spirit and flesh of American journalism at large in Cowes at this moment'. He was determined to find out more from proper sources, and he put his case well enough to officials to be allowed up the long drive and into the house for an interview with Sir Arthur Bigge. He pressed for more information, for more openness, but was rebuffed. The Queen's private secretary 'assured me that no information as to the Queen's health would be given in any other way than by bulletin, and that no deputations of pressmen, or anything of that kind, would be received'. It did not stop the speculation. Vincent, a clergyman's son with a classics degree from Christ Church, Oxford, would himself soon be among the pack talking to drivers and servants at the gate and quoting 'trustworthy sources' to piece together the progress of the Queen's illness, which he put down to 'a malady that some would call by the name of senile decay'. The reporters had to interpret for their readers the truth behind the bulletins. Was the Queen close to death? The world was waiting on their words. Forced to nail his colours to the masthead, the *Times* correspondent concluded that 'the case is critical in the extreme but not absolutely beyond hope'.

Inside the house, hope was slipping away. In the afternoon another bulletin was taken to the gate and posted for the reporters to see. 'Her Majesty's strength has been fairly maintained throughout the day,' it began optimistically, but went on, 'Although no fresh developments have taken place, the symptoms continue to cause anxiety.'

Reid and Powell were right to be anxious. The Queen lay quietly in the little bed, apathetic and hardly able to speak, though she was quite calm. Her pulse was strong, but her breathing was shallow and she now had trouble swallowing. As night fell she was barely conscious and Reid allowed the princesses back in to see her, knowing that their presence would not disturb her. They came in and stood round her, but she showed no signs of recognizing any of them.

In London that day all eyes were on the Kaiser. The train he had taken from Berlin outpaced the arrangements at the other end. The imperial yacht was supposed to meet him at the Dutch coast to ferry him across to England, but could not get there in time. The British cruiser *Minerva* was in full steam from Portsmouth to escort him across the sea, but she too was falling behind schedule. So he commandeered the mailboat, ran the imperial flag up the mast of a steamer of the Royal Zeeland Company, and dashed out of Flushing and across the

North Sea to Sheerness. A fierce head wind slowed him down and he was forty-five minutes late docking at Port Victoria pier. To Baron von Eckardstein, who went on board to greet him, he complained that he had been inundated with telegrams from his aunts at Osborne begging him to turn back. He had ignored them. He would never forgive himself if his grandmother died and he was not there.

A special train was waiting to take them to London, and they sat together discussing the possibility of a formal Anglo-German political alliance. There were fears in Berlin about the balance of power in Europe and the increasing cooperation between Russia and France, which threatened to squeeze Germany from both sides. Cementing relations with Britain would counteract this. The Baron had recently been having secret discussions with his high-level British contacts, among them Joseph Chamberlain and the Duke of Devonshire, about this prospect. He felt he was making progress, but he was anxious that the Kaiser might be too rash in pressing the matter with any British ministers he might meet. It was too soon, too delicate. He urged his headstrong Emperor to be discreet, and, surprisingly, the Kaiser agreed. It was a relief to Eckardstein's superiors back in Berlin. The Kaiser's mission of mercy could be a great boon. It could just as equally backfire if it ended in rows with his relations. 'I hope urgently the royal family will not get on the wrong side of the Kaiser with their usual lack of consideration,' the director of the political section of the Foreign Office, Fritz von Holstein, telegraphed Eckardstein. 'Do your best with the British ministers, or anyhow see that something is done to make them insist on courteous treatment for the Kaiser.' In the event – and to everyone's surprise – the Kaiser turned out to be his own best ambassador.

It was six in the evening as the train neared London. A large crowd had assembled at Charing Cross station, spilling on to the platform and getting perilously close to treading on the red carpet until the police took control and ushered them all back behind barriers. A procession of royal carriages began to arrive, skidding over the newly sanded roads and coming to a halt on the platform. The last one brought the Prince of Wales, who had arrived in the capital from the Isle of Wight just two hours earlier. Anxious crowds had been at Victoria to meet him too, wanting news. He was optimistic. The fact that he was in London was a good sign. 'You see they have let me come away,' he told inquiring courtiers before being driven away to prepare for his nephew's arrival. Their meeting at Charing Cross was cordial, and, raising their hats to the crowd, they were driven to Buckingham Palace through streets lined with spectators. There were no cheers, only a deep silence of respect, which was now the prevailing mood of the capital and the country. That night the Kaiser dined with his uncle and his cousin the Duke of York. At Victoria station a train was in steam and waiting, just in case.

The Bishop of Winchester could not avoid mentioning the Queen when he preached at Whippingham that evening. She had been in their prayers, the words 'thy servant, our queen' being substituted for 'this child' in the collect for a sick infant. But in his sermon he was guarded in his remarks. He knew she was very ill indeed – more so than the official bulletins indicated – and that the doctors thought there was little hope for her. But there must have been reporters among the congregation who knew he had just come from the house, and he was anxious not to be a source of stories for them.

Afterwards he went back to the rectory of St Mary's, Cowes, where he was staying as a guest of the vicar, the Revd Launce-lot Smith. A parcel of clean shirts had just arrived for him, sent by his wife from Farnham when she realized he had gone to the Isle of Wight without taking any clothes with him. He was most grateful. Shortly after 10 p.m. he sat down in the candlelight to write to her. The Queen was not likely to die that night, but she was 'very, very ill' and there was little hope of recovery, 'even in an impaired condition, which God forbid'. Tired by his long day, the Bishop put down his pen and went to bed at eleven o'clock, but he was woken an hour later by a carriage at the door. A messenger had an urgent note from Fritz Ponsonby at Osborne. The Queen had suddenly got much worse. He should come at once and be prepared to remain there.

He threw on his clothes, jumped into the waiting carriage, and was at the house within twenty-five minutes. There the Queen's doctors, Ponsonby and Lord Edward Clinton were having an urgent meeting with Sir Arthur Bigge in his room. They had just issued a midnight bulletin which made gloomy reading. 'The Queen's condition has late this evening become more serious, with increase of weakness and diminished power of taking nourishment.' Reid thought the end might even come in the night. They had to decide on practical steps.

The telephone line was open to Marlborough House, and the urgent issue was whether the Prince of Wales should leave straight away for Osborne. Reid had been in touch with Sir Francis Knollys, the Prince's private secretary, at intervals throughout the day. Now he told him that the Queen had taken a turn for the worse and he thought the end might not be far off. The Prince should not delay his return to Osborne too long. There was even an argument for his leaving London immediately and travelling through the night. Ponsonby had already contacted the captain of the *Alberta*, and she was on her way to Gosport to meet the train. But Knollys was reluctant. The Prince was exhausted. It was better for him to have a good night's sleep and leave first thing in the morning. He and the Kaiser would take the train at 8 a.m. and be in Osborne well before midday. Would there still be time? Reid conferred with Powell. Of course they could not be certain – in these situations, anything could happen – but they thought this would be all right.

Reid put the phone down, and the group at Osborne sat talking for another hour, even though the non-stop work of the last twenty-four hours had left them all desperate for sleep. Constitutional issues that had not raised their heads for more than sixty years were suddenly staring them in the face. Bigge thought that, if the Queen died before her son left London, the Prince would have to stay there and summon the Privy Council as King. They ran through this possibility and, as the Bishop recalled, 'many more problems of a like sort which nobody is clear about for lack of any precedents within people's memory or knowledge'. The reality, the magnitude, of what the Queen's death would mean was suddenly coming home to the courtiers, and they felt unprepared and untutored for it.

When the meeting broke up, Reid and Powell returned to the Queen's bedroom for a difficult night. They gave her more oxygen, and in the small, dark hours of the morning, as she struggled to breathe, they even thought she might not make it through to the dawn. Reid was surprised that none of the princesses came to check on their mother that night. But the Queen's daughters had long gone to bed, were deep in sleep after all their hours of vigil at her bedside, and were unaware until the morning that there had been so much concern during the night.

Meanwhile a room with a bed in it had somehow been found for the Bishop, even though the house was full, and there he began a new letter to his wife from 'one of the most solemn houses I am ever likely to spend time in'. He was overwhelmed by the historic moment. He thought of the Queen's accession (though it had been long before his own birth) and 'the great resolves she made before God as to what her life's work should be like'. He thought of his own part in her affairs – 'all the talks and talks and talks I have had with her in this house and at Windsor since I first came here almost on this day 18 years ago and thank God for what she has been to England and to the world'. He was glad he had come. 'I should never have forgiven myself if when they wanted me at the close I had been far away and I do think my talks this afternoon were of some good.' But 'it is so strange to find oneself in the midst of all the personal sorrow of a great family'.

One issue in particular troubled the Bishop, and he confided his thoughts to his wife. What would happen if the Queen did not die but her health was so damaged that she was unable to do her job any more? The spectre of mad George III, her grandfather, and the Regency was too recent to be forgotten. It had been a disaster for the monarchy. This was a thought that had worried the Queen too. Only a week ago, the day after Lord Roberts's last visit to Osborne, she had considered the matter and was determined that history would not repeat itself. 'They will want me to give in and to have a regency to do my work. But they are all wrong. I won't, for I know they would be doing things in my name without telling me.' That now seemed a most unlikely outcome. Before once more putting down his pen and going to sleep, the Bishop told his wife:

I cannot express how thankful I am to feel that so far as we can judge there is no prospect for her life being prolonged in a broken and marred condition. Dear old lady, she is simply worn out after 64 years of honest hard work for her people. How splendid that she should just end like this without ever putting off the armour. God bless her.

The Bishop was not the only one whose thoughts were churning through that dark night. Bigge and Ponsonby had decided it would be unwise for both of them to go to bed. One of them should be on hand instantly in case there was a sudden development. Ponsonby agreed to take the first watch and settled himself down in an armchair and read. At 4 a.m. he was so cold he wrapped himself in a rug.

Everything seemed ghostly and still but curiously enough I did not seem at all sleepy. As I sat there I thought of all the people crowded into Osborne House and what the Queen's death would mean to them, what would happen when the Prince of Wales came to the throne and what changes he would make. Gloomy thoughts in the small hours of the morning with only myself and a few policemen awake.

At six he was relieved by Bigge as agreed, and they had a cup of tea before Ponsonby went off to snatch a few hours' sleep.

While he slept, the rest of the house was slowly waking up to better news. The Queen had survived the night. In fact she showed signs of rallying. Randall Davidson was up at 7.30 after only a few hours' sleep and went quickly to find out what was happening. The house was quiet and at first he could only find a servant, who passed on the gossip that she was better. From Reid he learned that she was indeed stronger and that 'the urgency and the peril seems for the moment relieved'. But he was not one for false hope – 'of course it remains the same, au fond'.

This slight recovery worried the Bishop. 'I can't honestly say I am glad.' He could not shake off the thoughts he had had the night before about her surviving but being so ill that she would be just a ghost of her real self. It was very unlikely she could get back 'to her former level and I don't want a shattered life to go on with all the utter complications it would cause and the unhappiness to her and to others which would I fear be inevitable'. He must have felt uncomfortable with the views he had so honestly expressed in his letters to his wife – it might be thought that he was wishing for the Queen's death. It is not hard to sympathize with his attitude that she was better off dead than remaining alive but without her faculties. Nonetheless, when he later came to write up a formal account of events at Osborne he made no mention of the thoughts that had so concerned him at the time.

If he had known, the Bishop could have taken comfort in the fact that others felt the same way. Lord Esher thought 'the news from Osborne as sad as it can be. But what a comfort that the end of this long and splendid reign should come so rapidly. No lingering illness. The Queen drove out on Tuesday. Today she is at death's door.'[2]

The Monday papers had just one story to tell. 'God save the Queen! The world prays for her recovery. Her Majesty's condition critical.' The rest of the news was pushed down the page and very nearly off it – even the sensational story that one of England's best-known cricket umpires had accused the Indian batsman Prince Ranjitsinhji of lying and was under pressure from the MCC to apologize, or the swashbuckling account from France of the duel in which the Comte de Lubersac had been thrust through the chest by Baron Robert de Rothschild, with the result that the Queen was not the only one who was now in mortal danger.

From Osborne, the *Express*'s special correspondent wrote 'in the shadow of a great fear'. Column after column listed the anxiety at home and around the world. People were 'visibly affected' in Bradford; there was 'heartfelt sorrow' in Dover and 'universal sorrow' in Glasgow. New York was 'deeply moved', Vienna was 'touched', Canada felt 'deep sympathy', even among its French-speaking subjects, and there was 'gloom' in Gibraltar and in Cape Town.

The Queen remained drowsy through much of that Monday morning, but then came to and asked to play with her favourite dog, a white spitz known as Turi that she had brought back from Italy. Her request could not immediately be granted. There was a frantic search, but the dog was being walked in the grounds and only when he was brought back could she have him on her bed to stroke. She was pleased. At 11 a.m. Reid and Powell, who now had been joined by Sir Thomas Barlow, the Queen's physician extraordinary, signed a new bulletin. 'The Queen has slightly rallied since midnight. Her Majesty has taken more food, and has had some refreshing sleep. There is no further loss of strength. The symptoms that give rise to most anxiety are those which point to a local obstruction in the brain circulation.'

Barlow, a professor of clinical medicine, came to the conclusion that the Queen had not had a stroke as such. Her illness 'was really a failure of the vessels of the brain, not an apoplexy'. The arteries had been slowly damaged over the years, and the loss of circulation had now reached the point where it was affecting 'the centre of speech and the portion controlling the right side of the face'.

That morning the Prince of Wales and the Kaiser arrived, having breakfasted on the train from London to Gosport before going on board the *Alberta*. As the royal yacht was edged out into the stream by a tug, the band on the quayside played 'God Save the Queen!' and the Prince and his nephew stood to attention, their heads bared. As they crossed over to the island, the Prince of Wales's standard and the Emperor's standard flew beside each other on the masthead. True to form, the Kaiser was on the bridge for the crossing, while his

uncle sat in the saloon with his daughter-in-law, the Duchess
of York. There was no ceremony as they landed, no gun
salute, no guard of honour, just a small crowd who watched,
their caps doffed in deference, as the royal procession headed
off up the hill. Just as they reached the gates of Osborne, a
column of reserve soldiers from the Royal Rifle Regiment
was on a routine route march along the road, and the officer
in charge, Major Lord de L'Isle, brought his men swiftly to
attention to salute the royals.

Once inside the house, the Kaiser tackled his disapproving
aunts. 'My first wish is not to be in the way,' he told them,
'and I will return to London if you wish. I should like to see
Grandmama before she dies, but if that is impossible I shall
quite understand.' It was masterfully done. They did not have
the heart to send him away.

The new arrivals went in one by one to see the Queen.
They stood at the foot of the bed, but she did not see them.
She was asleep, but even if she had opened her eyes her vision
was so bad that she would not have taken in their faces. But
no one spoke and no attempt was made to rouse her.

In the afternoon, the Kaiser and the Prince walked together
through the grounds. Politics would have been on the agenda,
as it was for much of their time together. They found themselves in agreement. Both distrusted the Russians and the
French. They were nervous too about the growing influence
of the United States and what effect that would have on
Europe. The Kaiser felt that only his military strength was
maintaining the balance of power on the Continent. He
thought the time was past when England could stay aloof from
European affairs. Nothing concrete was discussed. The Kaiser
did not even use the word 'Germany', only ever referring to
'the Continent', but the mood of cooperation between them
was music to the ears of the Foreign Office in Berlin.[3]

As the two kings talked, the Duke of Connaught and the Duke of York strolled alongside. Their entourages were with them, and the party was easily spotted by the pressmen at the gates. They took heart from this, a sign that 'those who knew as much as can be known did not think the end was very near'. The royals seemed in reasonable spirits as they waved back to the onlookers and left the Osborne grounds to set off down the hill to the convalescent home for soldiers in East Cowes. There the matron showed them round, and the Kaiser sat for a long time by the bed of a gunner from the 66th Field Battery who had been badly wounded at Colenso, listening to his story. The royal party took tea before slipping out past the pack of reporters at the door. They clamoured round the matron for information, but she refused to say anything to them. The Kaiser and his uncle took their time returning to the house and some of the party extended their walk past the gates, again leaving the impression that there was no urgency. Another bulletin at 5 p.m. seemed to confirm this. 'The slight improvement of this morning is maintained.' Was there reason for hope?

Randall Davidson took up this very issue with the doctors. Finding them together in Powell's room, he asked whether there was good reason for the improved bulletin. They were embarrassed by the question, because, as they told the Bishop, it had been issued at the special request of the Prince of Wales and rather against their wishes. It was not untrue, they insisted, but they would not have made the news public in that form. They thought it might raise false hopes. So what was the truth about the Queen's condition? 'Well, there is some definite rally and there is more recognition and more life,' Powell said. Davidson pressed his point. 'Tell me, then, if it were the case of a Mrs Smith in Sloane Street and you were consulting over her, what prospect would you give?' The doctors went quiet. Reid refused an opinion, on the grounds that he had no experience of treating other patients. At last Powell said, 'I should expect her perhaps to live for four or five days.'

Even now, it seemed, the Prince of Wales was trying to deny the reality of his mother's imminent death, and it was this that had prompted the 5 p.m. bulletin. After it had been issued, he went in to see her on his own. The Queen and the heir to her throne spoke quietly to each other. She put her arms out and called his name – 'Bertie' – and he embraced her and broke down. Or so says Fritz Ponsonby in his account, but how he knew is unclear. However, there can be little doubt that there was great emotion on both sides. When the Prince left, Reid, who had waited outside, went back to the bed and was astonished when the Queen's hand reached out and grabbed his. She held it and kissed it, mistaking, in her befuddled state, her doctor for her son. She wanted the Prince back. He was sent for, and as he bent over her and whispered to her she said to him, 'Kiss my face.'

As the night drew in, those at Osborne gathered in anxious groups to talk and debate and worry. The Bishop found himself with the Kaiser and his uncle the Duke of Connaught, and told them what the doctors had told him.

We then discussed what it might mean both personally and politically if the Queen were to be going on with just a bare modicum of life. The Duke, very naturally, clung to all possible hope and would like her to remain alive anyhow. He was like an honest simple schoolboy. The Emperor, on the other hand, was (again characteristically) full of the terribleness of a life that is no real life and spoke with splendid enthusiasm about the Queen's greatness for 63 years and his wish that there might be no 'mean or unfitting' physical close.

The Kaiser approved of the swift way his grandfather, the Emperor William I, had died, and wished the same for his grandmother. They both had lived 'lives of iron and when iron is broken it doesn't waste away but goes "crack"'.

The Bishop found himself captivated by the Kaiser. 'He is a striking fellow, let people say what they will.' He had put aside his normal 'bossy' style and was telling everyone repeatedly that he was there as a grandson not an emperor. He was being nice, and it was appreciated. 'I think he has even won over the hostile princesses to his side,' the Bishop ventured, but his judgement was not totally right. They appreciated the kindness and tact their nephew was showing, but they wished he had shown the same consideration for their sister, his mother.

Reid had also managed a private conversation with the Kaiser, and received imperial thanks for having alerted him to his grandmother's condition. The Kaiser was anxious to see her alone if the doctor could possibly arrange it. There were things he wanted to tell her about his mother. He promised not to excite her, and Reid promised to do his best.

As the house began to settle down for the night, there was a sense that the drama was some way from reaching its climax. The Duke and Duchess of Connaught felt there was time enough for them to take their leave and go off to a cottage in the grounds where they could at least get a good night's sleep. Perhaps the doctors were right – this would go on for another four days, maybe five. Their midnight bulletin was non-committal: 'There is no material change in the Queen's condition. The slight improvement of the morning has been maintained throughout the day. Food has been taken fairly well, and some tranquil sleep secured.'

Tranquillity, though, had deserted the nation. Buckingham Palace was the focus for thousands of concerned Londoners, and they milled around its gates, reading the bulletins aloud to those pressing behind who could not get close enough to see. A constant stream of carriages pulled into the courtyard with visitors who wanted to sign the book of sympathy and concern that had been opened in the palace foyer. Page after page was filled with signatures, and officials were also overwhelmed with telegrams and telephone calls. In the City, bulletins went up at the Mansion House and the bankers and brokers crowded round for the latest news. A rumour went around that the Prime Minister was on his way to Osborne, but, though a train was constantly in steam at Victoria station to take ministers, it proved to be untrue. So many others were making their way to the Isle of Wight, however, that at Southampton docks the porter called out to ferry passengers 'Are you for Osborne?' rather than his usual 'Are you for Cowes?'

The morning papers tried to outshine each other in their eloquence. 'The life of lives is dropping towards the Valley of the Shadow,' the *Daily Telegraph* told its readers, 'and we who are the very children of her reign realize that the Sovereign and the mother to whose being we would cling as to our own, may be taken from us for ever.' She had rescued the monarchy after the 'choleric, wine-bibbing' William IV (as the *Daily News* described her uncle) and was irreplaceable. 'What successor could worthily fill her place?' asked the *Morning Advertiser*, and the *Star* agreed that 'Never shall we look on her like again. She has always been more than a monarch. She has been a great and a good woman. Great and good.' And not just in Britain. The newspapers took pride in her family connections to practically every royal house in Europe – one said she had no fewer than 233 blood relations still living.

The anxiety crossed all class boundaries, and it seemed to amaze the *Daily Express* that poor areas were as capable of concern as the better-off. A reporter it sent to the East End of London wandered from Houndsditch to Blackwall and found that 'rough men and women and hobbledehoys' were discussing the benefits of her long reign 'with an intelligence that would have astonished those who regard the East Ender as a blend of child and savage'.

Down in the docks, the latest rumours flew up and down the long quays. Men wheeling crates shouted them to men stacking timber, and men at the hatchways shouted them to men in the hold. In Wapping Wall at midday, four men tramped into a waterside tavern. They looked like workers from one of the neighbouring wharves, out for their dinner half-hour. ''Ere's God save her, mates!' said one and he raised his tankard. 'God save her!' said the other three. Without another word, the four rough Englishmen tramped out.

Sentimentality like this was everywhere, surpassed only by the first of the poems published to catch the mood for mawkishness. B. Fletcher Robinson's effort, also in the *Express*, was titled 'Her People Wait'.

> Along the thronging city street,
> Amid the traffic's roar,
> On board the anchored fishing fleet
> That wait the news from shore,
> Where Irish breakers churn the sand,
> Where leap the Irish deer,
> With anxious hearts her people stand
> Twixt sinking hope and fear.
>
> No moorland cot, however small,
> That shows the world apart,
> No stately mansion, proud and tall,

But holds an anxious heart.
No little seamstress, worn and white,
No lady wrapt in fur,
But falls upon her knees at night
And prays to God for her.

Each morn has brought a darker day
For her so loved, adored.
The answer to the prayers we pray
Is in thy hands, O Lord!
In mercy then Thy servant spare,
We plead before thy throne;
Yet if our woe 'tis right we bear,
Thy will, O Lord, be done.

Among the public, the demand for information was intense, and some concerned citizens were angry and frustrated by how difficult it was to obtain. 'The official mind does not seem to have gauged the intense anxiety of her Majesty's subjects to know her condition,' one reader wrote to *The Times*. On Monday morning he had looked in vain for an official bulletin at the post office, then walked to Buckingham Palace at 10 a.m. to find that the court officials had been slow and the latest notice displayed there was the one from the afternoon before. It was only when he made it to the Carlton Club in St James's and was allowed inside by the obliging doorkeeper to read the telegram posted in the hall that he felt properly informed. 'Surely a little more consideration and alertness might have been expected on so momentous an occasion,' he complained.

Outside London there was just as much concern. The sudden news of the Queen's illness was bringing the world to a halt. At Liverpool's normally bustling Cotton Exchange, prices were marked down and there was an air of despondency that observers said they had never seen before. In Birmingham, crowds poured in from the suburbs to wait outside the local newspaper offices for the latest news. Up and down the land, the newspapers were the unrivalled masters of information in this national crisis. The telegraph system gave the provincial morning and evening papers instant access to what was happening in Osborne and London. They turned out edition after edition, and the paper boys hardly had time to shout their wares in the streets before copies were grabbed from them. As the presses rolled inside, the latest pages were also pasted up in the office windows. Those too grand to join the throng expected a personal service. From his country home, Joseph Chamberlain sent numerous telegrams throughout the day to the editor of his local paper inquiring about the Queen.

This was an age of committees, telegrams and pomposity. No figure of substance, whether that substance was real or imagined, could let this moment pass without becoming part of it. At every official meeting, from city council to parish council and chamber of commerce to courthouse, chairmen, presidents, conveners, whatever their title, stood solemnly to meet the occasion. They made grand speeches, proposed and passed resolutions of hope and loyalty, and sent them humming down the wires. The Lord Mayor of Bristol was one of thousands whose messages were instantly on their way to Osborne. 'The Lord Mayor, high sheriff and citizens of Bristol have heard with deepest sorrow of their beloved Queen's illness and pray God she may soon be restored to health.' He duly got his reply, churned out by the frantic and by now overwhelmed courtiers and telegraph staff on the Isle of Wight: 'The Prince of Wales desires me to thank you for your kind expression of sympathy – Private Secretary.'

Some were more considerate. In Sheffield, a dinner of the

Crimean and Indian Mutiny Veterans debated whether to send a message but decided in the end that 'in this time of anxiety, it was inexpedient to trouble the royal family with telegrams, however kindly meant'.

Having sent its best wishes, the country then sat back to wait and worry. Everywhere, events were cancelled. The Duke of Devonshire put a pencil through all the forthcoming parties at Chatsworth. At the last moment, the lawyers of Lincoln's Inn called off their term dinner, and the Mayor of Fulham his reception at the town hall. The Lord Mayor of Leeds did the same. Sir Charles Warren called off his planned inspection of the Church Lads' Brigade. The list of casualties went on. The Admiral's dance at Sheerness and the Primrose League ball and a dinner for Colonel Webb MP in Wolverhampton were cancelled. In Somerset, the annual ploughing match of the Blagdon, Charterhouse and West Mendip Society was postponed. In the Midlands the Albrighton hunt met briefly, but they had no stomach for the kill that day and the hounds were sent back to the kennels.

For others, there were intensely practical matters to consider if the country was not to go to the dogs. The Queen's death, if it occurred, would mean recalling Parliament instantly. Or so the constitutional authorities believed, though it had been so long since such issues had arisen that they had to pore over precedent to be sure. 'The demise of the Crown is the only contingency upon which Parliament is required to meet without the usual summons,' the expert at *The Times* offered as his conclusion. Lord Esher was astounded by how unprepared everyone was. 'All has been confusion. The ignorance of historical precedent in men whose business it is to know is wonderful,' he wrote in his diary. Lingering hopes were not for him. He thought not of the past but of the future, the succession. He was Permanent Secretary to the Office of Works, and it was his job to ensure the smooth running of royal properties and even royal events. Three and a half years ago he had organized the Diamond Jubilee celebrations. Now there was work to do. 'I went to Windsor Castle and ordered everything to be ready for the end, and the beginning! I have had St James's Palace prepared for a Council. The men must work all night. Also the Houses of Parliament have to be made ready with all speed.'

It was the speed of events that drove others to a stunned inactivity. The *Standard* in London caught the mood. 'So rapidly has the Queen's disease run its course that millions of her subjects have only in the past few hours found themselves able to realize the irreparable loss with which they are threatened. The very suddenness of the calamity has added to the intensity with which it is felt.' Others realized that she had been unwell for much longer than had been admitted, but they attributed the reluctance to come clean about her true state of health to the Queen herself and her overwhelming concern for her people. 'A large number of persons have known for some time that the present crisis was imminent,' *The Times* wrote, 'but the Queen has been anxious that there should be no premature announcement of her condition.' It was a loyal line to take, and one appreciated by the public, even if it bore little relation to the facts.

But now the distress and anxiety from which she had apparently tried to save her people were everywhere, and spreading quickly through the Empire. In Kingston, Jamaica, the editor of the *Daily Gleaner* sent a boy round on a bicycle to stop at every church and give the pastor and congregation the latest information. In Calcutta, every telegram from London was anxiously awaited. *The Times* spoke of the silent grief that is felt among all the subjects of the British crown, among the daughter nations, our self-governing colonies, among the dark-skinned races, who under her rule have flourished in an atmosphere of integrity and equity previously unknown to them, among the subordinate princes and populations upon whom the Pax Britannica has conferred the immeasurable blessings of settled order and freedom from perpetual feuds. In every part of the Empire, the same sorrow prevails that has suspended all festivities at home and has even clogged the inexorable machine of business.

Even the nationalists in Ireland were prepared to suspend some of their hostility, though 'they take care to dissociate this personal sympathy for the Queen from any suspicion of loyalty to the throne and the constitution'.

After the sorrow came waves of fear about the future. What lay round the corner was the end of an era. Could it really be happening? How would they cope?

The Queen has been the most potent influence for stability and peace in our vexed and troubled age. No sovereign ever ruled whose loss could come home with so personal a sense of misfortune to her subjects, none for whom so many millions of men will utter the heartfelt prayer that the calamity which is clouding the threshold of the New Century may after all be postponed.

But it was a vain hope. The Victorian era was sleeping through its very last night.

# 6. Sunset

The Queen is slowly sinking . . .

Official bulletin

Randall Davidson spent the night at Kent House in the grounds of Osborne and planned a brisk start to the next day. He was going to finish another letter he had been writing to his wife just before he went to bed and then go to Osborne House for breakfast. Events overtook him. Just after eight o'clock a messenger arrived at the door with an urgent summons: he should go at once to the house. He stuffed the unfinished letter in his pocket and ran to the carriage that was waiting outside for him.

I went straight to the Queen's room. The Family were assembling, some of them not fully dressed. They knelt round the bed, the Prince of Wales on the Queen's right, the German Emperor on her left. About 10 or 12 others were there. The Queen was breathing with difficulty and moving somewhat restlessly. The nurse [Mary Soal, who had been brought in at the last minute] was kneeling behind her in the bed, holding up the pillows. The three doctors were present. Although the Queen's breathing was so difficult she clearly was quite conscious.

It was Tuesday 22 January, and the very deathbed scene that the Queen had always abhorred and expressly forbidden was assembling around her. She had once written to her daughter Vicky about the death of a Prussian relative and how dreadful it had been with everyone there. 'That I shall insist is never the case if I am dying.' But she was now in no position to protest.

Reid had not left her side that night. She had been half awake, half unconscious, in neither one place nor the other. From time to time she recognized him and called to him for reassurance. But she could not swallow and her lungs were congested. Her cough got weaker by the minute and, as she breathed, her windpipe rattled – a sure sign that she did not have long to live. He gave her oxygen and some liquid, but there was little more he could do. He scrawled out a morning bulletin, signed it along with Powell and Barlow, and it was issued at 8 a.m. It dispelled the vague hopes, the hints of 'slight improvement', that they had reluctantly put their names to just eight hours before. 'The Queen this morning shows signs of diminishing strength, and her Majesty's condition again assumes a more serious aspect,' it read.

Reid took a break, leaving Powell by her side as he hurried off to his own bedroom to wash his face and hands and change the clothes he had been in all night. There was a knock on the door and Powell burst in. She was dying. Come quickly. The same summons was going to rooms around the house. Dressing gowns were thrown hastily on, and the royal princes and princesses rushed downstairs and along the corridor to the Queen's room. Reid leaned over the small bed to give her oxygen. Davidson stood to one side reciting the prayers for the dead, though he found doing God's work at this critical time was made difficult because there were so many people crowded into the room, 'some of them giving way a good deal to emotion'. Amid their tears, her daughters called out their names – it's Lenchen, mama . . . and Baby's here . . . and

Louise – letting her know they were there, though her eyes could not see them. They named the others in the room too – everyone except the Kaiser, who was standing beside the bed.

He was put out by being excluded in this way and, seeing this, Reid turned to the Prince of Wales and whispered, 'Wouldn't it be well to tell her that her grandson the Emperor is here too?' The Prince was adamant that this would not be helpful. 'No, it would excite her too much,' he told the doctor. But another grandson, the Duke of York, was allowed to identify himself. He spoke up, telling his grandmother he was there and mentioning that so too was the Bishop of Winchester. 'Yes of course,' she said, 'and is Mr Smith here too?' Urgently a messenger was rushed off to Whippingham to bring back the vicar, Clement Smith.

Outside the gates of Osborne the journalists were filled with foreboding. The first bulletin of the day seemed to chime ominously with the grey weather and leaden skies over the island. As they trudged up the hill from Cowes, they were a little surprised that the flag on East Cowes Castle had not already dropped to half mast. They faced another day on watch, certain the end was in sight, aware that it was only a matter of time before the Queen's 'magnificent constitution' was overwhelmed by 'the great and invincible enemy'. Behind them they heard a bugle call from the barracks in East Cowes, a reminder of how normal life was carrying on despite the epoch-ending drama that was taking place in the house on the hill.

Their numbers had been growing day by day as the crisis developed – French, German and American reporters swelling the pack. They were in a complaining mood. The Osborne officials had been slow as usual in putting the morning bulletin up on the gate, and by the time the reporters had rushed back down to Cowes and telegraphed the details to their offices it was already old news in London. Now there was little to do. The occasional carriage came and went, a royal messenger raced by on a white horse, parties of navy officers came to sign the visitors' book in the lodge. The monotony was broken when three figures in bright silks and turbans – 'Hindoos who had journeyed to lay their tribute of sorrow at the feet of their great Maharani' – came up the hill from Cowes. The word went round that they were princes, but they failed to argue their way past the policemen at the gate, who allowed them to leave a message but refused to let them in. The reporters closed round them and heard that they were from Madras and had interrupted a lecture tour in England to come and see the Empress of India before she died, 'a desire which was doomed to the bitterest disappointment'. They expressed their annoyance at the 'conventionalities' that were standing in their way, and went off to their hotel in Cowes to await what they were sure would be a summons from the Munshi, the Queen's Indian servant, to visit her before it was too late.

That morning the watchers inside Osborne waited for her to slip away, but she fought back, astounding everyone by her will to live. It was phenomenal, Powell and Barlow agreed. Reid urged the family to leave the room and let her rest. He gave her some food in liquid form, and she began to talk to him more coherently than she had done for a while. Her mind seemed much clearer, and the doctor – who was still intent on doing the best he could to help the Kaiser – felt he could make one last effort to let her grandson see her in private. He left her sleeping, her maids watching over her, and went in search of the Emperor, who was still indignant at the way his presence had been glossed over as they stood around the bed. 'Did you notice that everybody's name in the room was mentioned to her except mine?' Reid nodded. 'Yes,' he said, 'and that is one reason why I specially wish to take you there.'

But it would not be a clandestine meeting. Having been expressly ordered not to let the Queen know the Kaiser was there, Reid was not about to defy the man who shortly would be his king. He went to the Prince of Wales and asked if he could now take the Kaiser in. The Prince relented. Reid led the way into the bedroom and ushered the Kaiser to her bedside. Reid leaned over the Queen and spoke softly. 'Your Majesty, your grandson the Emperor is here. He has come to see you as you are so ill.' She smiled. Reid stood aside and left the room, and for five minutes the Empress and the Emperor were alone in the small intimate world of grandmother and grandson. What he told her must have pleased her, because when he had gone away and Reid went back to her side she told him, 'The Emperor is very kind.' But which emperor was she referring to? Eckardstein, the German envoy, later reported that, barely conscious, she had mistaken the Kaiser for his father, the dead Frederick.

Others were allowed in at intervals as she slept. Her private staff slipped in through the door – her assistant secretary Fleetwood Edwards, McNeill, Clinton, Bigge – and paused for a moment as they took in her pale, thin face. The Bishop said more prayers. They left and walked quietly down the grand stairs to the drawing room to sit, heads bowed, and wait.

Reid was now the person she seemed mainly to focus her attention on. She smiled at him when he spoke, and when he asked her to take some food she was happy to follow his instructions. 'Anything you like,' she whispered, and the sound of her voice and the sadness of it all brought a lump to his throat. He was allowed to lift her and turn her from one side to the other when she needed it. Until then, that had been a task strictly for her dressers, but they told the doctor that the Queen liked him helping her in this way. Perhaps he had the 'strength, care, handiness and gentleness' of John Brown, whom she had decreed many years ago should be her only male helper when she was ill.

At midday a fresh bulletin was posted from the doctors. 'There is no change for the worse in the Queen's condition since this morning's bulletin. Her Majesty has recognized the several members of the royal family who are here. The Queen is now asleep.'

An hour later Reid felt confident she was not about to die. He scribbled a note to his wife, who was at their cottage on the Osborne estate. 'I can't help admiring her determination not to give up the struggle while she can. I hardly dare to hope she may yet win, though she deserves to.'

The optimism was heartfelt but short-lived. Just before 2 p.m. she began to go downhill again. Randall Davidson was having a late lunch with Clement Smith when he was called urgently. Taking the vicar with him, he hurried across the covered walk that linked the Household wing to the royal quarters and along the corridor to her bedroom. He could see that she was much weaker. There was no sign that this was just a temporary relapse, and at three the doctors sent for the family. The deathbed scene assembled once more. The Queen lay with her daughter-in-law, the Princess of Wales, holding her in her arms as Reid and Barlow held the oxygen mask to her face and tried to ease her breathing. To one side of the bed, the two clerics, Davidson and Smith, took it in turns to recite prayers and passages from the Scriptures, but it seemed she barely noticed them. Only the last verse of 'Lead, kindly Light' caught her attention, and the Bishop felt sure she had heard and appreciated it.

But still she clung on. For an hour they watched, the silence broken only by the prayers of the Bishop and the loud wails

of nine-year-old Prince Maurice of Battenberg, Princess Beatrice's youngest son, who had to be taken out. Reid decided
she needed to be made more comfortable in the bed, and he
asked everyone to leave while this was done. The princesses
made their way into the corridor and across into the Queen's
sitting room. Through the oval window the wintery light
outside was beginning to fade; it would soon be dark. They
took their seats on the sofa and around the circular table where
they had been so many times before to sew and read and
chatter as she sat at her desk – the one she had once shared
with Albert – writing letters. The Bishop moved quietly
among them, offering words of consolation. Next door, the
Prince of Wales and the other men had taken refuge in the
Prince Consort's dressing and writing room. A fire of beech
logs was burning in the grate, and above it a portrait of Albert
looked down on his sons and grandsons. They talked but there
was also work to do, and they sat at his desk in turns to write
letters and telegrams. They were full of foreboding. To the
Lord Mayor of London, it was the Prince's 'painful duty to
inform you that the life of the Queen is in the greatest danger'.

Reid came in for a quiet word with the Prince of Wales. He
was ministering as best as he could to the Queen's body, but
he was troubled by those in charge of her soul. The constant
round of prayers by the Bishop and the vicar was causing
distress. He wondered if they should be asked to stop until she
was actually dying. The Prince agreed. When the family were
summoned back into the Queen's bedroom, it would be better
if the Bishop stayed outside for the time being. He could come
in when the Prince sent for him. Reid passed the message to
the prelate. If Davidson, so proud of his role in the family's
affairs, was put out by being excluded in this way, he disguised
his feelings and agreed that this would be for the best.

'The Queen is slowly sinking' were the solemn words of

the four o'clock bulletin. The journalists who read it at the gate saw it as the end of all hope: she would be dead by sunset. After issuing it, Reid went back in to see her and then called for the family. They came in and took up positions around the bed, some standing, some kneeling, all anxiously leaning forward towards the tiny figure lying helplessly on the small divan in the middle of the room. Mrs Tuck and Nurse Soal were at the head of the bed.

The minutes ticked away in the hushed room. An hour passed. By now the numbers were swelling. The Duchess of York, the children of the Duke of Connaught, the Duke of Argyll, and Prince and Princess Louis of Battenberg had arrived from the mainland, and all of them joined the family group crowding into the room. Some found the emotion too much and went out from time to time to recover their composure in the sitting room, where the Bishop waited with comforting words and a sympathetic ear. But the Kaiser would not budge – not after coming all this way and in the teeth of such persistent opposition. He stood to the right of the bed, his eyes fixed on the Queen as her breathing became more laboured. 'My proper place is here,' he had told Davidson before going in. 'I could not be away.'

He had one more duty to perform, one more 'proper place' to be. He dropped to his knees at her side and, with his right arm – his good arm – underneath her, he supported her as she gasped and tried to speak. Reid was holding her on the other side, and it was to him that she kept turning. 'Sir James,' she said once and then again and again, 'I am very ill.' He whispered back to her, 'Your Majesty will soon be better.'

At six o'clock it was clear that the end was approaching. By now the Prince of Wales had drawn up a chair and was sitting at the left of the bed, just behind Reid. His sister Princess Louise was kneeling beside him, and the rest of the family were grouped around the room. One by one they came forward, each saying their name to the Queen and making their farewells before stepping aside to weep and wait. She showed signs of recognizing them, and her mind seemed clearer than at any other time during the day. Princess Louise felt the drama of the occasion, but she thought it 'stately' too. The only distressing part was her mother's laboured breathing, which was painful to see and hear, but otherwise she thought her peaceful enough in these last minutes. She was slipping away like 'a great three-decker ship sinking', according to the Princess's husband, the Duke of Argyll.

Davidson was still outside in the sitting room, and must have felt that his presence was now essential. But he was told that her breathing was now so difficult that it would be impossible for her to accept his religious ministrations. It was 6.25 when he was finally called in. He entered alone. For some unexplained reason – a call of nature perhaps – Clement Smith had chosen that moment to leave the sitting room where they had been waiting patiently for so long.

As he began his prayers, the Bishop was only just in time. The Queen was staring at Reid and at her son sitting behind him. Then her eyes seemed to move past them and fix on the figure of the dead Christ in the massive painting by Gustav Jäger that hung over the fireplace. 'Then came a great change of look and complete calmness,' according to Davidson. Through her tears, Princess Helena noticed it too – a 'look of radiance on her face'. 'She opened her dear eyes quite wide, and one felt and knew she saw beyond the Border land and had seen and met all her loved ones.' The Bishop had just finished the Aaronic blessing – 'The Lord bless thee, and keep thee. The Lord make his face shine upon thee, and be gracious unto thee. The Lord lift up his countenance upon thee, and give thee peace' – when, in the arms of her doctor and her grandson the Kaiser, she quietly drew her last breath. It was 'without struggle, a gentle fading away', according to Sir Thomas Barlow.

Reid let go of her wrist. He had been holding it for the past hour, constantly monitoring her pulse. It had been strong right up to the last moment, but now it faded away. He kissed her hand, then took his left arm from under her and let her body down on the pillow. The time was precisely 6.30 p.m. The Queen was dead.

Prompted by Reid, the King – which, in that instant, he now was – leaned forward and closed her eyes before he broke down with sorrow and grief. But his sister Helena stared intently at her mother, and she marvelled at what she saw. 'In death she was so beautiful, such peace and joy on her face – a radiance from Heaven.'

The news had to be stopped. This death was a momentous state event, and there were procedures. Slow as the authorities, both Crown and civil, had been to grasp what was happening, they at least knew that an announcement had to be made properly. They feared servants' tongues and tittle-tattle. The doors of Osborne had been locked, and Bigge had ordered policemen to be stationed outside and at all the gates so nobody could get out to leak the news unofficially. He also put a stop on all the telegraph wires from the house until the formal announcements had gone out to the Lord Chancellor, the Prime Minister, the Lord Mayor of London, the Archbishop of Canterbury and the crowned heads of Europe. Then and only then did the head of the Household police force, the Queen's personal detective, Superintendent Charles Fraser, walk up to the Osborne gates.

There the reporters were thinking of their approaching deadlines for sending reports back to London. The end was certainly coming, but when? It had been a long day, and an even longer night of waiting stretched ahead. As the sun began to sink, a discussion began. One of them put up the suggestion that the timing of death was often linked to natural events. He knew of a doctor who argued with some authority that the ebbing of human life and the ebbing of the tide were linked. It was all to do with the forces of nature. Tide tables were pulled out of jacket pockets. Out in the Solent, the waters were now near their lowest point. There was still a faint hint of red in the western sky, but it was suddenly dark over the island. A cold wind sprang up.

They were so involved in their speculation that at first they did not notice Fraser, not until he was standing on the steps of the stone-built lodge. Then they turned and rushed towards him. 'Gentlemen,' he announced, his head bowed, his voice strained with emotion, 'I grieve to say Her Majesty passed away at half-past six.'

There was a quick moment of respect as the men raised their hats. Women in the crowd of onlookers burst into tears. And then there was pandemonium. Reporters grabbed their bicycles or leaped into waiting carriages and raced off in the direction of the post office in East Cowes. Shouts went up from the reporters as they sped past people on the hill: 'The Queen is dead! The Queen is dead!' When he heard about it, Fritz Ponsonby thought the behaviour of the press 'disgraceful'. James Vincent, the *Times* correspondent, was overwhelmed by the rush. He had been in the town filing a holding story to London and had not been at the gates of Osborne for the announcement. He was driving up in a carriage as the mob came down, the noise they made like a fox-hunt in full cry. The journalists responsible for it were 'an outrage', he declared. 'This yelling stampede established a record in bad taste and inhumanity.'

Even the more down-to-earth *Daily Chronicle* reporter was astonished. 'I have seen many rushes of journalists to telegraph offices but never any like this.' As they reached the post office they leaped from their bicycles or threw themselves from their cabs, and more than one of them was injured in the mêlée as they pushed and shoved their way in. In a few minutes more the instruments were clicking off the momentous tidings to every quarter of the globe.

The news was sweeping through the small town, and people came out of their houses and gathered on the streets. At first they seemed unable to take in what they had heard, that 'their beloved Sovereign had passed from them for ever'. But then shopkeepers began to put up their shutters and hang out black crêpe as a mark of grief. Cowes, the Queen's holiday home, would show the world how to mourn a monarch.

As shops and businesses shut down, the newspapermen pressed on. The postmaster, Mr Mott, had brought in extra staff to man the wires, and forty of them were working through the night in shifts. The reporters had had hours of waiting in which to craft the words they sent. It was down to their grandiloquence to capture this great occasion. James Vincent could now update the story he had already sent. He scribbled out a new introduction to his report and passed it to the telegraph clerk: 'All day long the Angel of Death has been hovering over Osborne House. One could almost hear the beating of his wings. But at half past six those wings were folded and the Queen was at rest.'

Inside Osborne, the Bishop of Winchester had discreetly withdrawn from the Queen's bedroom to allow the family to be alone with her for the last time. He stood in the passage for a few minutes until the Prince of Wales came out all on his own. The Bishop bowed. 'Your Majesty,' he said, later recording with pride that he had been 'the first to greet him as Sovereign'. Then Davidson hurried off to the equerries' room, taking it upon himself to be the one to break the news of the Queen's death to Sir Arthur Bigge and the other senior members of the Household.

They must have known already, however, because the Earl of Clarendon, the Lord Chamberlain, was already with Bigge, and he had been in the Queen's bedroom when she died, to witness and record the event, as required by his office of state. Clarendon had arrived at Osborne just three hours earlier, sent from London in a great hurry as the administration in Whitehall and Westminster at last awoke to the fact of what was happening.

For more than a week, the seriousness of the Queen's condition and the distinct possibility that she would die had been well known in the most powerful homes in the land. Margot Asquith was in a house party at Chatsworth when her husband, Henry, let her into the secret. Going into her bedroom as she was dressing for dinner one night, he told her he had just had a telegram saying the Queen was very ill and 'he feared the worst'. But the news was 'a profound secret and I was to tell no one'.[1] It can hardly have been a close-kept secret. The other guests that weekend included Arthur Balfour, who had been tipped off by his private secretary months before that the Queen was seriously in decline, and Joseph Chamberlain, who had been at Osborne recently and had seen for himself.

But the Prime Minister, Lord Salisbury, appears to have shut his mind to the possibility that the sovereign was terminally ill. He froze. On Friday 18 January his niece by marriage, Lady Frances Balfour, had been to see her brother the Duke of Argyll and her sister-in-law, Princess Louise, at Kensington Palace and had learned the truth. She also 'knew Salisbury had no idea how serious it was'. She set off for Hatfield, his house in Hertfordshire, the next day, battling through a heavy storm in her determination that he should be told in no uncertain terms. He was still in London when she arrived, so she waited. The evening papers with their news of 'grave symptoms' confirmed her fears. She 'felt the clouds were closing in rapidly – all that stormy afternoon history was being made'. But the Prime Minister would not be told. When he arrived home he swept into his sitting room and closed the door. He would not be disturbed. She waited a while longer and then gave up. Back in London, she took a bus home from King's Cross and was struck by the anxiety of everyone around her, 'the absorbed looks, the questions of the working men, the universal buying of newspapers'. It was odd how everyone was moved – everyone, it seemed, except the Prime Minister.[2]

It was not until Tuesday, the day of the Queen's death, that action was taken. That morning Lady Frances saw the Duke of Argyll, who had just been telegraphed from Osborne with instructions to get there as soon as possible because the end was near. She drove with him to the station, and then went on to Downing Street to tell her brother-in-law Arthur that she thought he should go too. He had already had the same summons from the Prince of Wales and was getting dressed before leaving. She was amazed how unprepared everyone was. Balfour was the Leader of the House of Commons and the second most powerful politician in the land, yet he had only just discovered the first constitutional consequence of the Queen's death – that Parliament would have to meet immediately to swear allegiance to the new sovereign. He had an urgent paper prepared for the Prime Minister. But Salisbury had not read it and was astonished when he was pulled out of a committee meeting to be told. He was now, said Lady Frances, 'too shocked by his knowledge of the approaching calamity to look at the papers his private secretary had put out for him'.

Balfour at last hurried off to Osborne, travelling with the Duchess of York on a special train which left London at 2 p.m. When they arrived in the late afternoon, she was taken in to join the family around the Queen's bedside; he was left to kick his heels outside. In the hallway he was astounded to see official government boxes lined up, unopened and untouched for a week. The documents inside them would have to wait until eternity for her signature. But he knew that its absence was already creating problems. Many thousands of commissions for officers in the Army and Navy were awaiting the sovereign's consent. Even the administration of justice was being hampered, because judges needed the Queen's written authority before they could proceed with the assizes.

Now Balfour sat in the equerries' room listening to the Bishop's account of the Queen's last hours and minutes. There was an air of shock and uncertainty. Fritz Ponsonby admitted that 'no one seemed to know what the procedure was'. That evening in the private secretary's office at Osborne they rifled through as many old documents and books as they could lay their hands on to discover what had been done when George IV and William IV had died. The royal family were equally at a loss, feeling, according to Princess Helena's daughter, Princess Marie Louise, 'great consternation and bewilderment as to what was the correct mourning for the Sovereign. It was 64 [*sic*] years since such a tragic event had taken place.'[3]

The King had made his first decision as monarch. For the rest of that day he would remain the Prince of Wales. Out of respect for his mother, he did not wish to be addressed as the King until tomorrow. (His wife went further: she would not let anyone kiss her hand or call her Queen until after the funeral.) That was not all he wished to put off. From their

hurried constitutional readings, Bigge and Ponsonby concluded that the Privy Council must be summoned immediately, but the Prince of Wales was reluctant to leave Osborne
straight away. He was in no hurry to return to London and
put the private grief he felt on public display. But in the capital
the Prime Minister had taken a grip of himself and the situation
and sent Balfour a coded message that there must be no delay.

That night, the Prince and the rest of the royal family pored
over the instructions left by the Queen about what should
happen on her death. Her will, written just over three years
earlier, affirmed that

I die in peace with all, fully aware of my many faults, relying with
confidence on the love, mercy and goodness of my Heavenly Father
and His Blessed Son and earnestly trusting to be reunited to my
beloved Husband, my dearest Mother, my loved Children and 3
dear sons-in-law. And all who have been very near and dear to me
on earth. Also I hope to meet those who have so faithfully and so
devotedly served me, especially good John Brown and good Annie
Macdonald.[4]

They must have cringed at the mention of Brown's name –
fumed even. The Prince of Wales would not have wanted to
be reminded of him at a time like this, but he would have his
revenge on the awkward Highland servant who had treated
him with disdain and disrespect, refusing to acknowledge any
superior except the Queen herself, not even her eldest son
and heir. Later on, every memento of him he could lay his
hands on would be systematically destroyed.

With a thoroughness characteristic of her, the Queen's will
went on to decree everything, down to the style of her funeral
and what sort of coffin she wanted. Under no circumstances
was her body to be embalmed; there was to be no lying in

state; as the daughter of a soldier, she was to have a military funeral, borne to her grave on a gun carriage; purple and white, not black, were to be her colours in death. The coffin was to follow the model of those in the royal vault at St George's Chapel. It would be a triple casket – a wooden shell inside a lead coffin and an elaborate outer coffin. By tradition, these were made by Banting's, a firm of undertakers in St Paul's Churchyard in London, who had been carrying out royal business for two hundred years. The Prince asked Reid to sort the matter out, and the doctor wrote a note to Lord Clarendon, the Lord Chamberlain. Banting's should be instructed to go ahead with the coffin for the Queen, but should be sure to have the wooden inner shell at Osborne within thirty-six hours so that the Queen could be sealed inside it as quickly as possible.

The exhausted Reid had yet more work to do. He ate a hurried dinner and then went back to the Queen's bedroom to help her maids and the nurse prepare the body. They lifted her off the divan and back on to her proper bed, which they pushed back into its position against the back wall and under the towering green canopy. Reid took the opportunity to examine her physically – something that in twenty years he had never done before. He noted that she had a ventral hernia and a prolapse of the uterus: her womb had dropped and the muscles had stretched – no surprise in a woman who had given birth nine times, though the condition would have contributed to her abdominal aches and pains over the years.

Reid left the women to dress the Queen in a white gown and place her wedding veil over her face. Princess Beatrice, who more than the rest of the family had learned to understand her mother's ways in the years she had sat as her companion, brought in a crown of Wedgwood-blue hyacinths in dark-green foliage which she placed beside her mother. She was in a daze, unable to take in the fact that it was all over.[5]

Alone with their mistress, the dressers had a secret job to do. Mrs Tuck took out a letter that had been in her keeping for more than three years and opened it. On the envelope, in the Queen's unmistakable spidery handwriting, were the almost indecipherable words 'Instructions for my dressers to be opened directly after my death and to be always taken about and kept by the one who may be travelling with me'. It was dated December 1897. The letter inside, a dozen pages long, was as clear as could be – it had been dictated to Harriet Phipps, the Queen's secretary, and she had copied it out neatly and, to avoid confusion, with the last word of each page repeated at the top of the next. Mrs Tuck read the contents and then put the letter away until, obediently and lovingly, she could carry out her last duty to her Queen.

Downstairs in the drawing room, the Bishop of Winchester was doing his duty too. Earlier he had taken a moment or two off to record his role in history. Finding the unfinished letter to his wife in his pocket, he quickly scrawled a note in red ink across a double sheet at the end: 'Tues, 22nd. It is now 7 p.m. and since 9 a.m. I have been almost continuously in and about the Queen's room, ministering to her at intervals and I was present at her death 25 mins ago. So all must wait till I can get quiet to write. I am worn out now.'

He had recovered his energy and was now flitting from person to person and group to group, offering sympathy and comfort to Princess Helena and Princess Beatrice, whom he thought 'calm and sensible'. He chatted with Balfour, but found the politician wanted to talk about other matters, such as who Davidson thought should be the new Bishop of London. Then, at 10.15 p.m., the family gathered again in the Queen's bedroom for prayers, led by the Bishop. He looked at her 'lying in the bed where she had died, all beautifully arranged, with quantities of white lace and a few simple flowers; the little crucifix which had always hung over her head within the bed being in her hand; her face looking pale and quite calm and almost youthful'. Princess May, the Duchess of York (later Queen Mary), thought 'Grandmama looked so lovely and peaceful dressed all in white with lace and the bed covered with flowers.'

As they prayed for their mother, the family's thoughts turned to a missing member. In Germany, the eldest of the Queen's children was devastated when the news reached her. Bedridden Vicky's physical pain from the cancer was matched by the hurt in her heart and her 'agony of mind at this overwhelming sorrow. Oh my beloved Mama! Is she really gone? Gone from us all to whom she was such a comfort and support. To have lost her seems so impossible. What will life be without her?'

It was a question earnestly being asked everywhere in the land that night.

# 7. A World in Shock

*Thus, in its sad simplicity, falls the crushing blow at last . . .*

The *Daily Express*

Cinderella was sitting in her rags by the kitchen fire. The gaslights had just been dimmed in the auditorium of the Pavilion Theatre in the East End of London and there was a murmur of appreciation from the audience as the curtains pulled away to reveal the first tableau of the pantomime. Before she could speak, the lights flared up again and the theatre manager strode on, a telegram in his hand. 'Ladies and gentlemen, it is my sad duty to announce that Her Majesty the Queen is dead,' he said. The performance could not continue. A quiet sigh ran through the audience. Without a word, they got up and left. There would be no fairy-tale ending that night.

Outside in the streets, the news was being passed from mouth to mouth in the cold night air. Along the Whitechapel Road the word travelled, peeling off into dark, crowded alleys, shouted up to rooms in tenement buildings and down through gratings to homes in cellars. It was seven o'clock, and workers were pouring out of warehouses and factories. When they heard, they stopped, and groups gathered on the street corners. The conversation was quiet, shocked, reverent. 'She was a good old lady, and if ever anyone was mother to her country it was the Queen,' one workman, his hands and face still covered in grime from his day's labours, told those around him, and heads nodded in agreement.

Newspapers were now on the streets, and men 'hurried from omnibuses and rushed from restaurants and public houses, from shops and offices and even from private dwellings' to buy them. The news spread over the city like a flood, and its immediate aftermath was dramatic as blinds were drawn, curtains pulled down, lights extinguished.

In the Mile End Road, a congregation of five thousand at a mission meeting in the Great Assembly Hall wept as they were told the news. Then the organ began to play the *Dead March* and everyone stood, heads bowed, as the music caught the moment. The solemn strains from Handel's oratorio *Saul* were striking up everywhere. At the other end of the land, in a grand country house just outside Aberdeen, the pianist Mr Julian Clifford was about to give a concert to four hundred local music-lovers gathered in the splendid library at Dunecht House. He had travelled up from London to play at the invitation of Mr Pirie, the owner of the house, and the turnout was excellent. But, as he composed himself to begin, Mr Pirie put up his hand to stop him. A telegram had arrived – the Queen was dead. Quietly, everyone stood and filed to the chapel in the house, and, as they prayed, the pianist played Chopin's *Marche funèbre* and the *Dead March* on the organ. Neither in Dunecht nor in the Mile End Road could they have known that, in her will, which the royal family would shortly be reading in Osborne, the Queen had specifically forbade the playing of the *Dead March* to mark her death. 'Handel always tires me,' she had once said, 'and I won't pretend he doesn't.'

The news had reached Mr Pirie from the editor of his local paper, the *Aberdeen Journal*. It was a pattern repeated up and down the country as newspapers, the main source of information, everywhere played a crucial part in the national drama. The editor of the *Aberdeen Journal* was particularly busy. He had sent an urgent telegram not only to Mr Pirie, who was an important local figure, but to all the villages along the river Dee. At Ballater, the nearest town to Balmoral, the message was pinned up in the newsagent's window, and a tearful crowd gathered to stare at it. Meanwhile, in Liverpool, the local correspondent of the *Daily Express* was the first to give the news to the Lord Mayor, Alderman Arthur Crossthwaite, who at once drove to the town hall, where the flag was lowered to half mast and black cloth was draped over the balcony.

The curtains were falling everywhere. In Manchester, *Aladdin* was into its second scene at the Prince's Theatre when the manager, Mr Courtneidge, stepped solemnly on to the stage and announced that the Queen had died. Across at the Theatre Royal, *Little Red Riding Hood* ended after just twenty minutes. The St James's Theatre, though, was slower to act, and it was not until after 8 p.m., when the first act of *For The Colours* had ended, that the performance was abandoned. The orchestra broke into the *Dead March*.

More serious pursuits ground to a halt too. In Salford, a public lecture on 'The Engineering Triumphs of Our Age' was interrupted when Alderman Mandley held a whispered conference with other members of the Parks and Libraries Committee and stopped it there and then as a mark of respect. Before the audience filed out, Alderman Snape stood up to reminisce about the Queen's visit fifty years ago with Prince Albert and the Duke of Wellington. On the other side of the country, Mr Walter Runciman MA was just getting ready to deliver his talk on 'The Elizabethan Voyages' at the YMCA in Newcastle when a local MP, George Renwick, took the platform to announce the death of the Queen. He wanted to say some words but, unusually for a politician, felt unequal to the task at that time. The lecture was abandoned.

In the City of London, the Queen's death had been expected all day. That morning the crowds making their way to their offices had stopped outside the Mansion House, the home of the Lord Mayor, and pushed through to see the bulletin board for the latest news. There were so many of them that the police had to move them along to stop them spilling into the road and halting the traffic. The noon bulletin – 'There is no change for the worse' – had brought a slight hint of hope, and some had managed to raise a cheer, but in the afternoon all doubt had disappeared. One observer noted that 'a deep gloom fell over the City which even the ceaseless roar of traffic and the bustle of business failed to lighten'. Business, in fact, had virtually ceased, and the commonest trade was in words of sympathy and concern. 'The sorrow was too near and too personal for men to busy themselves about buying or selling,' the *Daily Chronicle* reported. 'Each one's thoughts were turned towards the death chamber at Osborne, and all were trying to realize the imminent loss which hung over London, Britain and the Empire at large. The great sorrow fell upon all classes and all ages. In factory and shop, in counting house and office, people expressed their fears for the worst.' There had been constant rumours until 'at last the word passed around that the end had come. There was a movement of the people like the swaying of a field of corn when a summer breeze passes over it, and all eyes were turned to the Mansion House.'

Thousands were gathered in the street when, just after seven o'clock, Frank Green, the Lord Mayor, appeared at the open window of his parlour in evening dress and black tie. There was a hush. All heads were instantly bared. Top hats and cloth caps alike were gripped. 'Fellow citizens, it is with deep sorrow I have to read you a telegram which has just reached me from the Prince of Wales: "Osborne, 6.45. My beloved mother, the Queen, has just passed away, surrounded by her children and grandchildren – Albert Edward."'

Not a sound was heard, not another voice spoke. The Lord Mayor left the window, and the blind was slowly pulled down. The crowd melted away, but others arrived to press round the noticeboard to read for themselves the announcement that was about to change their world. The silence was broken by a historic sound as Great Tom, one of the ancient bells of St Paul's Cathedral, began to toll, its mournful note echoing out across the city. The order for it to be rung had come from the Lord Mayor, at the request of the Home Secretary. The bell, first cast for Edward I, had hung for centuries in Westminster Hall and had been brought to Christopher Wren's rebuilt cathedral two hundred years earlier. It tolled rarely – it had last done so for Prince Albert – and had not announced the death of a monarch since 1837. The crowd on the cathedral steps wept openly. Over in Kensington, Lady Frances Balfour had heard the news and knew St Paul's would be marking the occasion. She stepped out into the night to listen, but no sound came from the east. The wind had changed direction.

At Buckingham Palace, another crowd looked on as the blinds came down. They were brand new, having been mysteriously installed in the windows at the front of the building only the day before. The purpose was now plain – they had been put up to be pulled down as a mark of respect. The palace had no bell to toll and, by tradition, its flagpole only ever carried the royal standard, and then only when the monarch was in residence, and this could never be at half mast. The falling blinds, cutting out all light from the windows, were the signal to those watching at the gates that the end had come. But the growing crowd had to wait another hour for official confirmation of what they already knew. A policeman walked across the wide quadrangle and tied a new board to the railings. Until now the boards had been of red cloth, but this one was black. 'The Queen died peacefully at six-thirty,' those nearest read out aloud for those at the back of the crowd to hear.

Across Green Park, in the gentlemen's clubs of St James's and Pall Mall, the members had waited around anxiously throughout the day, standing in quiet groups in their clubs or mingling outside the Russian cigarette shop to hear the latest rumour. The Guards Club was now deserted. As the news came through, every one of its officer members left, feeling that to be relaxing and at their ease was the wrong thing for military men to be doing at such a time. In their clubs, however, the politicians were deep in solemn discussion. At the National Liberal, they had gathered around the ticker tape in the smoking room to see the 'melancholy tidings'. The chairman, Earl Carrington, ordered the flag to be flown at half mast. At the Carlton, Athenaeum, Reform and Travellers', the same procedure was followed. There was conversation, but it was 'muffled', in the words of one clubman, 'as though the talkers were talking under their breath'.

There was a similar hush in the streets outside. The American writer Henry James walked down Pall Mall from the Reform and sensed real fear among the people around him, who were dazed by the news. Leaving his club, another gentleman was astonished that even the traffic seemed to be quieter. 'The customary maelstrom in Piccadilly Circus is abated. The cut-and-thrust proceedings of the theatre-going hansom cabs are conspicuous by their absence. The Strand is full but singularly quiet.' He was swept up in the crowd heading eastward, unsure of where he was going until

presently the dome of St Paul's shows up, and all about the Cathedral approaches the crowd waxes and stands silent, waiting for the sounding of the bell. The hold this sovereign lady of ours had upon the hearts of all her people is shown by the strange quiet that has fallen this night upon this eminently unsentimental and utilitarian metropolis. The silence that has lapped London these last hours seems to show more certainly than anything else how absolutely she was Queen of us all.[1]

By now, all the theatres in London and throughout the country had closed, without waiting for the formal order from the Lord Chamberlain telling them to do so. The managers of the West End theatres had prepared for this moment. They had been in touch with each other the day before and had agreed that they would all instantly halt their performances the moment her death was announced. Most had not even begun and theatre staff were able to turn their audiences away at the door. But there had been an early start for the pantomime at the Theatre Royal in Drury Lane, and the overture was two-thirds through, the actors dressed and waiting in the wings, when a halt was called. Leading actors, Beerbohm Tree and Charles Hawtrey among them, made their way to Wyndham's Theatre in Shaftesbury Avenue, where they composed a collective letter of condolence to send to the Prince of Wales. The audiences hurried away into the night, and by nine o'clock the West End, normally buzzing with activity and excitement, was a desert.

The crowds heading from the West End to St Paul's passed along Fleet Street, where the lights would burn through the night and early morning in newspaper offices and printing works. There was much to do. Reports were flooding in – not just of the events as they unfolded at Osborne and in London but of reactions to the Queen's death everywhere, from the smallest hamlet in the British Isles to the capital cities of the world's great nations. Every correspondent had a tale to tell, and, as their stories filled the telegraph wires, so the sub-editors and compositors filled the pages. They knew the demand on the streets tomorrow morning would be insatiable. The *Daily Mail* – which already claimed to have 'the largest circulation in the world' – would double its normal sales to one and a half million the next day.

At the Tudor Street offices of the *Express*, the *Mail*'s newest and deadliest rival, a sub-editor had gathered in front of him the reports telegraphed in from around the Empire. Most papers – *The Times* and the *Daily Telegraph*, for example – would print these verbatim, one after another, as a matter of record, no matter how repetitious. But the *Express* was altogether racier and pacier, an exponent of a new type of popular journalism for a new type of public. The sub-editor let his imagination take wing.

Through the green, unfathomable depths of all the seas the cables flashed last night their messages of sorrow, which plunged a world in grief. The sun had sunk when England heard the news but as the sun swept westward over the broad waters of the Atlantic the cables caught and passed him in the race, so it was but early afternoon when the great Dominion [Canada] knew the melancholy tidings. The bells jingle loudly in the streets of Ottawa as sleighs come dashing to learn the truth they feared, and as they hear it turn sadly away.

We leave the snow-clad north and drop southward to warmer climes. Bermuda has the sad news and sends it on to Turks Island, to the Windward Isles, to Jamaica and British Guiana. The merry, careless negroes will be mourning in their own fashion, crying bitter tears for her they loved so well . . . Once more we sweep on, across the Southern Seas, leaving behind the islands we own where the happy folk are splashing in the surf, ignorant of their loss since no cables pierce those waters till New Zealand bulks larger to the southward . . . The news has reached Calcutta at midnight and the crowded native quarters are awake mourning the death of her who embodied for them the power and honour of the British Raj.

It was a snapshot of Victorian imperialism that suited the *Express* and its readers. Patriotism and optimism were the paper's mission; 'our party is the British empire; the future is our heritage' was its self-proclaimed message. But readers' emotions needed to be tugged too, and for that the editor had commissioned a special poem. It was the centrepiece of page two.

> The vision pales and dies
> Which gladdened long our eyes,
> Great majesty in womanhood enshrining;
> She passes to her rest,
> Victoria the Blest,
> Her crown with a diviner lustre shining;
> And while her stricken people weep,
> She lays her sceptre down, and falls asleep.
>
> Hush! She is sleeping now –
> Smooth is the wrinkled brow –
> Closed are her eyes by Death's caressing fingers;
> Calm is the white, wan face,
> Where the endearing grace
> Of motherhood and widowhood still lingers.
> Silence the trumpet and the bell!
> The Queen doth slumber – wake her not! – all's well.
>
> Her gentle spirit drew
> As doth the sun the dew
> Our hearts to her, alike in joy and sorrow;

And when the daylight died
She took our hands and cried
'Be of good cheer, there is a bright tomorrow!'
She was our mother then, and more,
And loved us as no sons were ever loved before.

But when, at war's alarms,
She called her sons to arms,
Then was she Queen, defiant, lion-hearted.
Then was she King and lord,
Girt with her Empire's sword –
Seaward the lightnings of her legions darted;
War-worn they came again to her,
Who was their sovereign balm and sweetest comforter.

Not as we bring the bloom
To deck her kingly tomb
Shall we survey the splendour of her glory;
But in the after-years
When pride hath dried our tears
Our children shall be told her wondrous story.
Now let her rest, in Jesus sleeping –
God guard her ever in his holy keeping!

The paper was filling up. There was other news to report –
in Italy, Verdi was dying; in Wales, a woman miner who had
smoked all her life had died at the age of 103; a deadly outbreak
of plague in Hull had been contained – but these stories would
have to be crammed into a single column on page five.

Down in the composing room, the head printer had found
his blackest italic type and across the first two columns of the
front page he ran his history-making headline – 'Death of the
Queen – A world in mourning'. The sides of the page were

edged in black; thick funereal rules ran down between the empty columns – he waited for the words to fill the white space. Meanwhile, the paper's top 'colour' writer was at his desk. The obituary as such, the full history of her reign, had been written months before and had been lying around in type since the first hints of her illness, ready to be rushed into print. His job now was to try to catch the moment, to find the words that would convey the magnitude of the occasion.

He began well enough – 'Thus, in its sad simplicity, falls the crushing blow at last . . .'

But then he felt unequal to the task:

There is no living pen – probably none ever lived since writing began – which can do justice to the emotions agitating at this hour millions of throbbing breasts. The subject is too sacred, too private to every one of us, too intimately interwoven with all we possess of love and faith and understanding, to be laid bare for men to read about.

He quickly found the way to his readers' feelings:

Today it is not our national loss that we mourn. The bitterness of that affliction will not be fully realized until we miss the wise counsels, the ripe experience, the almost infallible judgement, and all else that was embodied in the person of the great good Queen who ruled a mighty Empire for more than sixty years, who had associated with the foremost intellects of that marvellous period, and who had never faltered in her devotion to duty or her fulfilment of responsibility. Queen Victoria was to a large extent the personal embodiment of our Empire and history, and our loss as a nation at her death is much as if we had been suddenly deprived of the accumulated wisdom of generations.

But our grief today is rather for the loss of a friend, a guide, and one who was intimately bound up with our daily lives and who reigned in all our hearts. That is the immediate, the heartbreaking blow. We can only endure it like men, remembering with gratitude, not so much the national loss we suffer by her death, as the national gain we have so long enjoyed in her precious life.

The *Express*'s readers may have been mourning the loss of a friend, but for the leader writer at *The Times* an entire era had died, and he crafted his words accordingly:

For nearly 64 years she has watched, at first with conscientious diffidence, later with ever-maturing experience but always with the sympathetic insight of a sensitive yet finely-balanced nature, over every development of national policy and destiny . . . Epochs sometimes find names that do not very accurately fit them but we can speak with accuracy of the Victorian age. Her reign coincides with a sort of second renaissance, an intellectual movement accomplishing in a brief term more than had been done in preceding centuries. Since the days of Elizabeth there has been no such awakening of the mind of the nation, no such remarkable stride in the path of progress, no such spreading abroad of the British race and British rule over the world at large, as in the period covered by the reign whose end we now have to deplore.

Her own life was one of almost austere simplicity and homeliness. Her court has been unsullied by the vices which had come to be regarded as the inseparable concomitants of courts, and if society at large has not quite reached her standard, at least it cannot plead the want of a shining example. Her whole life, public and private, has been a great and abiding lesson upon the paramount importance of character. No lesson is more needed in days when superficial cleverness or real ability untrammelled by scruples, too often fills the public eye by the meretricious aid of the self-advertisement which the Queen abhorred.

But the writer was anxious about the future, aware that Britain had lost some of its drive and was now facing serious challenges in the world:

At the close of the reign we find ourselves somewhat less secure of our position than we could desire, and somewhat less abreast of the problems of the age than we ought to be, considering the initial advantages we secured. Others have learned our lessons and bettered our instructions, while we have been too easily content to rely upon the methods which were effective a generation or two ago. In this way the Victorian age is defined at the end as well as at its beginning. The command of natural forces that made us great and rich has been superseded by newer discoveries and methods, and we have to open what may be called a new chapter. But if we now enter upon our work in the spirit embodied in the untiring vigilance and the perpetual openness of mind that distinguished the Queen, if, like her, we reverence knowledge and hold duty imperfectly discharged until we have brought all attainable knowledge to bear upon its performance, her descendants will witness advance not less important than that of her long and glorious reign.

If *The Times* felt uncertain about the future, many others in the land were lost for what to do in the present. They looked to the past for answers. At the College of Arms, officials were pulling out the records for 1837 to find precisely what ceremonies had marked the death of William IV. All they were prepared to say was that 'ancient usages would be repeated'. The same message came from the Dean and chapter at Westminster Abbey, who presumably expected the abbey to be the focal point of the nation's mourning as before. If so they were alone in their expectations, because it was well known that Windsor was where the Queen wished to be buried and, since she had died at Osborne, there might be no role at all for the capital city. But, undaunted, the Dean and canons were digging out documents to re-enact the past.

Of all the great state institutions, only the Lord Chamberlain's office acted decisively. Typically, it imposed a ban. The theatres had closed instantly, sending their audiences home in a spontaneous act of respect. The Lord Chamberlain made this official by revoking all their licences. That night, actors and actresses, stage hands and front-of-house staff had been happy to do the right thing. But it cost them a night's pay. They stood around by the stage doors mourning their Queen but worrying how long they would be out of work. The Lord Chamberlain had no advice to offer. The theatres could be dark until after the funeral, perhaps longer. When William IV died they had been shut for two weeks.

Edward George Saunders, owner of the Coronet in Notting Hill Gate and two other popular theatres in Camden and Brixton, was having none of this. He had shut his show that night but planned to open it again the next night and carry on, stopping only on the day of the funeral itself, whenever that might be. He was worried about the staff, and he sat down to write a letter to the *Standard* pleading for 'the thousands of employees and smaller members of the profession in the metropolitan theatres and music halls who are at the present entirely thrown out of work'. They were as loyal to the Crown as anyone, 'but in addition to the grief which they have sustained they are threatened with an almost general loss of employment for possibly a fortnight to come. This is at a time when great numbers of them are engaged in pantomime, which is their yearly harvest, and the distress which this class will undergo will be most severe.' He begged his fellow managers to follow his example and show real respect to 'the great dead' by not letting their poor employees and those dependent on them starve. It was the first clash of a new age

– the rights and welfare of the workers against tradition and protocol. There would be more in the days and weeks ahead. But at first no one could think of anything other than slavishly following the old ways, and for now Saunders was on his own.

He was not alone, however, in his concern about the effect of the Queen's death on business. The clothing trade expected to do very well out of a short period of mourning but to be devastated if it was dragged out for months. Overnight, everything except black disappeared from shop windows. For the big London stores, the third week of January was the start of the traditional White Sale of sheets, tablecloths and all other sorts of household linen. The shops were dressed accordingly. The announcement of the Queen's death in the early evening left the store owners with a problem – their customers would be horrified to walk down Regent Street and Bond Street the next day and see windows still in white. That night, the shop staff toiled to turn white into black, dyeing every piece of cloth they could lay their hands on and totally transforming the appearance of the stores by the next morning. It was a small miracle that became legendary among retailers.

Suddenly, everyone wanted black crape. The papers listed the mourning-dress code. This was simple enough for the men – 'a black hatband, a black tie and black gloves with garments of a dark hue' – but women needed 'black dresses, black jacket or mantle, black hat or bonnet and gloves, scarves and ruffles to match'. The smart ones would find ways to relieve the gloom. 'White may quite properly be used with black and, after a short interval, mauve and grey will be seen.' Jewels used to be ruled out for mourners, but now jet, opals, rubies and amethysts were considered socially acceptable. The stylish *Queen* magazine debated whether the old-fashioned black silk scarf would make a comeback, 'thrown carelessly about the shoulders, the ends allowed to fall to the feet'. It ran

pages of suggestions and illustrations of what was reasonable
to wear. It disapproved of the Parisian habit for too much
crape. 'There is no doubt in our modern days we are steering
a middle course between too much mourning and hardly
enough.'

But, whatever a woman chose to do, it would be costly –
particularly for those least able to afford it. The *Daily Telegraph*
was sympathetic about this: 'Every woman in the land, be she
ever so poor, will want a black gown in order to show
her respect for the venerable Queen and it follows that the
observance of mourning will affect the lower middle classes
more than any other since this article is not always possessed.'

To meet this demand, the most commercially astute wholesalers had taken a judgement on the Queen's health days ago
and had hauled in extra stocks of black crape. Their factories
in Yorkshire had gone into overdrive, and they had even
wired Continental suppliers in Saint-Étienne and Basle to
secure extra capacity. From Grenoble a large shipment of grey
and black gloves was already on order. But canny customers
had anticipated her death too, and even before it had happened
shops in the West End were already bursting to the seams with
orders for black made-to-measure crêpe-de-Chine dresses for
indoor wear and plain black cloth coats for going out. Those
happy to wear ready-made black skirts found they were soon
in short supply. One wholesaler in Leeds was landed with an
order for 1,000 black ties for immediate delivery.

There would be an immediate spending spree, but then
there would be a problem. 'A considerable dislocation of
trade will be involved,' the *Telegraph* reported. The trouble
was that wholesalers had stocked up with coloured goods for
the spring, and now these were likely to remain unsold. They
feared their business would be 'crippled'. 'The idea that a
period of national mourning is good for trade is incorrect,

even though it may occasion temporary pressure in warehouse and workroom.'

The key issue was how long the country would be ordered into mourning, and the precedents were closely scrutinized. The killjoys at the Lord Chamberlain's office had kept all the details. The death of William IV had plunged the court into black for three months, during which time the ladies were confined to 'black bombazines, plain muslins or long lawn linens, crape hoods, chamois shoes and crape fans' and the men to 'black cloth without buttons on the sleeves and pockets, plain muslin or long lawn cravats and weepers, crape hat bands and black swords and buckles'. For the general public the period of mourning had not been specified, but it was generally agreed to be six weeks. Victoria's reign had begun in black, and black had been its predominant colour since 1861. It was ending in the same sombre way.

It might also be ending in chaos. Viscount Esher had done his homework and looked in the *Annual Register* for 1837 to find out the ceremonial procedures that had been followed for the death of William IV. But others in high office were in danger of making silly mistakes. The Lord Chancellor and the Speaker of the House of Commons had talked privately and decided between them that they would take their oaths of allegiance to the King at their homes before the Privy Council met. Esher knew this would not do. The Council had to meet first, and it was the Lord Chancellor's first job to administer the oath to the new monarch at that meeting. Only when the King had been sworn could any of his subjects pledge their allegiance to him. Esher could not restrain his anger that those who should know better appeared to know nothing at all. He had learned, for example, that the Home Secretary had not been called to Osborne, though all the precedents suggested his presence was necessary to witness a royal death. 'I cannot describe the ignorance, the historical ignorance, of everyone, from top to bottom,' he fulminated. 'You would think that the English monarchy had been buried since the time of Alfred.'[2]

But it was the future rather than the past that excited him. 'What changes, political and social, this event will produce! It is like beginning to live again in a new world.'

# 8. Secret Last Wishes

She lay in her coffin wearing two wedding rings . . .

The new world that opened on 23 January 1901 was a black one. Thirteen-year-old Violet Asquith was holding tightly on to her nurse's hand as they battled through the crowds in a draper's shop in the centre of London to buy mourning clothes. 'From the hushed house we were sent into hushed streets where everyone, even the poorest, seemed to be already dressed in black.'[1] It was a Wednesday, but to another observer who walked those silent streets it seemed more like a Sunday. The traffic was lighter than usual, the throng on the pavements less pressing, many of the shops practically deserted. 'Friends greeted each other with a sense of common sorrow. In every group people exclaimed "God bless her!" '[2]

The hundreds of horse-drawn, open-top omnibuses bringing workers into the city bore signs of mourning, as did the ranks of hansom cabs. Their drivers had tied crape bows to their whips and had black bands around their hats. Flower girls wore black in their bonnets, and street sellers did a good trade in black shirt studs. In post offices there was a rush to buy sets of stamps with the Queen's head on them before they ran out. Only the shops selling black clothes were full. In one outfitters, mirrors had been ranged along the counter so the men who came in to buy a black tie could put it on there and then. People seemed in a hurry to look the part, 'as if ashamed to be seen without the evidence

1. Dynasty: Queen Victoria with her eldest son, later Edward VII (*right*), a grandson, later George V, and, on her knee, a great-grandson, later Edward VIII, *c.* 1900

2. Osborne House on the Isle of Wight

3. Always writing: the Queen with her
Indian servant, the Munshi, 1897

4. 'Baby': Princess Beatrice, with her
children, 1899

5. Riding out: in her pony carriage, 1896

6. 'Lenchen': Princess
Helena, 1883

7. Princess Louise, 1890

8. Vicky: the Queen's eldest daughter, on the arm of her son, the Kaiser

9. The doctor:
Sir James Reid

10. The bishop:
Randall Davidson

11. The equerry: Fritz Ponsonby (*middle*), next to
Dr Reid, 1900

12. The servant: John Brown, 1882

**Le Petit Journal**
SUPPLÉMENT ILLUSTRÉ
DIMANCHE 17 FÉVRIER 1901

FUNÉRAILLES DE LA REINE VICTORIA
La chapelle ardente

13. Queen Victoria on her death-bed,
by Sir Hubert von Herkomer

14. Honouring the coffin: the front cover
of *Le Petit Journal*

15. The last photograph of the Queen

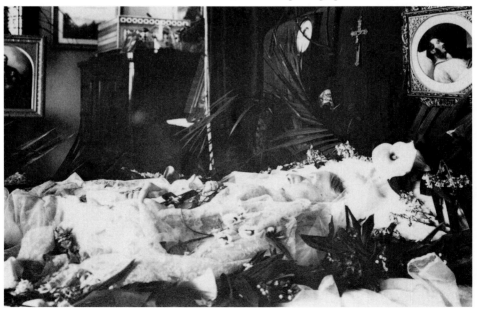

16. Slow march: the funeral procession at Hyde Park Corner

17. Sixty deep: the crowds in the park

18. Edward VII leads the royal mourners into Paddington station

19. The royal train waiting to carry the Queen's coffin to Windsor

20. The coffin nearly topples on the steps of St George's Chapel

21. The procession sets out for the mausoleum at Frogmore

of the sorrow which troubled every breast, young and old'.

In the City, the Stock Exchange opened and closed straight away. Business everywhere was reduced to 'slow and fluctuating movements', according to the financial press. 'Drawn blinds, shaded shops and the sombre trappings of woe may be observed everywhere.' Five thousand people took their places in St Paul's for a hurriedly called memorial service, while thousands more waited on the steps outside as the organist Sir George Martin played the *Dead March*.

Crowds built up around the newspaper stands to read in detail accounts of the deathbed scene at Osborne. Some were more fanciful than others, and the suggestion in one paper that, in her dying moment, the Queen had mistaken the Kaiser for Prince Albert was dismissed with contempt by its rivals. Less easy to disprove were the stories that her last words were 'Albert! Albert! Albert!', for which there was no evidence except their obvious plausibility. Or had her dying thought been 'Oh that peace may come!', a sentiment which was picked up with relish by the anti-war lobby.

For the serious-minded, the entire reign was described and analysed in lengthy obituaries. Less erudite readers could thrill at the coincidences. A lion, the royal beast, had died at London Zoo a week ago, an omen surely, and 'the superstitious had prophesied under their breath the loss which today we deplore'. Then there was Mrs Turner, who had worked at the Royal Nurseries in Slough, who was exactly the same age as the Queen and who died the same day of a similar complaint. Readers of the *Morning Post* were told what was by now obvious to them: that the country was 'plunged into mourning the like of which has not been seen before'. The *Daily Express* speculated on which members of the royal household were facing the sack and who was likely to replace them. The Duchess of Buccleuch was definitely out as Mistress of the

Robes, and the Duchess of Devonshire certain to take her place. The *Daily Mail* reflected a general sadness that the Queen had died with the war in South Africa unresolved: 'We could have prayed that she might not be gathered to her fathers till the contest had been won beyond dispute and till the ship of state had entered port. She has been taken from us when we can ill spare her ripe experience and her vast knowledge of measures and of men.'

Outside London, statues of the Queen in town and city centres became the focal point for mourning. They were quickly draped in black, and orderly queues formed to pass in front, bow the head, and mutter a prayer. In Liverpool, the death 'made a visible impression on strong men', a local reporter observed, 'a grief in every heart as if a member of one's family circle had been snatched away'. Even prisoners – colloquially known as 'guests of Her Majesty' – were affected, and at Walton jail it was reported that 'a sympathetic interest was evinced by those incarcerated'. Schoolchildren were sent home early in Leeds after an order went out from the education board that each head teacher should first inspire them with a talk on the Queen's life and character and lead them in a hymn, which was to be sung 'in a subdued tone'.

The speed with which she had gone from apparent rude health to death troubled the local press. The self-important London papers had tended to adopt a knowing tone – of course, they had been aware for a long time that she was unwell – but the provincial papers admitted their ignorance. 'Outside the family and household circles, no suspicion of a fatal illness was entertained a week ago,' the *Liverpool Mercury* told its readers. 'The demise has had the effect of an eclipse – as if a light which had ever been shining had been quenched, leaving us in darkness and with an unknown course before us.' The *Newcastle Daily Chronicle* believed the Queen had deliberately kept the news of her illness from the people so as not to spoil their Christmas and New Year celebrations – 'a self-abnegation which approaches the sublime'. But the *Leeds Mercury* thought her failing health had been kept secret so as not to upset her sick daughter, Vicky, the Empress Frederick.

The shock of her death was profound. 'We hardly yet can realize the full significance of the loss that marks so sadly the birth of the new century,' the *Birmingham Post* commented. But it was the simplest of things that brought home the reality. A phrase unheard for sixty years was awkwardly forming on everyone's lips – '*His* Majesty'. The novelist Thomas Hardy was not alone in finding it strange, awkward, unreal, that everyone would now have to sing 'God Save the King!'

At Osborne, His Majesty ordered the dining room, which was immediately below the bedroom where the Queen's body still lay, to be turned into a temporary chapel for his mother's coffin to rest in. As the King left for London – now *his* capital – the Bishop of Winchester took charge, but straight away found himself at odds with the princesses.

The dining room was a large, bright room with windows out on to the Italian terrace. Its walls were hung with portraits of the family, and it was these that caused the problem. The princesses saw no reason to move them. They felt that nothing could be nicer than for the Queen's children and grandchildren to be looking down upon her from the walls as she lay there in death. It was what she would have wanted.

Davidson was unhappy. He felt sure a more religious tone was called for, particularly since outsiders would be coming through the room to pay their respects. But it was clear that the princesses would not take down the family portraits. He could not overrule them, and it was not in his nature to argue with them face to face. He turned to the Kaiser for help, and

together they came up with a compromise plan. A section of
the room, including the part with a magnificent Winterhalter
painting of the Queen, Prince Albert and five of the children
on the wall, would be curtained off and left as it was. The
coffin would rest in the other part of the room, which would
be hung with red drapes covering the walls and the pictures.
Then religious paintings from other parts of the house would
be hung on the drapes.

The matter was discussed, and the Bishop and the Emperor
got their way. Arrangements were made for a firm in London
to rush down yards of crimson hangings and a gang of men to
help Mr Woodford, who was in charge of works at Osborne,
to put them up. They arrived that evening, and the Bishop
was astonished how 'in a marvellously short space of time that
part of the room which was to be used as a chapel was
beautifully draped from ceiling to floor'. Workmen carried an
altar from the Osborne chapel and placed it at one end of the
room. Over it was hung a painting of Jesus and his mother,
which they took from Prince Albert's study. In the centre of
the floor a small platform eighteen inches high was built and
covered with an Indian carpet. On top of this they draped the
royal ensign. Davidson felt something was missing, a touch of
grandeur. He remembered the four large candelabra he had
seen at the funeral of the Bishop of London just a week
ago. They had also been used at the funeral of the Duke of
Wellington. One in each corner would be magnificent. He
sent a priority telegram to St Paul's Cathedral asking for them
to be sent.

After lunch, the Bishop went to the Queen's bedroom and
was impressed by the simple way it had been laid out. He
thought her appearance had changed since last night, 'but she
still looked gentle, peaceful and dignified'. It was a time for
farewells. During the afternoon, those who had served her

most closely were allowed to pass through the room and to see her as she lay, 'so white and still and restful', as one of them put it. 'Her face is like wax and she looks younger than she has for 20 years.' Members of the Household were the first to go in, followed by the servants. Next came Admiral Fullerton and the officers of the royal yacht *Alberta*, their blue and gold uniforms a startling splash of colour amid the black ranks of the other mourners.

Finally the farmers, tenants and workers from the Osborne estate assembled in the entrance hall and waited in silence to be summoned. Soldiers, their heads lowered, lined the grand staircase as they filed slowly up to the first floor. They walked through her dressing room and then into the bedroom, where three of her Indian servants stood motionless by the bed. They stopped for a moment to look at the figure in white lying there, the face they knew clearly visible through the lace of her wedding veil. 'She looked so beautiful and good, just as she did when she patted my head in my childhood and spoke kindly to me,' one said afterwards. 'That's right,' said another, 'she was like she was when I was a lad and my father was in her service.' Dr Reid's wife, Susan, who had been a lady-in-waiting before her marriage, was overwhelmed. It was a sight she would never forget. Her face was 'like a lovely marble statue, no sign of illness or age, and she still looked "The Queen" – all so simple and grand'.

It was a look to capture for posterity, which is precisely what the Kaiser had arranged. He had sent for a sculptor from Berlin, Emile Fuchs, who now sat in the Queen's bedroom preparing to make a plaster cast of her face for a death mask. The princesses were very upset. Their mother would have shuddered at the very thought of this intrusion. It was such a horrid thing to do. The Kaiser's order had to be overruled. Fuchs was told he could make sketches only, and as he sat there drawing he was watched over by a maid whose instructions were to make sure he did not touch the body. He was never to be left unattended. As the artist worked, the Princess of Wales was desperately trying to reach her husband in London. It was not easy, but when she did get through to him on the telephone he agreed with her at once. There would be no death mask, though Fuchs was allowed his charcoal drawings.

Meanwhile, the Bishop of Winchester was in a panic. He had not had a reply from St Paul's. What was happening to his candelabra? He telephoned the Lord Chamberlain's office and asked that someone should find out. The prelate's plea for help was probably the last thing the overstretched officials there wanted to deal with, but they agreed. The message came back that the candelabra were on their way but the Bishop had not been told this because the telegraph lines into Osborne were totally blocked by the thousands of telegrams of condolence. The Bishop was relieved – but not for long. When the candelabra arrived that night, it was obvious straight away that they were too big. Even the disappointed Davidson, all his efforts wasted, had to admit that 'they dwarfed everything else in the room and we could not use them'.

The royal train carrying the first King of England for nearly sixty-four years steamed slowly into Victoria station on a fine winter's day. Thousands of Londoners gathered in the sunshine outside for a glimpse of him, but when they saw him as he stepped from the red carpet and into his carriage they were silent. There could be no cheering at a time like this. The reception from his subjects on his return from Osborne was dignified and restrained.

But underneath the crowd's self-control there was anxiety, which was all too clear to observers among them. A true sense of occasion had drawn them to stand and wait at any point they thought the new King might pass. They waited patiently for hours, hundreds standing in vain outside the Houses of Parliament after a rumour went round that he would be going there. Others gathered at Horse Guards in the belief that an eighty-one-gun salute was about to be fired on the parade ground, but they were disappointed. They pressed policemen for information, but the law was none the wiser.

It was not idle curiosity that drew them; they were not there to gawp. They were trying to grasp this moment of change as it was happening, and to be part of it. They knew they stood on a fault line in history, 'the inheritors of an era that was gone, looking forward with sympathetic curiosity to a reign that was dawning on the horizon'.[3]

They were overwhelmed with instant nostalgia. 'The Victorian age, the longest, the greatest and the noblest in our annals, closes and we begin not only a new century but a new reign under entirely new and different conditions,' wrote the *Spectator*. It had a 'dread' of what lay ahead, born of a realization that 'we have come to the end of a great and glorious epoch, that we have reached our zenith and that the nation must now begin to decline'.

For Thomas Hardy, like many others, the Queen had been a source of stability and certainty, and it was what he called the 'general sense of unknowing' about the future that now gave him pause. The poet Robert Bridges felt 'as though the keystone had fallen out of the arch of Heaven'. Henry James sensed 'a very curious' atmosphere that 'incalculable forces for possible ill' had suddenly been let loose.

There were worries about the new King – his moneyed friends, his frivolity, his extravagance, his mistresses. Twenty-six-year-old Winston Churchill was in Canada when the Queen died, and he wrote to his mother to express his curiosity about Edward. 'Will he sell his horses and scatter his Jews or will Reuben Sassoon be enshrined among the crown jewels? Will he become desperately serious? Will the Keppel be appointed first lady of the bedchamber?' But he was glad the Prince of Wales had 'got his innings at last'.[4]

As the King drove to Marlborough House, the onlookers lining the route raised their hats. He doffed his in response. They would give him the benefit of the doubt, though they thought of him still as the Prince of Wales – or the 'Son-King' as one observer dubbed him. But they felt for his predicament. His was a hard inheritance, the onerous task of 'succeeding a predecessor of exceptionally exalted character. The King must lead the rest of his life in ceaseless comparison with the noblest standard of monarchy ever uplifted,' as the Archdeacon of Westminster put it.

Once inside the house, the King changed into the uniform of a field marshal. In other parts of the capital, two hundred of the highest figures in the land were making similar preparations, taking out whatever uniform was appropriate for their position in readiness for a rare state occasion. In his room in the House of Lords, the Lord Chancellor, the Earl of Halsbury, put on his black gown, knee breeches and full-bottomed wig and made his way to St James's Palace. The Privy Council was assembling.

There was a time when the Privy Council of advisers to the monarch had had supreme powers, and in theory it still did. In practice its role was formal and its day-to-day function was largely to rubber-stamp decisions made in Parliament. Its members – there were several hundred of them – were politicians and churchmen, some still in office but many with their days in power behind them, their appointment an honour, a retirement gift from a grateful Establishment. The ceremony they were about to go through, however, was one of the

Council's last remnants of grandeur. In a throwback to Charles I and Elizabeth I and to the medieval kings beyond them, its job was to meet and to proclaim the new sovereign.

In the Banqueting Room at St James's Palace, a collection of what Lord Esher called 'curious old fossils' gathered.[5] The Prime Minister was there and all the members of his Cabinet, together with the Archbishop of Canterbury, the Lord Chief Justice and the Lord Chamberlain. Not all were privy councillors. Some of those present – the Lord Mayor of London, for example – were notables who had been invited as spectators of a moment of great tradition, a unique fusing of past and present.

At precisely 2 p.m. the Lord President, the Duke of Devonshire, stood up and formally announced the death of the Queen. A deputation was sent to the King, who was waiting in a side room, but before he arrived a draft of the proclamation announcing the start of his reign was read and approved. Halsbury picked up the Great Seal of England and attached it to the document. Then, to a formal cry of 'The King is coming!', the new monarch came into the council room, preceded by the Lord Chamberlain, the Lord Steward and the Master of the Horse, all walking slowly backwards.

A large crimson and gold chair, his throne for the occasion, had been placed at the head of the room, and he stood in front of it to address his people for the first time – his voice breaking a little as he began, but then getting stronger. He spoke without notes, which Esher thought showed 'great nerve', and at times he hesitated, as if he could not quite bring the correct word to mind. It was 'the saddest' of occasions, the loss of his mother was 'irreparable', but he would always try 'to walk in her footsteps'. He announced that he would be known as King Edward rather than by his first name of Albert. It was not a snub but a tribute to his father. 'In doing so I do not undervalue the name of Albert which I inherit from my ever lamented great and wise father, who by universal consent is deservedly known by the name of Albert the Good and I desire that his name should stand alone.'

Edward VII sat down as the Lord Chancellor read him the oath of allegiance. The King said nothing, but lifted his right hand to signal his assent before putting his signature – 'Edward R.' – on the parchment presented to him. Still sitting, he placed his right hand on a cushion for the royal dukes to come forward, one by one, to kneel and kiss his hand. His brother, the Duke of Connaught, his son, the Duke of York, and his brother-in-law, Prince Christian, did their duty in full, but the eighty-one-year-old Duke of Cambridge, born in the same year as his cousin Queen Victoria, was physically unable to bend the knee. He bowed as low as his frail body would allow. Another cushion was then placed at the King's left side, and the other members of the Council stepped forward to kiss that hand. It was arduous for the ageing Prime Minister, Lord Salisbury, and the King showed his respect by leaning forward to help him up.

After a little over an hour, the first act of the new reign was over. It had not impressed Viscount Esher, who thought the King dignified but the ceremony 'unimposing'. Perhaps the splendour of the occasion had been marred for him by the mistakes that crept into the proceedings. All the ministers had brought their seals of office with them, having been told they would have to hand them over and receive them back from the new monarch. They had been misinformed. The Lord Chamberlain's office had forgotten to station a shorthand writer in the room for the King's speech, and, since he had given it from memory and had no written record of it himself, history was in danger of being lost. They had to ask Lord Rosebery to write down the King's words as he remembered them, and it was an agreed version that was printed as the official record in the *London Gazette*. Then there was the confusion that broke out when the clerk of the Council asked all those who were not actually privy councillors to leave the room while certain privy business was processed. Some did; others stayed. One who went out was the Lord Mayor of London, left standing with his aldermen in an empty side room without even a chair to sit on and furious at having been expelled. Then the Archbishop of York tried to get back in and found the door shut against him. He missed the formal proclamation of the King, including the clerk of the Council's clanger. 'God save the Queen!' he called out at the end. 'King!' the Earl of Halsbury hissed at him, but hardly anyone else seemed to notice. Why should they? It was hard to break a habit of six decades overnight.

But change was happening. The Lord Chancellor and the Speaker of the House of Commons left St James's for the short journey back to the Palace of Westminster. Parliament had not been due to sit for another month and had been hurriedly summoned back early, as it had to be by law, on the Queen's death. As the first MPs arrived in the chamber of the House of Commons, they ran into the cleaners, dressed in white workmen's blouses, who were only just leaving.

At 4 p.m. the Speaker, William Gully, wearing black mourning bands, rose from his chair to tell the House that they had been called there to swear their allegiance to His Majesty the King. The very word sent a buzz of excitement along the green leather benches. 'I do swear that I will be faithful and bear true allegiance to His Majesty King Edward the Seventh, according to the law. So help me God,' he pronounced, and then summoned the Members in groups of four and five to take the same oath. But where was Balfour? He should have been the first. Anxious eyes searched the floor and the lobby, but there was no sign of him. The Chancellor of the Exchequer, Sir Henry Campbell-Bannerman, stepped up to the clerk's table and led Joseph Chamberlain and two others in the pledge of loyalty before signing his name underneath the Speaker's on the Roll of Parliament. Five minutes later a breathless Balfour arrived and was pushed ahead of the queue of MPs to swear. Then he took a pen and squeezed his signature on the Roll in the space above Campbell-Bannerman's before leaning back against the side of the Speaker's chair to chat to his friends while other Members swore and signed. Across in the House of Lords, a similar ceremony was under way, each peer swearing loyalty and then shaking hands with the Lord Chancellor.

In the Commons, the ceremony went on for two hours – until the last Member, Mr Samuel, approached the Speaker's chair and took the oath in Hebrew, wearing his hat on his head and with his hand on a copy of the Old Testament which he had brought specially. It was twenty-four hours since the Queen had died, and in that full day the loyalty of her legislators had passed seamlessly and completely to her son. As if to mark this moment, as the House adjourned and MPs milled around in the yard outside waiting for their carriages to take them home, their conversation was stopped as the eighty-one-gun salute, counting out the years of the dead Queen, finally boomed out over Whitehall from St James's Park.

'Seamless' was not the appropriate word at Osborne. A curious stand-off was taking place between the Queen's staff and those of the new King. The two households had always got on in a gentlemanly fashion, and continued to do so to such an extent that nobody was prepared to assume command. Fritz Ponsonby watched the post pile up. 'Whenever a telegram or a letter arrived no one would open it. The Prince of Wales's people hated the idea of taking everything over abruptly and we had ceased to hold any appointment.' Ponsonby filled in his time by offering to help Princess Louise with her paperwork. She had nearly three hundred telegrams to answer, and did not know where to start. He was used to churning them out – hundreds a day during the past week. He went through her pile with her, and she selected the ones for standard responses and the ones she wanted to reply to personally. She dictated, he took her words down in shorthand, and it was all sorted out in fifteen minutes. He went off to send the telegrams and the Princess, true to form, to moan to her sisters that she now had nothing to do.

The morning of 24 January saw the Bishop of Winchester up early and fussing round the temporary chapel to make sure the workmen who had come from London had done a proper job during the night. In the bedroom above, Fuchs was still sketching, but he had now been joined by another artist, Sir Hubert von Herkomer, a German by birth but now living and working in England. Herkomer knew he had to work fast. The coffin was expected later that day, and then the body would be placed in it and she would be lost from sight for ever. He focused on the ghostly whiteness of her wedding veil and tried to catch the way her face and hands and the cross she clutched appeared as if they were breaking through the surface of the sea. She seemed to float, anchored only by the flowers strewn around her – purple crocuses, snowdrops, and arum lilies with bright-yellow stamens. It was an ethereal and romantic picture, a true Victorian image of death.

Davidson had breakfast and was back in the chapel with Princess Beatrice and Princess Helena when they were told that the undertaker had arrived from Banting's in London. They assumed he had brought the shell coffin, as arranged, but they were in for a surprise. Davidson fetched Dr Reid and they met the man outside the Queen's bedroom. He was not the sombre gentleman that the Bishop had expected but 'rough and ordinary'. To their further amazement, he said he had not brought the coffin but was there just to take preliminary measurements of the body. Somehow the instructions that Reid had sent to the Lord Chamberlain immediately after the Queen died had been muddled, and instead of the coffin arriving at Osborne that morning, as the doctor had requested, there was just this altogether unsatisfactory-looking under-taker's assistant.

It was a disaster. The King was due back at Osborne that afternoon expecting to place his mother in her coffin and move her to the temporary chapel to lie in state. This was now impossible. The measurements would have to be sent to London before work could start on the shell, and the very earliest it could be finished was tomorrow afternoon. The man was less than helpful. He was just an assistant, he told them. He had been given his instructions when he left London, and he had no authority to do anything but follow them. It made no difference to him that the body in question was the Queen of England: he had his orders and he was going to stick to them. Reid and the Bishop confessed they 'were at a loss what to do'.

They asked the Kaiser, and between them they decided that the shell coffin would have to be made locally. The man from Banting's should take his measurements and then go to the leading undertaker in Cowes so that it could be made up on the spot. It had to be ready that evening without fail. The man argued. That was not what he had been told to do. His firm would make the coffin, not some local undertaker. It took the full fire of the German Kaiser's wrath to ram home the point to him. 'It is always like this,' he thundered at the little man. 'When an ordinary humble person dies everything is arranged quite easily and with reverence and care. When a "personage" dies, you fellows all lose your heads and make stupid mistakes which you ought to be ashamed of. The same happens in Germany. You are all alike!'

Davidson stifled a smile. 'If the occasion had been a less grave and solemn one, there would have been much that was humorous in the Emperor's harangue to the rather dull undertaker's assistant.' The terror tactics worked. 'The Emperor frightened the poor fellow into helpless obedience,' the Bishop recalled.

Reid and the Kaiser took the undertaker into the Queen's bedroom, with the Bishop tagging along behind. The man asked to be left alone to take his measurements, but Davidson said:

he was so unsuitable a person that we declined to leave him, and, as a matter of fact, the measurements were taken by the Emperor, Reid and myself, under the direction of the man, who stood by and told us exactly what he wanted. Subsequently the Queen's confidential dresser took some further measurements when none of us were there. It was altogether a curious scene.

Curious too was the Bishop's behaviour, or so Reid thought. Why had he barged his way into this intimate occasion? It was right and proper for the Queen's doctor and her grandson to carry out this task, but why was it a job for a bishop? In Davidson's own account he was, of course, a central figure in the proceedings, but Reid saw it differently. He 'seemed to think he ought to be there and he made himself prominent in giving directions', the doctor noted. The Kaiser was annoyed too, or so he told Reid later. The Bishop's interference and familiarity would have cost him his life in Germany, he bragged. 'If I were dead and my pastor came in the room like that he would be hauled out by the neck and shot in the courtyard.'

The King was now on his way back from London after his reign had been formally proclaimed to the people in ceremonies at St James's Palace and at Temple Bar at the entrance to the City of London. He did not attend in person, because his mother had given instructions that he was not to do so. She had been there when her name was shouted to the crowd through an open window at St James's in 1837 and had found it 'peculiarly painful'. The King had stayed in Marlborough House that morning while, across the road in neighbouring St James's Palace, the King of Arms, surrounded by heralds in brightly coloured tabards and trumpeters in gold tunics, made his grand announcement from the first-floor balcony to the crowd in the courtyard:

We do now hereby, with one voice and consent of tongue and heart, publish and proclaim that the high and mighty prince Albert Edward is now, by the death of our late sovereign of happy memory, become our only lawful and rightful liege lord Edward the Seventh, by the grace of God, king of the United Kingdom of Great Britain and Ireland, Defender of the Faith, Emperor of India . . . God save the King!

Below, the Commander-in-Chief of the Army, Lord Roberts, wearing the blue sash of the Order of the Garter – his last gift from the Queen – sat on his horse and led his troops in a salute as a band played the national anthem.

Before leaving London for Osborne, the King had sent a message that he wanted the Bishop to prepare Holy Communion for the royal family in the Queen's bedroom. Davidson queried the instruction. A service in the room by all means, with prayers and hymns, but surely Communion would be better in the chapel the next morning. He may have been motivated by old loyalties: he knew the Queen had been a regular churchgoer but a rare communicant – twice a year, at Christmas and Easter, was enough. He had also heard of the Queen's irritation when she was told how Christle, her favourite grandson, had taken Communion on his deathbed. But the Bishop was quickly reminded that there was now a new power in the land. The King wanted a celebration of Holy Communion beside his mother's bed, and that is what he would have.

It was not the only sign of the new order. As he returned to the Isle of Wight, the flag on the royal yacht was raised from its half-mast position in honour of the dead Queen to full mast for the living King. Around him, all the warships were dressed in bright flags to welcome the monarch and, in contrast to the silence that greeted his arrival just six days before, their guns roared out in salute. He stood on the after-deck of the *Alberta* under an awning, and for the first time that day the sun peeped out from behind the clouds.

Just before 4 p.m. the royal family crowded into the Queen's bedroom once again. With them were Harriet Phipps, three of the dead Queen's personal maids and a page-boy. The furniture was pushed away into the window to make a proper space around the bed, which the King knelt beside with his Queen. The Bishop was struck by the demeanour of all those present – 'perfectly silent, attentive, even eager. In the centre lay the little Queen with fresh flowers arranged on the bed, the small Imperial crown lying by the side, her face beginning to lose a little of the fine look it had the previous day, but most calm and peaceful.'

That night, there was a significant change in the Household. They sat down to dinner, then at ten o'clock the King sent for all the members of the late Queen's staff. He wanted to be

introduced to them properly. This was not a social occasion
but a symbolic one and, to emphasize the point, he chose the
most formal room in the house in which to greet them – the
council room, where the Queen had held audiences and
privy councils. Bigge, Edwards, Reid, Ponsonby, Clinton,
McNeill, they all waited in the corridor as if they were first-
time visitors. Then an equerry – one they barely knew –
summoned them in one by one and called out their names to
the King. They bowed and kissed his hand. He said a few
words to each of them and was 'kind and gracious' according
to Clinton. It was simple and dignified though a little too
formal, the Bishop of Winchester thought. He wondered how
the others were feeling in this unaccustomed secondary role.
They had been the keepers of the gate; now they were kept
waiting there themselves. It must have been 'strange' for them.
But the order was changing, and there in the council room at
Osborne – the Queen's lifeless body only a few hundred feet
away – they were the first to feel it.

By the time the audience was over, the shell coffin, made of
unpolished oak and covered in white satin, had arrived from
Mr Marvin, the undertaker in Cowes. Reid took charge as it
was carried into the bedroom and put down on the floor on
the far side of the bed. He had talked to the King and the
Queen, no doubt apologizing for the delay in its arrival, and
they had agreed that putting in the body could wait until the
morning. A party of sailors from the *Victoria and Albert*, the
second of the royal yachts, had come up from the dockside to
be on hand to carry the coffin downstairs to the chapel. They
had been waiting since the afternoon, but now they were
allowed into the bedroom to file past the body before going
back to their ship. Lieutenant Pelly, the officer in charge, was
ordered to have them back by ten o'clock the next morning.

The doctor could now give some thought to a secret task. The Queen had given precise instructions on how she was to be treated after death. Some of these the family knew – there was to be no lying in state, under no circumstances was her body to be embalmed, she was to have a military funeral. But some of her wishes were to be kept from them. These she had written down for her chief dresser, the loyal Mrs Tuck, who the night before had taken Reid aside. She wanted his help. There were certain items that the Queen wanted buried with her, some of which she did not want her family to know about. It cannot have been hard for the doctor to work out that this was something to do with John Brown, but he said nothing beyond agreeing to cooperate. He had made it his responsibility to see that everything she had commanded would be carried out. With the help of a nurse, he and Mrs Tuck cut the Queen's hair, dressed her in a white silk dressing gown, and fixed the Order of the Garter to it. Then they left her for the night.

The next morning Dr Reid began the very last act he could perform for his royal mistress. The undertakers had sprinkled charcoal in a layer an inch and a half deep over the bottom of the coffin, and on this he and Mrs Tuck and another of the maids arranged the items the Queen had insisted on being buried with her. The list was long. Albert's dressing gown was laid down first, alongside his cloak – a special one that had been embroidered for him by their second daughter, Princess Alice. It was a double memento of loved ones the Queen hoped to see again – the thirty-five-year-old Princess had been the first of her children to die. Various shawls and handkerchiefs belonging to members of the family came next, and then on top of this layer they placed a plaster model of Albert's hand, framed photographs, lockets and bracelets. They were trinkets she had collected all her life, and each one

had a particular memory. There was something, however
small, for virtually every member of her family, every special
servant and close friend. There was even a sprig of heather
from Balmoral. Mrs Tuck had the list, and checked it off to
make sure nothing had been missed. But, as he laid the
cushioned lining inside the coffin on top of the Queen's
mementoes, Reid kept two items back.

The coffin was moved to the other side of the room and
chocked up so that it was level with the body on the bed. The
King came in with the Princess of Wales, and they sat alone
with the dead Queen for a few minutes. Then the Princess
placed some more flowers on her mother-in-law's body and
left. Outside, the Kaiser, the Duke of Connaught and his son,
Prince Arthur, were waiting. The Duke of York should have
been there too, but he was ill. He had a temperature and a
cough, and was in pain; Reid had ordered him to bed with
what turned out to be a bad bout of German measles. The
solemn moment went ahead without him.

Inside the bedroom, the King, the Kaiser, the Duke and his
son stood on the left of the body, their hands on straps that
had been put underneath it earlier. On the other side, Mr
Woodford and two of his workmen from the house – the same
ones who had moved the dying Queen's bed and replaced it
with the small divan – took up position. Two of the Queen's
maids took her feet, Reid and Mrs Tuck her head, and, on a
command, they picked up Queen Victoria's almost weightless
body and put it gently into the waiting coffin.

The King and his royal relatives left the room, and Mrs
Tuck and the other two women busied themselves around
the coffin, arranging the dressing gown neatly, adjusting the
lace and the silk veil. Reid had his final duty to perform. Mrs
Tuck had given him the Queen's favourite photograph of
John Brown and a lock of his hair inside a small case. The

doctor had planned his secret mission well and had brought some tissue paper with him. He wrapped it around the two precious mementoes to stop prying eyes, particularly those of the Queen's children, from seeing what they were, then he placed the package in her left hand, precisely as she had instructed. He picked up the flowers the Princess of Wales had left and arranged them over and around her hand as a further cover.

He felt his job was done. He had made sure her last wishes were followed. He wrote in his journal, 'My duties were over with the Queen after twenty years' service!'

The women of the royal family were waiting downstairs in the drawing room when Reid came in and invited them to take their last look. The Princess of Wales – still refusing to be called the Queen – led the way up the grand staircase. The dead Queen's three daughters, her three other daughters-in-law and seven of her granddaughters came in procession behind. There were tears in the bedroom but briefly. After they had gone, there were others who had to make their farewells. Miss Phipps came in with another lady-in-waiting, then Bigge led the gentlemen of the Household past the coffin. The final visitor was the Munshi. When they had all left, only the men of the royal family remained, and, with the King at the front of the group, they watched in silence as the coffin was closed on the Queen. The lid was screwed down. At that moment they knew for sure they would never look on her like again.

Reid also knew that his secret mission was now certain to go undetected. With the coffin sealed, no one could stop the Queen being buried with the controversial mementoes of John Brown she had requested. Having made sure that her instructions were carried out to the letter, he knew too that she lay in her coffin wearing two wedding rings. One had been put on her finger on that happy day in February 1840 when she had married Albert in the Chapel Royal in St James's. The other she had worn for sorrow. It had belonged to John Brown. It had been his mother's wedding ring, and he had worn it himself for a short time before giving it to the Queen, and she had worn it constantly for nearly eighteen years, from the day of his death in 1883. Her instruction had been that, along with several rings from her 'beloved husband' and others from her family, it was to be on her finger when she was buried. (See the Appendix on page 294.)

A white pall was put over the coffin. It was a temporary covering. At the Royal School of Needlework, in South Kensington in London, the students had started the day before on a white satin pall lined with silk. In each corner, they were painstakingly embroidering the royal arms and the crown of England, to a design they had been given by Princess Helena. She had telegraphed her instructions to the principal, and forty students were working their fingers to the bone in shifts day and night to finish it by Saturday.

The coffin was lifted and eased out of the bedroom and into the narrow passage outside. Lieutenant Pelly's party of sailors had returned as ordered, and the eight petty officers took the coffin on their shoulders and slowly marched down the stairs. The whole house stood in the hall at the foot of the stairs as the coffin was carried into the dining room and placed on the raised platform in the middle.

The temporary chapel – the '*chapelle ardente*' as it was generally known – was everything the Bishop of Winchester had expected. Blinds shut off the three windows in the semicircular bay, and sunlight penetrated the room only when the double doors to the drawing room were opened to let someone in or out. Electric lights threw a dim glow round the room, augmented by six large candles in tall silver holders that had been found to replace the ones sent from St Paul's but rejected because of their size. The crimson of the drapes on the wall was broken by a huge German tapestry on one side and a silk Union Jack, taken from one of the royal yachts, that dropped from ceiling to floor on the other. Andrea del Verrocchio's *Madonna and Child* hung over the altar, and another Renaissance painting of a religious scene over the mantelpiece.

On the coffin lay the Queen's velvet robe of the Order of the Garter, trimmed with ermine, and at the head a small diamond crown. The Garter robe was yellowing in places with age. Flowers, wreaths and palms filled the room to such an extent that Fritz Ponsonby found the strong scent of the gardenias sickly and oppressive. There were red azaleas from Princess Helena, tied with ribbons and marked with an H, white lilies from Louise, marked with an L, and Beatrice's blue hyacinths. Red, white and blue. Alongside, a tiny posy of spring flowers carried a card which said, 'Dear Gan-gan, from Elizabeth of Hesse'.

The Queen was never alone. In one corner, in turban and robes, stood her Indian servants; in another were the kilted Scottish contingent, among them a faithful Brown – not John, but his nephew William, as close as she could get in death to what had been her heart's desire. She had a military escort too, though it had been assembled in haste and was painfully unsure of the job it had to do. The right to stand guard on the dead monarch belonged to the Queen's Company of the Grenadier Guards and, on the instructions of the Duke of Connaught, they had been sent for. Until they arrived, the only military unit close by, a reserve regiment of the King's Royal Rifles stationed at Parkhurst Barracks, would have to do the job. To Ponsonby's disgust, the riflemen were clueless. What were their duties? It was explained that a soldier was to stand at each corner of the coffin, head bowed, rifle reversed.

But they had never been drilled in the movements for reversing arms. For guidance, their captain sought out Ponsonby, who after all was a guardsman with experience on the parade grounds of India, but he could find nothing in the training manuals. Like so much that followed the Queen's death, no one was quite sure of the correct procedure. But they had no time to dither, and Ponsonby, the Rifles officer and Sir John McNeill quickly worked out a ceremonial drill for changing the guard. They found it had to be done every hour, because the overpowering scent from the flowers upset the men if they had to endure it for longer than that.

That afternoon, sixty men and three officers from the 1st Grenadiers arrived at East Cowes and took over duties in the house and around the coffin. They were an imposing unit, the tallest in the entire Army – one of them just short of seven foot. At first they had no more idea of what to do than the men they replaced, so they copied the same drill. But that was smartened up the next day, when their commanding officer came with proper instructions. From then on, the changing of the sentries was immaculate – 'a most impressive sight', according to Ponsonby, 'all done in slow time'. In bright-red tunics, black busbies on their head, they stood around the coffin, silent and unmoving as the grave, head down, hands crossed over the butt of the rifle, muzzle resting on the toe of the boot. As each new watch took over, the officer standing down solemnly declared to his replacement, 'I commit to you the charge of the body of her late Majesty Queen Victoria, Queen of Great Britain and Ireland, Empress of India.'

Despite appearances, what was happening in the *chapelle ardente* was no official lying-in-state. The Queen's will had specifically ruled that out. But servants and Osborne estate tenants were allowed a last look and, ushered in by footmen who had swapped their scarlet liveries for black uniforms, 250 of them filed past the coffin. Their thoughts were of 'a true friend who made her people's joys and sorrows her own', as one Whippingham farmer put it. He remembered how she would come to his cottage, refuse to sit down, but stand by the parlour table for a quarter of an hour asking about every member of the family and knowing them all by name. Princess Beatrice was usually with her, making a fuss of the dogs and cats. Others recalled the children's parties at Christmas and the annual gift of a plum pudding and ten pounds of beef, the harvest suppers on the Prince Consort's birthday, the signed photograph of her they had each received on her Golden Jubilee. Each stood for a minute or so beside the coffin, the memories clouding their eyes with tears, before they were let out through the drawing room and on to the terrace.

Afterwards, members of the royal family chose their moment to slip in. The Duchess of York thought the scene in the chapel 'so impressive and fine yet so simple. We go from time to time, and the feeling of peace in that room is most soothing to one's feelings.' Princess Marie Louise had the same experience. As she knelt in front of the coffin, she was overwhelmed with a sense of 'peace and awe'.

But the private grief at Osborne was causing anxiety in the rest of the country. The royal family, the Household, the servants could not hang on to the Queen indefinitely. The news that a privileged few were filing past her coffin brought thousands of people to the Isle of Wight in the hope of seeing her too. They packed the ferries to Cowes and landed in such numbers that the Marine Hotel, which had closed for the winter, reopened to take in visitors. The rumour was fuelled by a mistaken report in the local newspaper in nearby Newport that islanders would be admitted. The fact that it had apparently been said by Sir Arthur Bigge and had been published in the *County Press*, which everyone knew had impeccable royal contacts, convinced the locals that it was true and they trudged up the hill in their Sunday best, only to be turned away at the gates. Some were allowed through – friends who had been on the Queen's personal visiting list, the island's mayors, naval and army officers in uniform – but the rest were kept at bay. When were the people, her subjects, to get their chance?

The *Daily Telegraph* feared not at all. There was even talk that she might never return to her capital but be taken directly to Windsor. With deep respect, the paper made its position clear. 'To carry the Queen's remains in semi-privacy from one country place to another – from the royal residence in the Isle of Wight to the Royal Mausoleum at Frogmore – is quite impossible.' It demanded – again with deep respect to the Queen's wishes and to those of her son – 'a stately and elaborate funeral'.

It must give the widest opportunity for as many as possible of her Majesty's subjects to testify to the full their admiration, their respect and their love. The greater the publicity that can be attained, the greater, we feel sure, will be the satisfaction of the English people. Let the cortege, with all the melancholy pomp and circumstance of death, pass from station to station, from Osborne to Portsmouth, from Portsmouth to London, from London to Windsor, everywhere encircled and guarded by those crowds of anxious, tearful mourners who from every class and rank of our community desire to give the most marvellous tribute which any monarch could seek to possess of enduring and deathless loyalty.

Nothing less than this could meet or satisfy the paramount emotion of the moment.

The paper's leader writer even invoked the ghost of the legendary El Cid, the eleventh-century knight of Castile, to make his case:

His dead body was led forth upon his horse at the head of the Christian army, and by its presence obtained a splendid victory. As her body passes to the tomb, her beloved Majesty may and will inspire, encourage, comfort, fortify and confirm the lessons of her long reign in this its closing scene. To miss such an opportunity would be more than a mistake. It would be a public loss and an Imperial disaster.

The state had a right to bury its Queen with full honours. Sooner or later the private mourners of Osborne would have to give up their dead.

# 9. In Memoriam

We feel that the end of a great epoch has come . . .

Arthur Balfour to the House of Commons

The Mayor, Mr Daniels, and the other three magistrates on duty in the ancient market town of Oswestry in Shropshire stared at the list of defendants whose misdemeanours they would have to pass judgement on at the petty sessions. The night before, the doleful news about the death of the Queen had reached them by telegraph. It was a calamity, no doubt of that, they agreed among themselves. What could they do to mark this historic occasion? Their town, just a few miles from the Welsh border, had a royal tradition that went all the way back to its charter of freedom from Richard II, and even beyond him to King Offa in the ninth century. They ran their eyes over the day's cases – the usual run of drunks and petty thieves and some more serious charges involving bodily harm. The Mayor ventured an idea to his fellow Justices of the Peace. They should honour the Queen's memory by tempering justice with mercy.

Putting on his chain of office over his black robes, he walked into the courtroom and took his seat in the middle of the bench. Then he called for all seventeen of the day's offenders to be brought before him. They were bundled into the dock and told, to their amazement, that the case against every one of them would be dismissed – even the mother who had been

accused of neglecting her children and the father who was on
a charge of persistent cruelty. 'There are cases here which
deserve punishment,' he told them, 'and in the ordinary way
there would be convictions. But we feel that, in the presence
of the death of the Queen, it would be a gracious act on our
part to dismiss you all.'

Before they could slink away, unable to believe their good
fortune, they were sternly warned not to think that being let
off in any way condoned their wrong-doings. They owed
their freedom to the Queen, and they should never forget it.
'We are poorer by her death,' the Mayor intoned, though, as
they walked free, the lucky seventeen must have felt enriched.

Elsewhere, magistrates preferred lectures to leniency.
Gravely aware that history was watching them, and drawing
on all the importance that the moment gave them, they were
the self-appointed mouthpieces for everyone's feelings. 'It
is fitting that anyone occupying a public position should
endeavour to give expression to the profound grief which has
befallen us all,' the chief magistrate told Southwark police
court, speaking from beneath a royal coat of arms draped in
black. 'I feel I cannot proceed to the business of the court
today without referring to the grievous news,' the judge at
Birmingham County Court announced; it was 'a terrible
blow, an unspeakable loss'. At North London police court,
His Worship Mr Haden Corser was minded to adjourn straight
away, but then he thought about the Queen's devotion to
duty and knew he had to carry on.

But the Shropshire lads were not the only ones to get
away scot-free in the late Queen's name. In Glasgow, Baillie
Wilcock discharged all of the prisoners at the Northern police
court except for two whose crimes were thought too serious
for clemency. Across at the Eastern court, Baillie Maclay gave
all the prisoners a lecture about the Queen before sending

away unpunished all those up before him for minor offences. Unusually, the notorious Barlinnie jail received no new prisoners at all that day.

Such generosity was seen as a proper tribute to the Queen. After all, on the very day she died, the chairman of Sheerness Urban District Council had received a letter from her enclosing a postal order for three pounds. He had written to her about John Harfoot, a civilian clerk working in the offices of the Commander-in-Chief of the Nore, whose five sons were all serving in Her Majesty's Navy. The money was her thanks to a family of exceptional loyalty.

Loyalty was also the issue in Ireland, but differently perceived. Demands for Home Rule were as divisive as ever. Gladstone's Liberal government had spectacularly failed to solve the problem – his attempt to free Ireland (or to surrender it, depending on your point of view) had brought down his administration. The Queen, unwilling to see her kingdom diminished, had been delighted. She had chosen to visit the island in the summer of 1900, making an arduous tour which had exhausted her, despite the rapturous welcome she had received in Dublin. It had proved to be her last major outing, and one which some even thought had hastened her death.

Ireland now paid tribute to her. In Dublin, ships in the docks were dressed at half mast, and in the city centre Messrs Forrest & Sons, who for more than fifty years had held the royal warrant for Irish goods, put up mourning shutters and draped the whole inside of the shop in black. But an unseemly row broke out at a meeting of the local corporation when a Nationalist councillor, Timothy Harrington, challenged the Unionist Lord Mayor's motion of condolence. He harangued the Unionists. 'Without in any way detracting from the high personal qualities of the deceased, this council must decline in the present political condition of Ireland to take part in any demonstrations of loyalty to the English throne.' The Unionists hurled back their disgust at his lack of taste, his appalling manners, his attempt to make political capital out of bereavement. By a slim eight-vote majority, the republican was defeated by the royalists, and Dublin's condolences were finally sent to the new King at Osborne.

Harrington's stand was typical of the republican response. Republicans were caught in two minds about Queen Victoria. In mourning her, the *Cork Examiner* also mourned 'the millions who during her reign sank into the grave as paupers or were thrust from our shores unequipped for the struggle of life in a strange land'. But it had never held her responsible for 'the wrongs we suffered while she was our ruler. She was but the figurehead of the State. We do not regard her as one that wilfully injured this country or could be described as our enemy.' On the other hand, 'it would be hypocrisy on our part to profess to participate in the sorrow that will be experienced in other lands. During her long reign, while she had shown conspicuous favour to Scotland, she never gave the slightest indication of any interest in this country.'

The *Irish Daily Independent* condemned her as 'an opportunist' and of limited intellectual capacity.

As the sovereign of Ireland she was eminently forgetful of her obligations . . . No reign was more destructive for our people or more ruinous since the time of the Tudor queen. When famine scourged the land and our people were flying in hundreds of thousands to seek homes in distant lands, she could spare less from her privy purse for the relief of distress in our midst than the Sultan of Turkey deemed it desirable to offer.

But it absolved her of personal responsibility and blamed her attitude to Ireland on Prince Albert, 'who once famously encouraged the government to apply the same processes on the Irish as the Russians had to the Poles'.

There were others too who chose to use the Queen's death to attack Britain. The press in St Petersburg and Moscow linked her to the evil effects of the Boer War, 'that much-condemned enterprise'. *Novosti* said her death was an opportunity for England to 'mend the wrongs of her ways and make peace'. Another Russian paper, the *Exchange Gazette*, with complete misunderstanding of the British constitution, urged the new King to dissolve Parliament and give the people the chance to impeach the ministers who had led the country astray. In New York, the Dutch Mayor caused a storm of protest when he refused to have the flag on City Hall lowered to half mast.

These were exceptional reactions. The rest of the world expressed its grief. In Washington, President McKinley heard the news of the Queen's death with shock, and the flag at the White House was lowered to half mast — the first time ever for a foreign ruler. The Senate and the House of Representatives both voted unanimously to send their condolences to the royal family. Sympathies were extended even to those not directly involved in her death: the New York Chamber of Commerce telegraphed the London Chamber of Commerce to express its sorrow 'on the loss of your illustrious Queen'.

Her personal popularity transcended political differences. The British Embassy in Paris was besieged by well-wishers, willing to suspend their anger over the war in South Africa for a while. In South Africa itself, the strangest tribute of all came from Boer prisoners of war in the Greenpoint detention camp, who, far from glorying in the death of their enemy, decided to 'suspend their usual amusements' for a period of mourning. It was hard to think what those amusements were — they were unlikely to be 'very amusing', an anti-war newspaper pointed out. It seized the opportunity to make a political point:

The Boers are a brave and chivalrous people with whom it is a great misfortune to be at war. Her Majesty was to them the symbol of the country with which they are engaged in a deadly struggle. These prisoners do not know what has become of their farms, their wives or their children. Yet they desire to pay her memory the only mark of respect in their power. It is a wonderful proof of the influence which the Queen's character had in every race and every clime. But it is also a signal proof that the Boers are the exact opposite of the barbarous and brutal savages they have been called in our Yellow Press. They are men with whom an honourable peace might at any time be made in the full assurance that they would keep their word.[1]

Oceans away from South Africa, the British residents of Shanghai went into mourning for a month and the Japanese court for three weeks. Hong Kong thundered to the roar of an eighty-one-gun salute from the British fleet there, accompanied by a German battleship and four cruisers, three warships from the United States, and a Portuguese cruiser which had steamed across the South China Sea from Macao to pay tribute. The municipal council of Athens decided to name one of the squares in the city after her. In Uganda, the five-year-old boy King was taken by his regents and tribal chiefs and a large gathering of 'native followers' to commiserate with the protectorate's special commissioner. The Austrian Emperor Franz Joseph sent flowers to Osborne from his own conservatory. The King of the Belgians ordered two months of mourning – an unprecedented tribute – and then put his royal yacht on standby. He, like the leaders of much of the rest of the world, was preparing to go to one of the most moving and impressive funerals that would ever be seen.

The Earl of Clarendon was convinced he ought to be in charge. As Lord Chamberlain, he was responsible for cere-monial occasions, and he put the case for his masterminding the funeral when he sat down with the King and the royal dukes to discuss the arrangements. He lost the argument. The Duke of Norfolk was forceful in claiming the traditional right as Hereditary Earl Marshal of England, and, though there were doubts about his abilities, he was the man to whom the King turned.[2] It meant following orders: the Queen had, of course, decided every detail in her will.

Lord Esher's imaginative suggestion for what he called 'a sea procession' had to be vetoed. It would have been splendid – bringing the Queen to London from the Isle of Wight, out along the Solent, up through the Strait of Dover and round to the Thames estuary, then magnificently along the river to her capital city, escorted all the way by the finest ships of her Navy. It would have been a statement that Britannia still ruled the waves, despite the growing battle fleets elsewhere – particularly the Kaiser's. 'However, she seems to have given certain directions which are to be followed,' he noted with regret. The date was fixed for Saturday 2 February, which gave them ten days to get everything ready. The preparations would be 'mighty'; he set to work.

The outline of the funeral was set, and so was its colour. The Queen, having worn black for so much of her life, wanted none of it for her death. She was a widow going to meet her husband, and she would be buried in white, like a bride. She was an empress, and she would be surrounded by the imperial colour. Purple was the order from beyond the grave. Above all, the funeral would be a military occasion, beginning with the coffin being carried from Cowes to Gosport in the royal yacht *Alberta* through a line of warships that would stretch almost the entire width of the Solent. Then it would be taken by train to London and solemnly borne through the streets on a gun carriage from Victoria station to Paddington. From there another royal train would take it to Windsor and a funeral service in St George's Chapel before the last leg from the chapel to the mausoleum at Frogmore.

London would get a chance to honour the Queen, and its leading citizens were duly grateful. According to one observer, it would be the capital's saddest but grandest day since the burial of Lord Nelson in the crypt at St Paul's nearly a century earlier. But there were worries about the popular reaction. A London crowd – a 'mob', some would call it – was unpredictable. It could be witty and wisecracking and full of good humour but quickly turn to annoyance and anger. It distrusted any form of authority – particularly the police, as any constable trying to do his job in the East End knew full well. If he tried to arrest a drunk or stop a brawl in a public house, he was likely to be on the end of a savage beating as friends and neighbours piled in to protect one of their own. No one doubted the loyalty of these people, but there was a danger of the occasion losing its dignity or turning into an unseemly demonstration of jingoism of the sort that the popular support for the war had so often provoked.

At the heart of the fears was the uncomfortable fact that, for all the proclaimed unity of late-Victorian society, London was two cities in one, and the two halves rarely met. The well-off in the West hardly ever ventured further east than the smart shops around St Paul's Churchyard and the offices in the City, and East Enders kept away from the fashionable end of town except to sell flowers on street corners, drive buses, carts and cabs, and clean up after the horses. What

would happen when East Enders crushed into the West End
of London? Would they behave properly? Would socialist
agitators exploit the crowds? And what about the tide flowing
in from the suburbs on the underground and overground
trains? It was all so unpredictable.

The *Standard* decided to put aside its distrust and promised
that 'the inhabitants of London will bear themselves as
becomes members of a great nation at a very solemn time. An
element in our character of which we have no reason to be
proud and which has come unpleasantly to the surface within
recent months, will be wholly invisible.' It called for 'gravity
and silence'. 'The prevailing thought must be of what is due
to her whom we have lost, to her bereaved children and
grandchildren and to the English people.'

There must be no idle gawping. 'The country will be
disgraced if there is any trace of mere sight-seeing curiosity
among the tens of thousands who will collect to watch the
long line of princes and representatives of kings and states, of
sailors, soldiers and heralds and statesmen as it makes its slow
progress along the streets.'

Others worried about the crowds getting out of control
through no fault of their own. There would be real dangers
to life and limb if, as seemed possible, people could not see
properly. 'When the Duke of Wellington passed through the
streets of London to be buried in St Paul's, the coffin was
elevated on a car above the line of sight, so that those at
the back of the crowds could see it as distinctly as those in the
front,' one man with memories of 1852 told readers of the
*Daily Chronicle*. 'Consequently everyone stood quietly in his
place. But if the Queen is borne on a gun carriage, all behind
the front rank will struggle to obtain a passing glance. What
may occur then?'

There were some who went further and disapproved of a

military funeral altogether, even though that was what the Queen had specified. A peace-loving correspondent thought it entirely the wrong thing. 'The Queen has conquered more than Wellington and Napoleon put together – not by conflict but by love and virtue. Let there be no gun carriage – that is not suggestive of love. Let the coffin be raised high and uncovered, or, if there must be something upon it, let it be her widow's cap.'

Such a humble suggestion was dismissed as the state planners began to assemble the pageant. The Duke of Norfolk had made his way to Osborne to spend hours with the King and Lord Roberts planning the details. The Bishop of Winchester was drawn into the discussions after the King put him in charge of the service at Windsor. He was taken aback by the Duke's lack of basic knowledge. 'He was curiously ignorant of many of the things that everybody else knew,' the Bishop noted. The geography of Windsor itself had the Duke completely stumped. He had drawn up an initial blueprint for a procession so long that if it went directly from the station to the castle, as he intended, the front would be past the chapel before the coffin on its gun carriage had even started. The Bishop, who had once been Dean of Windsor and knew the town well, pointed out that the procession would be unable to move at all, an observation that left the Duke 'nonplussed'. With the Bishop's help, a longer route was devised, going round the town before heading up the hill to the castle.

While the planners were planning, the doers were doing. In Windsor Castle, the clerk of the works, Mr Nutt, had his band of carpenters at work inside St George's Chapel building tiers of seating and installing a grey carpet along the nave from the main door to the altar. He had instructions that there should be no black drapery inside the chapel, only purple, but what happened outside the castle was beyond his control. In the High Street, the columns of the Guildhall were being covered in black and trailed with ivy, despite the heavy rain that was pouring down and forcing the workmen to take shelter.

Nutt was soon faced with a more perplexing problem. After Prince Albert's death, his likeness had been sculpted by the Italian artist Carlo Marochetti for the sarcophagus in the Frogmore Mausolem. It lay there on his tomb, waiting for his loved one to join him. What was not generally known was that the sculptor had made a similar image of the Queen at the same time. She had thrown herself fully into the job of planning and preparing the mausoleum – it had eased her grief – and she had seen in her mind's eye her own effigy eventually lying beside her husband's. The artist's eye and hand had done the rest. The result was perfect. It was a comfort to know that she and Albert would be immortalized together in the prime of their lives. But now, nearly four decades on, who even knew of its existence? Lord Esher, but only because the last time the Queen was at Windsor she had taken him aside and told him. What he did not ask her was where the sculpture was. How could he? Since he was the Crown official in charge of the Office of Works, he would have been expected to know such a detail. And, if he had asked her, it was unlikely she would have had the answer. Was this a matter for monarchs?

But now the moment of truth had come. The effigy was needed, and Esher had to admit he did not have a clue where to look. Surely Nutt would know. But, to the nobleman's horror, Nutt knew nothing. He had never even heard of it, and nor had anyone else on the staff at Windsor. There was no record of it in the archives or in the lists of art work, no mention of it anywhere. It was utterly perplexing. The thought flashed through Esher's head that perhaps it did not exist at all. Had the Queen imagined it? Had she not been in her right mind when she told him her secret? She had been so forgetful in those last months, not all there all of the time. Nutt carried on questioning the workers and finally found an old man whose memory went back far enough. Yes, he remembered the Queen's effigy – beautiful in white stone, made by some Italian, just like the Prince Consort's, the one in the mausoleum. But where was it? He took them to the stores and pointed to a wall. With pickaxes they knocked away the bricks, and there was the Queen, safe and ready for her last resting place. The funeral could go to plan after all.[3]

Lord Salisbury knew what had killed the Queen, but he kept his thoughts to himself and those closest to him. He knew because, although he was ten years younger than her, he felt worn down, just as she had. His eyesight was poor, he dropped off to sleep when he shouldn't, and he was weighed down by personal bereavement. But the longest shadow that lay over him was the war in South Africa. He backed it to the hilt, never showing any sign of wavering, but the casualties and the cost troubled him. None of this could he admit publicly, but in private he would say of the Queen, in his melancholy fashion, 'The war killed her, but she never flinched.' It was as if he was writing his own epitaph.

When he stood up in the House of Lords three days after her death to pay tribute to her, he was clearly in some distress. It was 'the saddest duty' that he had had to perform. He faltered. His customary vigour and directness seemed to desert him. To those who watched, he gave the impression that he was 'almost overpowered by the tragedy of the situation'.

He could find no fault with the way the Queen had conducted business, he told his fellow peers. The position of a constitutional sovereign was not easy. 'Duties have to be reconciled which sometimes seem far apart. Much has to be accepted which may not be pleasant.' But she understood the limits of her powers while at the same time maintaining a steady and persistent influence on the actions of her ministers which no one could mistake. 'She left on my mind the conviction that it was always a dangerous matter to press on her any course of expediency of which she was not thoroughly convinced. No minister in her long reign ever disregarded her advice without afterwards feeling that he had incurred a dangerous responsibility.' He praised her wisdom and her instinctive understanding of her people. 'She had an extraordinary knowledge of what they would want. When I knew what the Queen thought, I knew certainly what view her subjects would take, especially the middle class.'

As the Lords listened, breaking into the Prime Minister's oration only with their murmurs of agreement, MPs in the Commons were caught up by his nephew Balfour's rhetoric. There too a constitutional ritual was being enacted that symbolized the independence of Parliament from the Crown. The monarch was forbidden to step on to the floor of the House of Commons. His First Minister had to be his messenger. Balfour entered the House from the lobby and stood at the bar, the line across the floor that delineates the confines of the chamber and over which no outsider can step. The benches were packed as he announced in a slow and clear voice, almost spelling out the words, that he had 'a message from the King'. That word again. It set off another buzz of comment. He walked forward and handed the document he was carrying to the Speaker, who read out the message. 'The King is fully assured that the House will share the deep sorrow which has befallen His Majesty and the nation by the lamented death of his Majesty's mother, the late Queen.'

Then Balfour leaned against the dispatch box and began what Lady Frances, who was sitting in the visitors' gallery, thought was the finest speech she had ever heard him make. 'The emotion under which he laboured was great,' she said, and it affected his voice, which was higher-pitched than usual, not so full, less booming.

He was shocked by the suddenness of the Queen's death. 'I can hardly yet realize the magnitude of the blow that has fallen upon the country. In all the history of the British monarchy there never has been a case in which the feeling of national grief was so deep-seated, so universal, so spontaneous. We feel that the end of a great epoch has come.'

He praised her unstinting hard work, which she had carried out to the end. He had seen the evidence of it with his own eyes:

Short as was the interval between the last trembling signature affixed to a public document and final rest, it was yet long enough to clog the wheels of administration. I remember when I saw a vast mass of untouched documents which awaited the hand of the sovereign it was brought vividly before my mind how admirable was the unostentatious patience with which she carried out her share in the government of this great Empire. For her there was no holiday, no intermission of toil.

Her death, he ventured, had been 'a happy ending'. She had kept her people's love and affection right to the end. Other monarchs had seen their popularity wane. Not her. 'She passed away without a single enemy in the world, for even those who loved not England loved her.'

At least one observer thought the praise from Salisbury and Balfour excessive. *The Times* felt it should have been tempered with a little more realism. It did not dispute that 'the character of the great sovereign we have lost has left an indelible impression on the nation over which she ruled', but it could not agree that her reign had been trouble-free. 'Perhaps the historian of the future will say that the eulogies passed in this hour of public sorrow are too unqualified. Thirty or forty years hence it may become commonplace with critics that the extraordinary prosperity of the second half of the nineteenth century was not without its drawbacks.'

*The Times* was cautious in its criticism, but it was not the only paper which sensed that the nation was in danger of going to excess in its veneration of the dead Queen. The *Saturday Review* was perturbed by the overt displays of mourning. 'The nation has been deeply moved,' it declared, but 'deep grief is silent. Let us therefore take our sorrow with restraint and reasonable reticence.' It reminded its readers that her death was hardly unexpected nor a tragedy. This was the case of an old lady dying after a long and good life. Her death was not premature or untimely. 'There was no sense of incompleteness.' And it urged everyone to pay their respects and quickly get back to normal. 'The sooner this mournful ceremony is over the better, for a great many poor people will suffer considerably in the interval. Closing shops and theatres and the like involves loss to humble wage-earners.'

The Irish-born playwright George Bernard Shaw – always ready with an opinion to shock the Establishment – also wanted her disposed of quickly. He complained that keeping her coffin at Osborne for a week and more was 'insanitary'. His social principles demanded that she be quickly cremated or buried in a shallow grave in a coffin that, like her, would swiftly decompose.

But speed was not on the minds of those in power. They wanted time to see her properly to her grave and time to grieve for her. The Lord Chamberlain had now issued his official instructions for court mourning. Ladies were to wear black dresses, trimmed with crape, and black shoes and gloves, with black fans, feathers and ornaments, the gentlemen black court dress with black swords and buckles. Then came the sting that was to cause considerable hurt: this was to last for six months. Although the order applied only to the court, there was every chance that many others would follow this lead. The fears of the rag trade appeared to be justified. The dress code would be relaxed at the end of six months, but only marginally. For the rest of the year, women would be allowed the option of black dresses with coloured ribbons or white dresses with black ribbons. Twelve months of black would have the textile industry in Lancashire and the garment-makers of the East End in the red long before that period was up.

It also caused concern that the order from court was vague about how long the rest of the population was expected to be in mourning. A letter to a newspaper complained, 'Women whose incomes have to be very carefully eked out would like to know the exact period of time, so that they may decide whether it is necessary to expend their money on a certain number of new garments or whether, by careful management, they can make a much smaller stock last.' It was signed 'A woman of limited income'.

She was not the only one carefully counting the cost of the monarch's death. Up in Balmoral, the local people were anxious that the Queen's home on the Dee would now be downgraded as a royal residence. She had loved it, spent large parts of the year there, and brought all the paraphernalia of the court to the area. The presence of the Crown put money in people's pockets – suppliers, shopkeepers, drivers, cleaners, beaters, cooks and maids all did well when the family was in residence. However frugally she might think she was living in her Highland hideaway, she had been good for business in the area. Her son, though, was known to have much less regard for Balmoral, and the locals felt it 'not at all likely that he will honour it much with his presence'. In Ballater and Braemar they feared the stream of tourists would run dry, and along the banks of the Dee house prices would slump as the properties there 'would be less sought after as a place of residence by wealthy Englishmen and Americans, despite all those rugged beauties that so much captivated Byron'.[4]

But what was a loss for some was inevitably a profit for others. On the very day of her death, William Baker had secured the most prominent place on the front page of the *Daily Telegraph* to advertise his 'Mourning Warehouses, Borough High Street. Also at Upper Street, Islington'. He had paid a premium to be at the very top, above the normal columns, in the space to the left of the paper's masthead. In the classified advertisements of another paper, an enterprising jeweller from Rye in Sussex was selling mourning watches at 22s. 6d. each, 'engraved with VR and bearing the dates 1837–1901'.

The newspapers soon devised their own ways of cashing in on the national tragedy with what today would be called 'special offers'. The *Daily Express* was quickly in the market with a plaster bust of the Queen 'modelled from life'. The 'most lifelike representation ever offered to the public', it had been sculpted by a Miss Gedowski 'with realistic fidelity' and the original bronze had been destined for the Queen herself. Only a limited number were available. Send immediately to be sure of having one of these treasured mementoes. Exclusive price to *Express* readers – the nominal sum of 2s. 6d.! Can be forwarded to any address in the United Kingdom, securely packed and carriage paid.

Considerably more expensive was the portrait of the Queen on offer to the readers of the *Illustrated London News*, which boasted that it had acquired five hundred proofs of a portrait of the Queen by the artist Benjamin Constant that had been displayed at the Paris Exhibition. They were a snip at ten guineas each. For those priced out of this market, however, there was a special double issue of the magazine. It had a complete illustrated life of Her Majesty, the full story of her death, and copious notes on the doctors who attended her, along with their pictures. The events at Osborne were shown with wonderful sketches 'by our special artist Mr S. Begg', drawn from life. And there was more. As a special bonus – which also reflected the speed of the modern media – the issue would contain photographs of an event that had only just happened: the proclamation of the King at St James's Palace. And all for just one shilling.

Mementoes were on offer everywhere, and the *Bristol Times and Mirror* was one of many local papers that produced special supplements. On the front was a full-page drawing of a weeping Britannia, helmeted head in hands, a sorrowful lion at her feet and an hourglass in which the sand had run out. Inside were page after page of history, but the public's obsession with the minutiae of royal life even then, a century ago, meant that it was the personal anecdotes that pulled in the readers, anxious to think themselves in the know. A 'lady of position who was persona grata with the Queen' described meeting her: 'I was very nervous the first time I had an audience, but down the corridor came the diminutive little lady, quietly dressed in black. I was struck by her exceeding dignity and amiability.'

There was little dignity, though, in the spat between two newspapers on the south coast over which of them had been first to break the news of the Queen's death. The *Southern Daily Mail* at Portsmouth knew it had won the race but said it was reluctant to trumpet this fact because to do so would be in 'very bad taste'. It broke its silence when its rival, the Portsmouth *Evening News*, claimed triumphantly that it had been the first. The *Southern Daily Mail* replied that the *Evening News* had not only been beaten but had admitted as much in its own report. It had heard the news from Superintendent Fraser at the gates of Osborne at eight minutes past seven, but that same news 'was wired to us from the Mansion House at 6.58 and the *Mail* was selling in the streets with it before the clock struck seven'.

Every local paper retold in detail the times the Queen had visited its area. The disgraceful fact that she had never set foot in South Wales did not stop the *South Wales Daily News* from recalling how her yacht had once moored off Milford Haven overnight. She did not land, though 'a very pretty dairymaid in complete Welsh costume' was rowed out and went on board to be admired. Others she had ignored sought excuses. She had hated Brighton, with all its unwelcome Regency associations, which prompted the local *Gazette* to argue that 'neglected as we were, it was not the fault of the town but certain reminiscences of the past that accounted for her estrangement. How much George IV did to make or unmake Brighton is a matter of argument.'

The readers had their say too – often, appallingly, in verse. The *Birmingham Daily Gazette* was overwhelmed with poems from readers, so many that it could not acknowledge them individually. It decided not to run any of them, arguing that to pick and choose would be 'invidious'. In fact, it was the standard of the writing that put off the editor. 'It is not given to many persons to express in imperishable verse the great sorrow of a nation,' he wrote.

Even the most gifted are apt under such circumstances to mistake the will for the deed. Our collection contains some specimens of pure pathos written by persons of considerable culture and distinction, who may bless us six months hence for barring poetry on this occasion. On the other hand some ill-written illiterate scrawls have the germ of a true poetic thought in them. But we sadly conclude that an author of the In Memoriam that shall be worthy of our great and beloved Queen has not yet revealed himself.

The *Bristol Mercury* had no such qualms, and subjected its readers to:

> Victoria's righteous sway
> From us has passed away
> And left us sad;
> But influence bright and clear
> Doth linger ever near
> For though her conflict's past
> Her works will last.

That weekend, hundreds of specialist journals were published, and each one dedicated column after column to her and her part in its particular field. She was a friend of the farmers, the nurses, the Army and the Navy. In her death, everyone claimed a piece of her life. The *Local Government Chronicle* looked back on 'the chief municipal events with which her late Majesty identified herself'. The *Railway Times* took pride in the fact that 'the whole of the development of the iron road took place within the late Queen's reign. Having overcome her first reluctance to adopt railway travelling she became a regular patron and was most keenly appreciative of the special efforts made by all railway officials for her safety and comfort.' The metaphors used were often well chosen. 'The reaper gathers in his harvest with relentless hand, and in his sheaf he binds the young and old, the great and the lowly,' was the *Farmer*'s description of her end.

But one notable group in the land deliberately did not claim the Queen as their own, and it led to a great row. Cardinal Vaughan, the Archbishop of Westminster and head of the Roman Catholic Church in England, issued an order to his clergy that there should be no Masses for the dead Queen's soul. The Cardinal's logic and his theology were impeccable. She was a Protestant, and there was nothing in the Catholic liturgy that allowed Mass to be said for those who were not of the faith. It saddened him to make this ruling. 'None will mourn more than the Catholics the loss of the good Queen.' They could pray for her, and indeed he urged them to do so. Bells at Catholic churches could be tolled and flags hung at half mast. 'Gladly and eagerly shall we join in the purely civil and social mourning.' But no Masses. And, 'of other rites for the dead, the church has none'. Privately, the new King was furious, telling his nephew the Kaiser confidentially of his anger.[5] His mother, while drawn instinctively to the simple faith of the Scottish Presbyterians, had actively and ecumenically embraced her Catholic subjects – 'I am their Queen and I must look after them,' she had once declared.

There was a bitter correspondence in the newspapers that went on for weeks, long after she had been buried. Catholics were appalled that their Church was so rigid, so stubborn. It cast doubt on their loyalty to the Crown and resurrected all the suspicions about them that they hoped had been laid to rest. Roman Catholics had had equal rights in the land for little more than a century. Until 1793 they had been refused the vote, and before 1829 they could not stand for Parliament. There were still plenty of Protestant diehards who would have denied them all these gains. They would see the Cardinal's decree as justification for their bigotry.

As the Catholics bickered, the Anglicans turned to their God in huge numbers. Church attendances had been falling for much of the Queen's reign as science and scepticism ate away at simple faith, materialism made a mockery of the spiritual, and the promise of salvation in the hereafter sounded increasingly hollow in the city slums. A national survey had revealed that only one in ten went to church in the major conurbations of London, Liverpool, Birmingham and Manchester. 'The masses of our working population are never or but seldom seen in our religious congregations,' the statistician who had run the census concluded.[6] But that Sunday after the Queen's death there was not an empty pew to be found anywhere, High Church or Low, cathedral or chapel. Many were decked out in black. At St Martin-in-the-Fields in the centre of London, draperies hung from the pulpit, the lectern, the balconies and the main door. At St Clement Danes they covered the choir stalls as well. Preaching to full houses, the clergy seized the opportunity to lavish unstinting praise.

The new Central Railway put on extra underground trains to take more than eight thousand Londoners to St Paul's to hear the Archbishop of Canterbury marvel at how the Queen had 'elevated the whole tone of society by her perpetual conscientious adherence to that law of right which she always had before her eyes. She was a ruler whom the people might copy – might follow with glad hearts and with nothing to distress their minds.' Again, the organist and choirmaster, Sir George Martin, played the *Dead March* from *Saul*. At Westminster Abbey, its choir screen and altar draped in purple, Canon Duckworth said, 'Probably no sovereign who has ever reigned combined in such a happy proportion masculine strength and tenacity of will with feminine tenderness.'

The Revd J. Hasloch Potter, vicar of St Saviour's in Southwark, offered up the opinion that the Prime Minister had not dared to voice. The war had killed her. 'It was reported that she had seldom smiled since it began. Might it not be said that she died a martyr to it?' But Canon Gore, preaching at

St Margaret's, Westminster, refused to canonize her in this way. She was not to be likened to Joan of Arc, St Teresa or St Catherine. 'Her goodness was of a homely quality, the goodness of a wife and mother, the sort of goodness that opened her heart to all the English race.'

The whole country seemed to be in church that Sunday. 'Father, in thy gracious keeping leave thy servant sleeping,' sang the choristers in a church in Hull, a black bow pinned at the heart of their white surplices. Outside, the wind howled its own requiem as the congregation mourned, their eyes drawn to the pulpit, the lectern and the organ all draped in black. His head bowed, one worshipper 'thought of the still chamber at Osborne, and of another Crown, not an earthly one'.

Commentators sought for meaning in this outpouring of religious fervour. It was marvellous to see how 'when the nation is deeply moved it turns by instinct to the sacred ordinances of religion'. This cast a significant light on 'the so-called disintegrating forces of the age, its alleged scepticism, its professed pessimism, its reputed recklessness or despair', according to the *Daily Telegraph*. This 'sudden awakening' was a tribute to the essential goodness of the Queen, the 'miracle' of her amazing strength of character.

On the Isle of Wight, the Bishop of Winchester also had a full congregation at Whippingham church, and one that even he found a little daunting. Sitting there in front of him, in pews screened off from the rest of the church, was the entire royal family – the King and Queen, the German Emperor, and some twenty other princes and princesses, dukes and duchesses. They had slipped in quietly from a side entrance, and the rest of the congregation were not even aware of their presence. Towards the back of the church he could see Lord

Roberts and members of the Household sitting among the local villagers and the few visitors from Cowes who had managed to squeeze in. The weather was gloomy and, though it was midday, candles had been lit inside the church.

Davidson had spent all of Saturday trying to write his sermon, but had been constantly distracted. The King had wanted to talk to him more than once; his advice had been sought continually. His wife had arrived, and he took her to see the coffin in the *chapelle ardente*. Then his presence at dinner at Osborne had been demanded. It was not until eleven at night, when he should have been asleep, that he got round to drafting anything – 'rather a serious matter considering the difficulty of the occasion'.

But, as always, he was fast on his feet. 'My friends,' he began, 'what can I say? What could any man say standing where I stand this morning at such an hour in such surround-ings? We are blankly bewildered. And though people are feeling this all the world through, there is here in Whip-pingham, for all of us, for all of you, something more direct and personal.' The sun was breaking through, and shafts of light filled the church as he paid the Queen a simple tribute that caught the intimacy of the moment for this very special congregation. 'She was our own, we loved her so and she has gone.'

That afternoon, the press was allowed into the chapel where the Queen's coffin lay at rest. At the personal invitation of the King, forty journalists filed past, open-mouthed and over-awed, taking in every detail, thrilled at the privilege of being there. Fritz Ponsonby was taking his turn as a member of the Household to stand in watch over his dead mistress. He was not comfortable. The strong smell from the flowers heaped around the room upset him. He also had a lot of work to do. The King, perhaps aware from the Bishop of Winchester that the Earl Marshal was vague about the layout at Windsor, had asked him to organize the procession and the military side of the funeral there, and he was itching to be off. He would have to be quick, because he could stay there only a few days before rushing back to the Isle of Wight to play his part in the ceremonial when the cortège left Osborne on the first leg of its journey. However devoted he had been to the Queen, standing here beside her coffin was hardly the best use of his time.

As the journalists left the chapel, a crimson curtain thrown back to let them out into the drawing room and on to the terrace, a handful stayed behind. They were illustrators whose job, with press photography still in its infancy, was to capture the image for the popular newspapers and magazines. They sat sketching quietly until the King's private secretary came into the hushed and darkened room. His Majesty had forbidden this. They must put down their pads and pencils and leave straight away. They did as they were told, even the two who had expressly been given permission. The King later realized there had been a misunderstanding and asked them to come back, but by then they had all left. Most already had on paper the outline and the details they needed. They finished their work elsewhere.

Out on the terrace, the reporters were comparing notes and looking out across to the waters of the Solent, where there was a new wonder to see. The Kaiser's imperial yacht, the *Hohenzollern*, had arrived. Large and white, she could have been mistaken for one of the Castle liners which regularly left Southampton for South Africa. There was a crucial difference, though. Her bow was shaped liked a ram, and she was armed with light weapons – a warship masquerading as a pleasure boat. Crown Prince William had also arrived from Germany, and the Kaiser had crossed to Gosport in the *Alberta* to greet his son. It was the Emperor's forty-second birthday, and as he passed the *Hohenzollern* on his way back the German sailors lined the rails to cheer him. When they landed at Cowes, he spotted three of the soldiers he had met on his visit to the convalescent home near Osborne on the day before the Queen died. He lifted his hat and smiled at them. They were thrilled. 'There ain't no side about him. He's the right sort,' one of them later told anyone who cared to listen.

The German Emperor – the man who just thirteen years later would take his country into the horror of a world war with Britain – was doing everything to make himself the most popular man in England. He had won over his uncles and aunts. The King wrote to his sister Vicky that her son 'William's touching and simple demeanour will never be forgotten by me or anyone.' Now he was wooing the people. And he was succeeding. The newspapers were full of praise for him and the way he had rushed to the side of his dying grandmother. 'His spontaneous action at this time will be remembered by the people of this country,' said *The Times*, '*for ever.*' Berlin's envoy in London, Baron von Eckardstein, was delighted. 'For a time, the Kaiser was, in the eyes of almost every Englishman, a most popular personage.' This rapprochement unsettled diplomats elsewhere. There were concerns in Paris and St Petersburg – 'nervousness' was the word – about the 'sudden courtesies' between Britain and Germany. But Washington welcomed the prospects for peace 'fittingly ratified at the death bed and bier beside which the King and Emperor stood'.

To honour his nephew's birthday, the King appointed the Kaiser a field marshal of the British Army. The next morning, 28 January, there was a ceremony which cemented relations between the British and German royal families even more. The Crown Prince, a nervous lad of eighteen who continually looked to his father for reassurance, was invested with the Garter.

The Bishop of Winchester, who was the Order's chaplain, had not brought his robes of office and had to put on the only formal clothes he had with him – his evening suit. There were a surprising number of Garter knights at Osborne – the King, the Duke of York, the Duke of Connaught, the Emperor, Prince Christian, the Duke of Norfolk and Lord Roberts. With the exception of the Duke of York, still confined to bed with German measles, they assembled in the audience room in full uniform. The officers from the *Hohenzollern* had also been invited, and they lined the room as, 'with great dignity and even pomp, so far as pomp was possible in the circumstances', the King presented the German Crown Prince with the badge, ribbons and cloak of the highest honour a British sovereign could bestow. The King's speech was fulsome. He spoke of the close ties between the two royal families and hoped that it could be extended to the nations as a whole, working together in pursuit of peace. He praised the Kaiser's devotion, which 'aroused a profound and permanent sentiment of gratitude and respect not only in the family circle but throughout the whole British race'.[7]

Afterwards, Lord Roberts and the Duke of Norfolk left hurriedly for London, where, that afternoon, with less than four full days to go, final plans were being drawn up for what the *Morning Post* described as 'the most victorious pageant of any sceptred monarch'.

The next day the King too was on his way back to the capital, travelling in appalling weather. Rain and sleet lashed the royal yacht as it stood waiting for him to come on board, and the winds were nearing hurricane force. As he walked from his carriage, a crowd cheered and he doffed his hat. The *Daily News* reporter who saw this was horrified at the King going bareheaded in the cold and the wet. 'Courtesy from the monarch is gratifying to subjects,' he wrote, 'but he need not carry that quality so far as to risk his health.' The country had no wish to lose a second monarch before it had buried the first.

Shortly after the King left the island, a ferry docked at East Cowes and there was a hush among the passengers as a large, heavy package was heaved off. It was thickly covered with black wrappings, but they knew what they were witnessing. Banting's in London had done their work. The Queen's coffin had arrived.

For the return journey across to the mainland there was another poignant piece of cargo. The Queen's little pony carriage in which she had so often driven round the grounds of Osborne, pulled by a white donkey, was on its way back to Windsor. It was not needed for her last ride.

# 10. Crossing the Bar

The ships like dark messengers of death sent to summon the
Queen . . .

The Revd Cosmo Lang

Flowers had started arriving at Osborne within hours of the
Queen's death. The wreath from the King of Portugal, a crown
of lilies and orchids on a cushion of violets, was spectacular but
so big it could not be carried through the door of the temporary
chapel and had to remain outside in the entrance hall. The
island was in danger of being overwhelmed, and an urgent
request was issued through the newspapers that wreaths should
be sent to Windsor.

Where had all the flowers come from? Remarkably, given
the time of year, apart from the violets and orchids that came
from the South of France, most were locally grown. The
florists in London were under siege, but they were grateful.
There had been a fashion lately for 'no flowers by request' at
funerals. Now they were back in business. Money seemed to
be no object. Amounts between £30 and £70 (equivalent to
£2,000 to £5,000 today) were normal, and it was estimated
that London alone would spend more than £50,000 (£3.5
million) on flowers for the Queen. It would have been better
sent to charity, one *Times* reader thought, especially since most
of the blooms were dead long before they reached their
destination. The editor of another paper thought the waste of

money 'appalling'. A new hospital wing could have been built with the amount 'squandered'.

At the market in Covent Garden, work was going on around the clock to meet the demand. Finished wreaths were boxed up in packing cases which were stacked all along the central aisle, waiting to be loaded into vans for Windsor. In Bond Street, one shop owner had to call the police to move on the crowd pressing their noses against his window to watch elaborate wreaths being made up.

The problem for the florists was that the bulk of their customers were official bodies rather than individuals, and few of them were content with just a simple, straightforward wreath. They insisted on a design that reflected who or what they were. The officers of the 7th Hussars demanded a floral tribute in the shape of the regimental shield. It was eight feet wide and eight feet high and required sixty thousand violets, each separately wired. The Freemasons ordered a *cœur de lion*, the music-hall artistes a harp of lilies, the City of London its civic shield with a cross of red carnations and a background of white camellias. Trinity House's tribute was in the shape of the Eddystone Lighthouse; the Royal Mint's had bands of silver and gold.

Elsewhere, wreaths and floral tributes appeared around statues of the Queen in city centres or at any other spot that was deemed to have an association with her. Birmingham was typical. There the men, women and children from the Italian community marched in procession in national costume to lay a wreath with the inscription 'The Italian residents in Birmingham humbly place this small token of affection and respect in loving memory.' The city council, naturally, took pride of place around the statue with its offering, but there were humbler tributes too. 'A token of love from a Reservist's child,' read one note round a spray of flowers. The actors at

the Theatre Royal sent a wreath, and so did the girls of the
King Edward VI School and the children from the Royal
Institution for the Deaf and Dumb.

Back in London, there was panic at Paddington. The borough
council knew the main-line station in their area was the
destination for the funeral procession, but they hadn't been
told precisely what route it would take and when. They were
most put out. They felt, as the responsible local body, they
were entitled to know. Civic pride was at stake. The clerk
had written to the Duke of Norfolk asking for official advice
and on 29 January had received a rather dusty answer. 'For
route, see today's *Times* — Earl Marshal,' he had telegraphed
back. He had kings and generals to worry about. He wasn't
going to waste much time on a handful of self-important
aldermen.

The council met to consider its position, and decided that
it should at the very least secure the best seats for itself. The
members voted to have a stand built in a prime position at
Burwood Place, halfway between Marble Arch and the station,
for themselves and their friends. They deliberated on who
should pay, and came to the conclusion that the cost would
have to be met from their personal pockets. But not the
wreath. That was an official matter and could quite properly
come out of public funds.

The route through the capital had been much discussed at
the meeting called by the Earl Marshal the day before. Sir
Edward Bradford, the Commissioner of Police, was worried
that the journey might be too short. If the vast numbers came
that he expected, too many spectators would be bunched
together in too limited a space. Taking the procession through
the open space of Hyde Park rather than up the narrow and
crooked Park Lane would be a great help, but he also needed

the whole route to be longer to ease the congestion on the pavements. So, instead of taking a direct line from Victoria to Hyde Park Corner and through the park to Paddington, a distance of just over two miles, the cortège would make a detour past Buckingham Palace, along The Mall to St James's and Piccadilly. This would add an extra mile, which eased the Commissioner's worries.

A rush began to secure the best positions to see the Queen's last ride through her capital. Shopkeepers and householders along the way could expect to make a small fortune by renting out their front windows and balconies, even more if they built small stands and packed in as many spectators as they could. The price would be high for such vantage points. A window in St James's Street, close to the palace, was immediately up for hire, with five tiers of seats. The owner was asking ten guineas each for seats in the front two rows, eight guineas for the third row, and five guineas for the ones at the back.

For the privileged few, there were special arrangements. Admirals and generals were allotted space in Friary Court at the front of St James's Palace. A stand was to be erected in The Mall for members of the House of Lords and House of Commons, but they had just twenty-four hours to get in their applications and there would be only two seats each. But the real issue for those in Parliament was whether they could join in the procession rather than just watch it. But it was a military occasion and there was no role for them, nor for the judges and the Lord Mayor and all sorts of bodies with links to the Queen who felt certain they should be represented. The Earl Marshal was firm. They could not just tag on behind. This was to be a mighty pageant, not a jamboree.

Meanwhile, hurried plans were being made for the many distinguished foreign visitors due to arrive for the funeral, and Buckingham Palace was already running out of rooms for them all. The Duke of Portland put his London home at the disposal of the court for any of the overspill. The King of Portugal was on his way, the Crown Prince of Denmark, the King of Greece, the Grand Duke Michael of Russia. 'The mother of dynasties will be borne to the sepulchre with all the dynasties around her pall,' the *Daily Telegraph* proudly proclaimed. 'Each of the royal arrivals reminds us of the wonderful relationships and associations with nearly all courts which gave the great Queen her unexampled place in the eyes of Europe. When our company of princely guests is assembled, we shall have with us the actual holders or immediate heirs of well-nigh 20 thrones.'

The list was growing all the time – the Crown Prince of Siam was now expected – and must have seemed endless to the customs officials at Dover, who had to make special arrangements to welcome each dignitary into the country on arrival across the Channel from Calais. Special trains were laid on to bring the visitors to London, and crowned heads had to be greeted at Victoria with all the trappings and fanfares that protocol demanded.

There was no fanfare, however, for the soldiers who would line the route of the procession. Thirty thousand were ordered to London, drawn from units all over the country, and, with all the barracks filled with troops based locally, Lord Roberts's staff had problems finding somewhere to billet them. They were relieved when the owners of the Earls Court exhibition area offered their site at Olympia as a temporary home for seven thousand of them, but the rest had to be scattered in drill halls all over the capital.

The horses would get better treatment. The Kaiser sent for half a dozen of his chargers, each specially trained for his use, to be brought over from Berlin so he could select one to ride in the procession. They were to be stabled in the mews at Buckingham Palace alongside eight cream artillery horses belonging to the Queen which would pull the gun carriage through the streets of London. The horses would definitely not be sporting black plumes, which had become the fashion in civilian funerals, though seen by some as rather common. As for the gun carriage, it, like the ones that would be used on the Isle of Wight and at Windsor, was getting a fresh coat of khaki paint and was being fitted with rubber tyres to deaden the sound – something the Queen had specifically ordered in the instructions she had left. Gun carriages were 'noisy', and she was concerned to minimize the 'very rough jolting', as if worried she might be uncomfortable on her final journey.

By now the issue of mourning had finally been settled. The King had heard the arguments from the clothing industry and ordered that full public mourning should last just six weeks. 'After the sixth day of March next it will not be desired or expected that the public should appear in deep mourning,' the *London Gazette* announced, but asked for 'half mourning' for a further six weeks after that. *The Times* welcomed this as 'a generous and enlightened concession'. The King had bowed to those who had argued that a prolonged period would inflict great hardship on the garment-makers and the shopkeepers who had accumulated stocks of coloured articles for the spring and summer. It felt the person they were mourning would have approved. 'Widespread and heartfelt grief still hangs like a heavy cloud over the nation, but the Queen, with her high sense of duty, would not have desired that her people should be turned aside from the stern tasks of everyday life by an excessive indulgence in the luxury of mourning.' *The Economist* agreed, and, as the funeral neared, it urged the nation to make its farewells and get back to work. For too long 'the nation has attended to nothing except accounts of widespread

grief, and the papers have all seemed to be edited by undertakers. We are not so prosperous that we can all indulge like
widows in a protracted luxury of tears. The business of the
country presses hard and must be done.' This was strongly
endorsed in the manufacturing heartland of the Midlands,
where the *Birmingham Daily Post* congratulated the new King
for 'so promptly removing what threatened to become a
serious strain and a grievous sacrifice'. Business must come
first. It was the clarion cry of the twentieth century.

One problem was resolved, but officialdom created another
one. The Lord Mayor of London sought clarification on the
colour buildings should be draped in for the funeral. The royal
Office of Works was emphatic – purple, as the Queen had
requested, not black. It was easier said than done. London,
indeed the whole country, had covered itself in black crape
from the moment her death had been announced. It was an
expensive business. Draping the entire frontage of a house could
use more than 100 yards of cloth, at a cost of £25 to £30. There
was a cheaper alternative – by covering just the balcony, a
householder could get away with 15 yards in a single drop of
plain cloth with no valance or border for just under £3.

Now the preference for purple caused fresh consternation
in the textile trade. The situation was impossible, according
to the boss of a firm in the City specializing in decoration.
'We will not be able to get purple at all. I have scores of
orders,' he complained, 'but there is not a yard left. It is a
colour we do not stock, largely because it is never wanted,
and we cannot get supplies now either from Yorkshire or
Germany, our only two sources.'

Even black was in short supply, and he advised those who
wanted that to cover their buildings to get on with it. Some
had been shilly-shallying:

Everybody here in the City wants to blossom out into mourning of some kind, but they have been waiting to see what each will do. Our black stuff is going fast, and the big houses, the banks and hotels, will find themselves in an awkward plight if they are not careful. Three days are enough for us to cover half the City, but we cannot do it if everybody leaves it till Friday.

He also knew some companies who were trying to get their mourning on the cheap. 'One big firm gave us an order for £22 10s.; then altered their minds, and tried to get the building done for less than 5s. per window. When that failed they decided to do the job themselves.' Others resorted to scavenging. The decorator had used 120 yards of material to cover the small frontage of his own workshop, but when parts of the drapery 'came away from their moorings in a gale, our neighbours calmly annexed the portion that blew on their premises'.[1]

The Saturday of the funeral was decreed as a day of national mourning, on the orders of the King. The problems this would cause had never crossed the royal mind or the minds of his advisers. Most factories normally worked until noon on Saturday. If the workers stayed at home, would they be paid for the time they had lost? Of course not. Saturday was also traditionally pay day, giving families the afternoon to shop for food for the weekend. Would they get their wages early? And, if the shops shut on Saturday – as most throughout the country agreed instantly that they should – how would ordinary people stock up?

A more acrimonious debate began over the pubs. Why should they close at a time when people were off work and demanding somewhere to go? Should they close in the day and reopen when the funeral was over? What would be

the right time for them to throw open their doors again?
Arguments went on in local authorities and chambers of
commerce everywhere. In the East End the landlords planned
to shut from 10 a.m. until 3 p.m., but in Liverpool it would
be six o'clock before they reopened. Rhymney in Wales
would be dry for the entire day, as would Glasgow, but the
publicans in Nottingham refused to follow this example. They
would not be stopped from opening once the funeral procession was over in London. The local paper was contemptuous. 'A more despicable exhibition of selfishness it would be
impossible to imagine,' it thundered. 'Such is the patriotism
of the pot house.'

There was furious debate too about whether to give school-
boys time off from Saturday lessons to be in London to watch
this undoubted moment of history. A man signing himself
'Pater' wrote from the New University Club in St James's to
urge headmasters of the great public schools to give boys
whose parents lived in the capital the day off. Pupils from
Eton would be in the crowds lining the streets of Windsor. It
would be only fair if others had the same opportunity, 'in view
of the historical interest which will attach to this mournful
pageant'. The idea horrified one Scrooge-like correspondent.
'Why should an occasion of national mourning be an occasion
of general schoolboy holidays? All schoolmasters know that
means mischief.' The headmaster of Winchester, for one, was
having none of this. He had been asked by parents if their sons
could be allowed out to see 'a wonderful sight', 'a splendid
spectacle'. He refused. It was a time when the school should
be united not scattered, and they would remember the Queen
in a service they could all join in at the cathedral.

At Windsor, the air was thick with the scent from the flowers
stacking up inside the castle walls. They had been arriving in

carts, trucks, wagons and vans for two days. A visitor felt faint in the presence of 'priceless blooms which ought only to be seen in midsummer'. At first tourists were allowed in to see them, but so many came that the gates had to be closed. Inside St George's Chapel, Nutt and his men had finished building the tiers of seating in the side aisles and now had to test them for safety. He summoned a company of guardsmen who were parading in their scarlet tunics and busbies, called them inside the chapel, and sat them down. Then, on his command, they jumped up and down, while he checked the struts and the joints until he was satisfied that the structure was perfectly sound.

Fritz Ponsonby felt equally confident about the arrangements he found when he arrived in the town from Osborne to carry out the King's instruction to check the plans for Windsor. He talked to the Mayor, the police and the officer commanding the troops, approved the extension of the route of the procession suggested by the Bishop of Winchester, and was happy that everything was in hand for controlling the crowds along the way. He headed back to Osborne, where he asked to be shown the details of the procession itself, which the Earl Marshal was supposed to be drawing up. To his horror, there was nothing to be seen. The Earl Marshal's office was still frantically working on the London end and had not even begun planning for Windsor. Ponsonby felt a wave of panic. Had he misunderstood the King's instructions? Was he supposed to be organizing the procession himself? He took the 9.20 a.m. boat out of Cowes on Thursday morning and a fast train to London.

At the Earl Marshal's office he walked into a scene of chaos. The heralds from the College of Arms – an unprepossessing lot, described by one courtier as 'ghastly cads, not a gent among them' – were dithering. They were used to doing everything by the history book – and in their own time – but there was a shortage of precedent to refer to and time was running out. He could see no system in the way they were working. Each was concentrating on whatever small detail of procedure suited him. Clerks were waiting around to take notes and do the paperwork, but they were not being used. Ponsonby crossly asked for the programme for Windsor. 'We haven't finished Osborne and London yet,' came an anguished shout in reply. It was less than twenty-four hours before the cortège set off from Osborne, he hurled back. What was going on? What did they think they were doing? His anger was fuelled by his realization that, if Windsor turned out to be a disaster, he would get the blame. He wanted to carry on at court, to get a job in the new King's Household. His chances would be ruined unless he took control.

Ponsonby strode to the Duke of Norfolk's office and demanded to see him. He was ushered in and, to his surprise, he found the Duke 'a thoroughly businesslike and capable man, dealing with telegrams, letters, ceremonials, enquiries from the Lord Chamberlain, Lord Steward, Master of the Horse, telephone messages from the Foreign, India and Colonial Offices, but quite unconscious that the work he was delegating to his subordinates was not being done'. He thought a skeleton programme for Windsor had been drawn up, and was rattled when Ponsonby told him it had not even been started. It was not his fault, he told the equerry. He kept getting new lists of kings and princes who wanted to come to the funeral, and this was making it impossible to finalize the London arrangements. He had five crowned heads, eight crown princes, and twenty other princes and archdukes to deal with, and their entourages too. There was nothing he could do about Windsor. Ponsonby had better go as quickly as he could to see Lord Roberts and draw up a plan with him.

At the War Office, the Commander-in-Chief could not be disturbed. Ponsonby sent in his card with a message scrawled on it – 'Funeral arrangements – urgent' – and was allowed in. Roberts was sympathetic when he heard that nothing had been settled at Windsor, and he gave Ponsonby the authority to issue any orders he thought necessary, with the Commander-in-Chief's backing, to get matters moving. Back at the Earl Marshal's office, the equerry worked out a timetable and a programme of events as best he could given the shortage of firm information about who would be there and dictated it to a shorthand writer, who typed it up. At least they now had something on paper, even if it had to be modified later. He took this to the Duke of Norfolk, who ran his eye over it, looking up from time to time to tell Ponsonby how he had upset the heralds. They thought he had been rude to them and had cast doubt on their efficiency, all of which was true, as Ponsonby admitted by way of apology, excusing himself on the grounds that without him no orders would have been issued at all.

The Duke made some amendments and nodded his approval, and Ponsonby left to have the programme printed and circulated to all those involved. He then took copies to the War Office and the Admiralty to explain the orders, before taking a late train back to the Isle of Wight. It was two in the morning before he crawled into bed, and he had to be up at dawn the next day to prepare for the departure of the funeral cortège from Osborne. But at least Windsor was more or less settled. A disaster had been headed off.

The Bishop of Winchester had been heading off disasters too. As the burden of the planning had moved from Osborne to London, he had been able to ease up and even take a long walk through the grounds and down to the sea with his wife.

He had led the royal family in a number of services for the Queen, helped by choristers from Windsor and their choirmaster, Walter Parratt. With Parratt's help, he had been preparing the order of service for the funeral at St George's and had come across a request from the Queen's daughters for an anthem, 'Give rest, O Christ, to thy servant with thy saints', which was from the Prayers for the Dead liturgy of the Russian Orthodox Church. Davidson thought there was a real danger this would give offence to many devout Anglicans and even more to the Methodists, the Presbyterians and the other Non-conformists.

He took his problem to the King, and 'the moment I explained the matter he saw it and felt that it must be altered but that his sisters would make objections'. The King and the Bishop went to see the princesses, and there was a fierce row. Yes, they most certainly wanted the anthem. Their mother had loved it, and it had been used before, both in the mausoleum and at Whippingham. Indeed it had, but, the Bishop reminded them, those occasions had caused a great deal of comment at the time, which he had deflected only with the argument that these services were private family affairs. But the funeral at Windsor would be a great national event, and the eyes of the world would be on them. Did they really want to introduce such a note of controversy to the occasion? The Russian anthem would offend the puritan and the old-fashioned and raise questions about the King's religious preferences almost before his reign had begun. The princesses were not convinced by Davidson's argument and backed down only when their brother insisted and sharply put an end to the argument.

Davidson now had to act fast. The order of service with the offending anthem in it was on the point of being printed. He telephoned the Lord Chamberlain's office in London to order it to stop the print run, and then rushed to the Osborne telegraph office to dictate the words of a substitute anthem. Within five minutes a clash between Church and Crown had been averted, but it had been 'a near shave'.

But the next day there was another altercation about the Windsor arrangements. The King had agreed that Madame Emma Albani, lead soprano with the New York Metropolitan Opera and one of the Queen's favourites, should be allowed to sing a solo at the chapel, at a private service on the day after the funeral. Davidson had strong objections to this. 'Not only would it be the first occasion of an outside professional singer (a lady) taking a solo in St George's at a Sunday service, but Madame Albani is a Roman Catholic.' Emboldened by his success over the Russian anthem, Davidson went to see the King again, but this time with a compromise to suggest. Wouldn't it be better if Madame Albani sang over the coffin at a special service for the family in the Albert Memorial Chapel at St George's? She would probably regard this as a much greater honour anyway. The King was not pleased, but in the end was persuaded and, as Davidson noted, 'ultimately it was carried out in the way I proposed and Albani was delighted'.

The moment had come. Out in the Solent on Friday 1 February it was an early start for the crews of the thirty British battleships and cruisers that had been lining up for the past two days, forming an unequalled naval guard of honour over the eight miles of sea from Cowes to Portsmouth. They were just five hundred yards apart, swaying at anchor in a gentle breeze on a cold and grey morning, from HMS *Alexandra* immediately off Cowes to HMS *Prince George* and HMS *Majestic* nearest to the mainland. A light mist made it impossible to see from one end of the line to the other. They were battle-grey and battle-hard, symbols of dreadnought power and the increasing mechanization of war.

More than one observer was wistfully dreaming of how much more beautiful a sight this would have been in the not-so-distant days of sail early in Victoria's reign. 'Now everything tends to power rather than beauty,' sighed the *Daily Telegraph* correspondent. But here was Britannia's modern might on display as never before, and it was awesome. The *Standard* could barely contain itself. Its naval correspondent thought it 'fitting that such a powerful fleet should assemble to salute the last great sea journey of her who had been Ruler of a world-wide empire and Mistress of the Seas. There is no parallel for such a pageant. It may well be counted among the greatest scenes of English history, to live in our annals for ever more.' It sent out a signal, 'an impression of power and a sense of dominion'.

On board the warships, officers were quickly into full dress uniform of long coat with gold epaulettes, laced trousers, cocked hats, swords, decorations and medals. The petty officers, men and boys put on their No. 1 dress of serge frock with gold badges, collars, cloth trousers and white straw hats. As the blood-red sun came up into a cloudless sky, it turned to bright gold, its rays picking out the frost dusting the rooftops of Cowes. On the hills above and on the common at Southsea on the mainland, crowds were already gathering. All was very still.

Foreign ships made up one end of a second, shorter, line – the Kaiser's squadron of two battleships and two cruisers, and cruisers from France, Japan and Portugal. There was a gap where the Spanish cruiser *Charles V* was expected at any minute, but she would never make it. Her boilers had broken down as she crossed the Bay of Biscay from Corunna and she had limped back to port for repairs. The Government in

Madrid felt humiliated and ordered an urgent investigation. Even more distasteful for Spanish pride was that, as news arrived that she had turned back, her place in the line to honour the dead Queen was taken by the royal yacht of the paltry Prince of Monaco.

Out on the water, there was a constant traffic of small boats. Paddle steamers and launches were setting out from Portsmouth with official parties – the press in one, members of the House of Lords and the House of Commons with their wives in others. On board the parliamentary boat was Keir Hardie, founding father of the embryonic Labour Party, and for now one of the House's two socialist MPs. (In five years' time there would be thirty; in ten years more than forty). Some might query the presence of such a republican-minded radical, but, as Philip Snowden, Hardie's co-founder of the party, explained, though he would have preferred a democratic republic to a monarchy, he had great admiration for Queen Victoria personally.[2]

A German torpedo boat hurried importantly through the waves to lie alongside one of the Kaiser's battleships. There was an exclusion zone around the fleet, policed by fast naval pinnaces, but local boatmen were trying to take up positions that would give their paying passengers a good view. They were charging ten shillings a seat, which annoyed the high-minded *Daily Chronicle*, fearful that 'cheap excursions' would turn this solemn occasion into a gala. 'All this is presumably unavoidable but there seems something about it that jars,' it said.

As noon approached, the guns on the warships were made ready for the salute that each one would give as the royal yacht carrying the Queen's coffin passed. An hour later the band began to form on each foredeck, under orders to play nothing but Chopin and Beethoven funeral marches. Away on the headland above Cowes another band marched into position. In the long drive at Osborne House, Lieutenant George Miller was assembling his Royal Marine bandsmen in their white pith helmets, their drums wreathed in black, for the mournful march down to the sea. He was there by special request. He and his men had often played for the Queen. She liked them. They would see her safely home.

Curiously, at that very moment, on a remote island five hundred miles to the north, the news of her death was just being broken to the last of her subjects to be told. Heavy storms had raged around North Ronaldsay in the Orkneys for a fortnight, and no fisherman dared risk the fearsome tide to cross the three-mile strait from Sanday, particularly since there was no pier to tie up at and the only way to get ashore was to run up on the beach. There was no telegraph on the island, and so it was only when the winds slackened that a boat could get across and tell the islanders what the rest of the world had known for a week and a half.

Inside Osborne House, the final preparations had been made. Reid supervised as the outer coffin of lead-lined oak was carried into the temporary chapel and the shell coffin with the Queen's body in it was lifted from the plinth and placed inside. The sides of the shell were packed with charcoal before the lead cover was soldered on. A silver plate had been prepared with a Latin inscription: 'Depositum Serenissimae Potentissimae et Excellentissimae Principis Victoriae . . .' – 'Here lies the body of the most serene, most powerful and the most excellent Queen Victoria, by the grace of God Queen of Britain, Defender of the Faith and Empress of India. Departed this life 22nd of January in the year of our Lord 1901, in the 82nd year of her age and the 64th year of her reign.' The plate was fixed to the lead cover and then the oak lid was screwed on to the top of the coffin. Finally, a square brass plate with the same inscription was fixed on the wooden lid. Then the completed coffin – weighing half a ton – was hauled on to a trolley.

The whole operation had taken an hour and a quarter, and now it was left to the Bishop of Winchester to complete matters. He and the Revd Clement Smith laid out purple cushions on top of the coffin and placed the great State Crown, the sceptre and two orbs on them. The guard of honour had been dismissed and the two clergymen were alone with the Queen, their thoughts and their prayers. Davidson thought it 'as solemn a time as any we had had'.

At 1.30 the coffin was wheeled out into the hall at the foot of the staircase opposite the main entrance, and the royal family gathered for a short service, a reading from St John, and a few special prayers. Then sailors in their blue jackets shouldered the coffin and, with kilted Highlanders, foresters from Balmoral, holding the pall, they marched it outside to the waiting gun carriage. Under a cloudless blue sky, the Solent gleaming in the distance for all the world like the Mediterranean that had been Prince Albert's inspiration for Osborne, they slid it into place.

Under the portico, the princesses gathered, all dressed alike in long black cashmere dresses trimmed with crape. They had worried about what to wear and had searched for a suitable look for mourning – one that was in keeping with the occasion but not as old-fashioned as the images they had found in prints and pictures of the last funeral of a sovereign. If they followed the precedent of sixty-three years ago, they would be wearing ridiculous large coal-scuttle hats. Princess Marie Louise suggested something less obtrusive – a Mary Stuart cap, as she called it, coming to a peak on the forehead and covered with a crape veil that dropped over the face. It was 'most becoming!'

she thought as they stepped out into the quadrangle to line up
in twos and threes behind the gun carriage. There was a shout
of command, and the riders on the dark horses in the traces
kicked them into action.

Along the path to the main gate stood soldiers, rifles reversed
on their boots, heads bowed, an avenue of mourning down
which the procession began slowly to move. Fritz Ponsonby
was in his place with Sir Arthur Bigge and other senior
aides and equerries alongside the gun carriage. Outside them
marched the Queen's Company of the Grenadier Guards.
Immediately behind the coffin walked the King, dressed in
the uniform of an Admiral of the Fleet, his nephew the Kaiser
and his brother, the Duke of Connaught, beside him. The
other princes followed, then the princesses. To one side was
Mr Woodford, the Osborne carpenter, carrying a wreath on
behalf of the King, his civilian clothes an oddity among the
scarlet tunics, blue uniforms, gold decorations and plumed
hats. Sir James Reid and the Bishop of Winchester were with
other members of the Household bringing up the rear.

The silence was shattered as the bagpipes of the Black
Watch gasped and broke out into the wailing 'Flowers of the
Forest'. James Vincent, standing under an ilex tree in an
enclosure on the lawn among schoolchildren from Whippingham, estate workers and servants, was struck by the small-
ness of the royal group 'by contrast with the amount of majesty
it embodied'. This was a great state occasion, but at the heart
of it was a family, grieving for a mother and grandmother.

As the cortège passed out of the grounds of Osborne and
on to the tree-lined avenue down to Cowes, the pipes ceased
and the massed bands, their drums muffled, took over with
Chopin and Beethoven. In the crowds on the footpath,
women curtsied and men tugged their hats from their heads
and bowed. The gardens of the little suburban houses with

views over the road were black with people. Hardly a word was spoken. One man dared to call out loudly to a friend and was silenced by the icy stares from everyone around him.

Down the hill the procession swayed at an achingly slow pace. It took its toll on the mourners. Onlookers thought Princess Beatrice seemed crushed by her grief. Then, on reaching the town, it was clear from the leaden way she was walking that the Princess of Wales was tired out. Princess Maud found it 'rather trying and exhausting' too, and had to be given a helping hand by her sister-in-law, the Duchess of York, who was under a double burden already – deeply saddened by the occasion, but also worrying about her husband, who had stayed behind at Osborne, still seriously ill with German measles. Even Dr Reid found the walk a strain and was glad when it was over.

At Trinity Pier, the cortège came to a halt alongside the royal yacht *Alberta*. Watched by the royal mourners, the coffin was carried on board and placed on a crimson platform under an awning on the stern deck. At each corner an officer stood at attention. Above, the royal standard hung at half mast. A small group of aides, among them Harriet Phipps, accompanied the coffin while the royal family were taken in steam launches to the *Victoria and Albert*, which was anchored a little off shore. There the royal standard was hoisted to the top of her main mast as the King boarded.

The *Alberta* slipped her moorings and, her paddles churning, moved out into the stream and picked up speed to six knots. The Duchess of York, who had left the family group and gone quickly back up the hill to be with her husband, watched from the tower at Osborne as a flotilla of eight small destroyers led the way out of Cowes. The funeral procession swept into the Solent and passed HMS *Alexandra*, the first of the line of warships stretching out as far as the eye could see. It was 'one of the saddest finest things I have ever seen,' she wrote to her aunt Augusta, Grand Duchess of Mecklenburg-Strelitz, 'a mixture of great splendour and great simplicity, a never to be forgotten sight on the most perfect of sunny days'. Churning her way up through the line, the tiny *Alberta* was dwarfed by the battleships and cruisers, a toy boat against their height, might and armour plating. The first gun salute echoed across the waters, then another and another, a minute apart but merging into each other in a continuous fusillade. Some claimed to hear the noise – 'as of distant thunder' – more than a hundred miles away in the Cotswolds. Columns of smoke from the gunpowder billowed out across the channel. On each ship the *Alberta* passed, sailors linked hands along the deck and the bands beat out their mournful music. The marine guards presented arms and the officers saluted.

Behind came the *Victoria and Albert*, a third royal yacht, the *Osborne*, and then the Kaiser's gleaming white ship, the *Hohenzollern*. On the deck of the *Victoria and Albert*, Princess Maud was amazed at the beauty of the occasion and the 'divine weather, calm and clear, just perfect'. As they passed HMS *Colossus* and then HMS *Nile*, Dr Reid glanced back at the island and tried to spot his wife among the crowd on the beach at Osborne Bay, but could not make her out. Standing nearby, the Bishop of Winchester kept his eyes ahead on the line of ships and was deeply moved. He felt tears on his face as he gazed at

the calm sea, the slow motion of the vessels, which seemed to glide without visible propelling power, the little 'Alberta' going first through the broad avenue of towering battle-ships booming out their salutes, the enormous mass of perfectly silent black-clothed crowds covering Southsea Common and the beach. I do not envy the man who could pass through such a scene dry-eyed.

It took an hour for the cortège to cross, and by the time the *Alberta* was level with HMS *Majestic*, the last in the line, and ready to turn into the entrance to Portsmouth harbour it was late afternoon. The sun was beginning to set. The sky turned red and gold, and the historian Sir George Arthur was just one of many who instantly thought of Turner's painting *The Fighting Temeraire*, 'towed to her last berth bathed in a light glowing and serene and about to enter a haven of perpetual rest'. Another lyrical observer wrote of

the shimmering silver sea, the sun sinking to the horizon in a still greater blaze of glory but still catching the *Alberta* in its track. Above her the moon, almost full, showed faintly in the sky. It was a scene for the canvas of a Turner. No other could have done justice to the intolerable glory of that sunset.

As the *Alberta* disappeared out of sight, a strange chill and desolation was in the air. The Queen had gone for ever, and the eyes that had gazed their last on her turned reluctantly to confront a darker and a poorer world. The sun went down, the lights began to twinkle from the ships, and the sea shivered into ashen grey. The bright day was done, and the night had come.[3]

On the shore at Portsmouth, the Revd Cosmo Lang caught sight of the small torpedo-destroyers leading the procession into the harbour and thought they were 'like dark messengers of death sent to summon the Queen'. He had been waiting with other dignitaries among the vast crowd, all dressed in black, and was amazed at the uncanny silence, 'the strangest I have ever known; it could literally be felt'. Two children had started to chatter hundreds of yards away from him, and he and others felt the embarrassment. As the *Alberta* came closer the sun was setting, and he too marvelled at the moment. It seemed divinely inspired. Behind him a retired general, choking back the emotion, muttered, 'No one will persuade me that Providence didn't arrange that!' The battery at the local garrison welcomed the flotilla with booming guns, and a single bell tolled from the parish church as the boats passed HMS *Victory*. On the poop deck of Nelson's wooden flagship, a military band struck up a funeral march as the *Alberta* tied up at Clarence Yard, the traditional landing pier for the royal yachts, which had a railway line behind and a small station where the royal family boarded their special trains.

The Queen had reached the mainland on the first leg of her journey to her grave. She would wait moored there overnight, a guard of honour around the catafalque, sentries sealing off the area, and picket boats patrolling the water to keep sightseers away.

The King and his family spent the night on the *Victoria and Albert*, anchored in the harbour, but the weather had turned, the wind was up, and it was bitterly cold. Few of them would get much sleep. Nor would Fritz Ponsonby, though it was worry and work that kept him awake. After the magnificent crossing from Cowes, he had gone to the cabin reserved for him on the auxiliary royal yacht, the *Osborne*, grateful for the chance of some rest. He had grabbed only a few hours sleep the night before, and the day had been physically and emotionally exhausting. Others in the dead Queen's Household were taking their ease, Reid was writing a letter to his wife, but Ponsonby's hope of relaxation was disturbed by a message from the *Victoria and Albert*: the King wanted to see him. He was ferried across in a pinnace and shown into the royal stateroom, where the King had a last-minute task for him. No one had made any preparations for the final part of the funeral. After the service at St George's Chapel on Saturday afternoon, the coffin would rest until Monday morning, when the family would accompany it to the mausoleum to be interred. Ponsonby was asked to organize the procession from the castle and the service at the tomb. The King was impatient for it to be done. It was now Friday night, and he wanted to see a printed order paper first thing on Sunday morning.

Ponsonby bowed and left, crossed back to his quarters, and sat there head in hands at the hopelessness of his task. What was he going to do? He was out on the water with no access to elaborate communications. He had no one to ask about precedents and no precise idea of who was expected to attend the Frogmore ceremony. Tomorrow he would have to spend most of the day walking alongside the cortège through London and then overseeing the procession at Windsor. To make matters worse, businesses would be shut on Saturday for the official day of mourning and his chances of getting anything printed were remote. If he didn't act now it would be a fiasco and, again, 'what little chance I had of being taken on by King Edward would evaporate'.

Spurred on by the wish to save his neck, he used the ship's telegraph to send a message to the printers at Windsor telling them to be on standby to work on Saturday evening. Then he sent a telegram to the Household office, asking urgently for a list of everyone scheduled to be staying at the castle for the weekend. The King's order was that only they would go to the mausoleum for what was to be a small family occasion.

He had a hurried dinner and then sat alone in his cabin to plan Monday's ceremony. It meant throwing caution to the wind. He just had to make it up there and then, all on his own, and hope it worked. All his years of service to the Queen, meticulously copying out her letters, observing her, absorbing from her the proper way for things to be done, paid off. The ceremony took shape in his head and then on paper, and when the list of guests arrived by telegram from Windsor he was able to fill in many of the gaps. But it was very late before he finished writing out the instructions to the printer, sealed them in an envelope, and left this for the royal messenger who had been ordered to pick it up first thing in the morning for delivery to Windsor.

He snatched some sleep before rising long before dawn for another arduous day of mourning.

# 11. The People's Farewell

The crowds of people . . . and not a single sound . . .

Princess Maud

A million people were preparing to make their way to the centre of London, a greater crowd than ever before – bigger even than for the Queen's two jubilee celebrations. The funeral was an occasion that cut across class barriers. Rich and poor alike, whether from smart West End homes, villas in the suburbs or city slums, all felt a compulsion to be there. The newspapers left no one in doubt about the significance of the moment. As the *Morning Advertiser* put it, 'The day will be one which must long dwell in the memories. It will mark the close of an era, the most wonderful and pregnant that this nation has passed through, as the greatest Queen the world has ever known passes by to her final rest.'

Arthur Conan Doyle, writing for an American newspaper, went even further with his tribute, describing the Queen as 'the dead saint'.[1] If that was taking praise too far, it was a fair reflection of the emotional mood of the people. There were few if any dissenting voices. Anyone who dared to argue risked being branded a cad. *The Times* was right when it said that 'love of the Queen has become one of the great silent and abiding factors in our national life'.

The sense of loss was tangible. 'We find it hard to reconcile ourselves to a world in which never again will a figure to which we owe so much be seen by mortal eye,' the *Standard* told its readers. London, it went on,

is almost a City of the dead, in which the minds of the living are monopolized by thoughts of one who is no more. It is as if a magician's hand had suddenly arrested the swift vitality that courses through the veins of the great City. It is genuine and spontaneous and springs from an emotion which has seldom been matched for the intensity with which it is felt by all classes. There are few people who are not affected by a sense of personal bereavement and regret. It is not often that any public calamity can touch us as closely as our private and domestic sorrows but this is one of those exceptional cases. Queen Victoria has left as many mourners as she had subjects.

And as many as found it physically possible to get to her funeral would leave their homes and go.

In the event, most of them were to miss the actual procession. The crowds were so dense that only one in a dozen could have even glimpsed the coffin as it went by. They craned their heads in crowds sixty deep in places; they stood packed together in the side streets too, with no hope of seeing anything at all. But they felt they had to be there, to be part of the occasion. They could not stay at home on the day the great Queen was to be buried. 'There was a feeling that generations yet unborn would speak of this day as one of the greatest in history, and everyone seemed to wish in a humble way to be worthy of it. They were conscious of her greatness and of the greatness of the Empire which rose to its present height during her reign.'[2]

Conan Doyle, looking at the sad and bewildered faces on the street that day, knew he was not alone in wondering where England would stand now that she was gone. 'It is a great and serious hour and it is felt so completely by all England,' G. K. Chesterton wrote. A man not known for giving way to tears, he had broken down and wept when he heard of the Queen's death. He called her 'the noblest Englishwoman I have ever known'. He loathed the Boer War, and was one of the few journalists who vehemently objected to it and the gung-ho patriotism it provoked. But her passing led him to renew his patriotic vow 'to do my best for this country of mine which I love with a love passing the love of Jingoes'. Such was the passion she had inspired in millions, and it would be the overwhelming sentiment on the streets of London that day. Oddly, Chesterton would not be one of them. He felt so deeply that he had decided to stay at home.

I like a crowd when I am triumphant or excited, for a crowd is the only thing that can cheer, as much as a cock is the only thing that can crow. Can anything be more absurd than the idea of a man cheering in his back bedroom? But I think reverence is better expressed by one man than a million. There is something unnatural and impossible, even grotesque, in the idea of a vast crowd of human beings all assuming an air of delicacy.[3]

Unnatural it certainly was, but it was not impossible, as the day proved. Staying at home to mourn, Chesterton missed a mass outpouring of popular grief that was without precedent or parallel in its dignity. The *Daily Telegraph* explained:

There have been times when the formal mourning of Courts has meant nothing to the minds of the people. There have been monarchs in England who never possessed the heart of their subjects. There have been some who lived to see passionate devotion perish and fervent loyalty grow cold. But nothing was so wonderful a vindication of her woman's spirit and her long sovereignty as the sorrow of her people when her coffin was carried through their midst.

★

One of those who watched and wept was Miss Etta Close, an intrepid young lady who lived in Belgravia. She had grown up imbibing that 'woman's spirit', and it spurred her into action when, a week before the funeral, she realized that the streets of London would be bare of decoration for the procession. Surely there should be wreaths to mark the Queen's passage – dark-green laurel, hanging, perhaps, from the lamp-posts. She discovered that the local authorities responsible for the roads along which the cortège would pass had no plans. Sitting in her parents' grand house in Eaton Square, she decided that if no one else was going to take up the challenge then it would be up to her. It was typical of the independence of mind and determination that later in life would take her on lone expeditions to Africa and then lead her to set up on her own there.

The first thing she did, naturally, was to form a committee of ladies. She sent notes to friends and acquaintances, she told them her idea, and within no time she had an enthusiastic group around her. Then she wrote to the local councils with her proposal for a wreath on every lamp-post, 'tied with stout string and of uniform size – 4 ft in diameter (outside measurement) and 9 ins wide'. Permission was given. Now there was no time to lose. They walked the route and counted eight hundred lamp-posts along the way. Could they really drum up enough interest to decorate every one? Through the newspapers, they appealed for wreaths, and to their astonishment they had reached their target by Wednesday night and, with two full days to go, more were flooding in.

Wreaths were brought in private carriages, in donkey carts and in vans from the railway stations and piled up in a mews behind a house in Upper Belgrave Street until the stables were filled to overflowing and the latest arrivals had to be stacked outside on the cobbles. The idea had caught the public imagination. There were contributions from peers and MPs, from street sellers and farm labourers, from schoolchildren and university students. They came not just from London but from all over the country – in one village, every inhabitant had picked a sprig of laurel or ivy and these had been woven together. The decorating began on Friday morning, the day before the funeral, but even after *two* wreaths had been put on every lamp-post there were still nearly fifteen hundred left over, and these were sent to hospitals.

On Friday the route was not only decked with boughs of evergreen, it was black with people. On a fine sunny day, despite some lingering wisps of fog, thousands tramped the streets from Victoria to Paddington, stopping to watch shop-keepers emptying their front windows to make way for tiers of seats or to look up at workmen festooning the fronts of buildings in black and purple. At Victoria station, where the coffin would arrive from Osborne, the pillars supporting the glass roof were painted so they looked like new. Advertisement hoardings were covered up or removed, so that no hint of commercial activity could interfere with the dignity of the occasion. But business was business for the street hawkers – 'gutter merchants', one paper called them – and they were trading on sentiment among the crowd, selling portraits and penny-dreadful biographies of the Queen by the hundred. Black-and-purple rosettes with a picture of the Queen in the middle cost a penny.

But the real business of the day was being done by those with seats to sell. In Buckingham Palace Road it was still possible to buy a reserved seat with a restricted view for two and a half guineas, but six to ten guineas was a more normal price and these places were going fast. Prices rocketed in Piccadilly. There, front-row seats at twenty-five guineas were all sold out, and one hotel with a particularly good view along the road was said to have let out a room for a staggering £500. It was only further along the route, in Edgware Road, that signs were still up offering 'Seats to let' – one with the added inducement of 'a sitting room fire and other comforts'. It was in this area that St Marylebone Borough Council ran into trouble with the residents. The councillors had voted to erect a stand to seat themselves and their friends across the entrance of a side road, Nutford Place, thereby blocking the view of the householders in that street. Fifty of the residents sent a letter protesting at this abuse of power at the expense of ordinary ratepayers, but they were unable to make any impression on civic pomposity. As Alderman Dennis told the council when they met to discuss the matter, council members 'could not be expected to stand huddled among a crowd at a street corner'.

As the members of the royal family rose from their disturbed nights for an early breakfast on Saturday, snow was falling on the *Victoria and Albert* and the wind began to gust violently. It quickly turned to sleet and then to pelting rain, which put the princesses in a state of anxiety in case their mourning clothes were soaked and they had nothing to change into. Onshore, the pier at Clarence Yard was filling with lines of soldiers and sailors. Riflemen formed a guard of honour along the railway line that headed from the special royal platform at Gosport and on to London. The royal train lay waiting with five carriages behind it, the middle one painted white. This was a carriage the Queen had often occupied when travelling to Balmoral or to Windsor, but now it had been stripped of seats. Purple and white velvet hangings covered the walls. A small platform was in the middle, ready for the coffin to rest on.

From out in the Solent a stream of pinnaces brought the

captains from every one of the warships that had lined the Queen's passage across the sea from the Isle of Wight yesterday. Each one climbed the ladder to the deck of the *Alberta*, marched to the middle, stood to salute the coffin, then crossed to the other side to stand in line awaiting the King. He was alone on the deck of the *Victoria and Albert*, taking a private moment for himself before the public business of the day began. A quarter of a mile away, a daring reporter from the *Daily Chronicle* trained a telescope on him and caught 'a face so white and very set, the real king, unaware that any man could see him, intensely melancholy, intensely sad'. It was a moment of truth, but the reporter was horrified at his own intrusion. He had gone too far. 'It came to me that it was sacrilege to gaze, and I turned away the glass and looked no more.'

A pinnace flying the royal standard took the King across the water to the *Alberta*. As he stepped on deck, a steam launch set out from the *Hohenzollern* with the Kaiser, cocksure and impulsive as ever, at the helm. There were askance looks from the Royal Navy contingent watching from the *Alberta*. What a time to be showing off! Would he pay the price for his bravado? 'He expects to bring her alongside, but he doesn't know the tide or the currents,' an admiral standing on deck muttered to the Revd Cosmo Lang. But the accident did not happen. The German Emperor powered the steam launch expertly through the strong current, brought her smartly alongside the *Alberta*, and stood up, dropped the controls and stepped off all in one go. Lang, for one, was impressed.

The royal family stood round the coffin as Lang led them in prayers. Afterwards the family began to move off, across the gangplank to wait on the quayside. The King was about to follow, but he paused and, as if glad to have this last chance of privacy with his mother, knelt at the foot of the coffin alone. Turning round, the Kaiser saw what was happening, stopped, and went back to kneel beside his uncle – 'the German Emperor and the English king side by side by the body of Queen Victoria', Lang thought to himself. It made him feel safe and sure about the future of relations between England and Germany.

As the two monarchs stood up and made their way off the yacht, a party of ten petty officers stepped forward and took the coffin on their shoulders. Slowly they marched from the deck to the shore and along a covered passageway to the train. They passed through an honour guard of senior army and navy officers, and Lang, walking in front of the coffin, had no doubt he saw a tear in every one of their battle-hardened faces as they saluted her towards her grave. 'Certainly,' he admitted, 'there were tears in mine.'

Torrents of rain were falling as the train steamed out of the station, taking Queen Victoria to her capital for the last time. But the cold and the wet made no impression on the men, women and children who stood in the Hampshire fields alongside the track to pay their last respects. Then, as the train passed through Carshalton in Surrey, the rain eased, the sun burst through, and a rainbow arched across the sky, seeming to crown it with a halo. The line of watchers, heads bared and voices stilled, was almost unbroken for the whole seventy miles of the journey. In the carriage behind the funeral car, the King looked out of the window and was touched by the dignity and respect shown by his subjects. Would they ever feel as much devotion to him?

The night horse trams brought the first Londoners from the suburbs to the centre of the capital while it was still dark. Mourners from other parts of the country had arrived at the main-line stations in the middle of the night and were wandering the streets, trying to keep warm in the bitter cold. A reporter from the *Daily Telegraph* easily spotted one such group in Piccadilly – 'their desire for information and guidance, their anxiety for instruction in minor details, their half-wondering contemplation of the long, shining avenue dotted by lamplights in the gathering haze, showed these were folk to whom green lanes and happy hamlets were familiar'. They would have been used to fresher air too, and the early-morning fog, fuelled by the smoke from hundreds of thousands of chimneys, made them cough. One man had the answer – he had wisely brought a respirator to filter out the noxious city fumes and, a mask over his face, was breathing normally.

As dawn broke on a bitingly cold day, the city was already on the move – but not in its usual way. Shops and businesses stayed shut and shuttered. There were no tradesmen's carts in the street. Instead, horse-drawn omnibuses and cabs, all crammed from top to bottom, filled the roads, alongside long lines of people walking. Many, knowing they could not rely on buses and trams, had set out on foot from their homes in the suburbs at 4 a.m. In Edgware Road, the morning milk cart was making its round as men and women began claiming their places, spreading rugs on the pavement and laying out food for the day. The high ground in Hyde Park had already been claimed and the steps and the slope around the statue of Achilles were full. In Piccadilly, carpenters putting the finishing touches to stands and hanging purple coverings were working in their Sunday-best suits so they could join the spectators when their job was finished.

From 8 a.m. troops in grey greatcoats with haversacks on their backs were in position lining the route, both as a guard of honour and to hold back the crowds, which by now were already eight deep in Hyde Park. The soldiers were under orders not to get too friendly with the spectators. An officer had appealed to the public not to give drinks to the men on parade. This had happened during an early-morning rehearsal a few days earlier and had led to 'several cases of misbehaviour, entailing the severest punishment on our return to barracks'. But, as the day wore on and the sun resolutely refused to come out to give even a hint of warmth, the men must have been sorely tempted to take a nip if it was offered. The cold was so intense that one soldier on duty in Hyde Park reckoned it was worse than 'when sleeping out upon the high South African veldt in midwinter'.

At railway stations on the outskirts of London the platforms were thick with people, and when the trains arrived they jammed themselves in, sixteen to a carriage intended for eight. They sat on laps and hung from the straps; they stood in the guard's van. No one complained at the inconvenience. There was little chatter, and the atmosphere was quiet and contemplative. This was not an outing; it was a solemn duty. The look on their faces was one of 'vague dread' at what lay ahead.

Now the trains were pulling into Charing Cross, King's Cross, Marylebone, and the crowds spilled out on to the streets to join the throng going westward. Thousands streamed across Westminster Bridge and Waterloo Bridge, heading for Victoria and St James's. In St James's Street every balcony was occupied by men in black coats and black ties and women in crape bonnets and black feathers. Up on the rooftops and among the chimney stacks stood servants and workers. In Piccadilly it was impossible to find a space on the pavement after nine o'clock, and the masses still pouring in were ushered down the middle of the road towards the park. But even this flow was too great and had to be stopped. Soldiers and police formed lines across the side streets to stop the crowds coming through, but the pressure was so great that more than once the human barricades gave way. Some were hurt, and St John's

Ambulance volunteers were called in to take away those who
had fainted or been bruised in the crush.

Further north, Oxford Street was a solid sea of humanity,
all dressed in black, moving slowly towards the park, then
halted by a bottleneck at Marble Arch as thousands more came
up the stairs and out on to the street from the underground
railway station. This was as close to the procession as most
would get. Horse Guards and mounted police held the crowd
back, but as people strained forward in a vain attempt to find
a vantage point the line here also broke on more than one
occasion.

Many in the crowd carried stepladders and soapboxes to
stand on and give themselves a few extra inches and a better
view from the roadside, but the police were wise to this.
Fearing accidents, the Commissioner had ordered a ban on
boxes, and the constables politely but firmly turned away
anyone who was carrying one. Some got through, however.
The cunning wrapped brown paper round a small wooden
block and tucked it under their arm as if it were a parcel. At
the last minute, as the procession approached, they would
put it down on the ground and stand on it before the law
could stop them. For others, mainly young men and boys, trees
gave the best vantage point. Opposite Buckingham Palace, a
single small thorn tree had seven people clinging precariously
to it. Those on high were not always as considerate as they
might be. In Hyde Park, a spectator in a tree carelessly tossed
away a match and set fire to the soft felt hat of a man
underneath.

As the numbers built up on the pavements, it became
increasingly difficult for those who had bought seats to get to
them. In Edgware Road the crowd swept one woman past
the front door of the house where she was expected. There
was no way she could force her way back against the flow,

and she had to go into another house further along the street and then climb out along the roof to reach her place. Some were not so lucky and failed to get to the seats they had paid for. Others had been conned. An argument broke out when too many people turned up at a house on the corner of Buckingham Palace Road and Victoria Street and it was discovered that the seats had been sold several times over. Fraudsters were out on the streets too. One man did a brisk trade selling 'official funeral programmes' for a penny. There was no such thing. When the buyers opened up the folded sheet of paper, they found themselves gazing at the details of the funeral of Mr Gladstone nearly three years earlier.

These incidents were exceptional. The overwhelming mood of the crowd was kind and cooperative. If people pushed forward, it was out of eagerness not impatience. And when they could go no further they stopped where they were, crushed together but content just to be there. There was no band music to entertain them, and this was no time for sing-songs. They stood in silence, just waiting. They were packed so tightly that it was impossible to put a hand in the pocket. 'The strength of our ribs was put to rather a severe test,' one of those in Hyde Park recalled. *The Times* was full of admiration.

It might easily have been forgiven if there had been some manifestations of impatience or intractableness. A stationary position for nearly five hours, herded together so that it was difficult, in some cases absolutely impossible, to move a single member of the body, with a keen wind blowing all the time, are not conditions conducive to amiability and good temper. Yet these were the two characteristics which distinguished the immense crowd.

As the hours ticked by, along the road from Victoria station and up as far as St James's the procession was beginning to form, with the band of the Household Cavalry at the front and half a mile of foot soldiers and cavalry before it reached even the generals and the high officers of state. Lord Roberts rode its length giving last-minute orders, making sure his Army would do its best for the Queen to the very last.

On a carpet of deep purple laid over the platform at Victoria station, kings and princes, grand dukes and diplomats were assembling. The Bishop of Winchester had once described the Queen's influence over the thrones of Europe as unique in the history of Christendom. Here, on her death, was the living proof. It had been Prince Albert's dream to create the ultimate royal family, an interlinked dynasty of relatives whose ties of kinship would preserve peace. On a day like this it almost seemed possible.

'Queen of an Empire, she has the Kings of the earth to attend her funeral, and, for the moment, no whisper of international jealousy breaks this hush encircling a Sovereign's repose,' wrote one commentator, overcome with goodwill. It was not strictly true. The German diplomat Baron von Eckardstein, for one, was not going to let down his guard, however friendly the occasion. He was keeping his eye on the King of the Belgians, the 'sly old fox', as he put it, who had scented the rapprochement between King Edward and the Kaiser – Britain and Germany – and was desperate to disrupt it. Political rivalries had also kept some away. Prince Ferdinand of Bulgaria had declined an invitation, fearing he would not be treated with the dignity he deserved.

But the Tsarevich was there, Michael, representing his absent older brother, Tsar Nicholas, also concerned about the overt overfriendliness between Britain and Germany. Though the Romanovs were now family, they were scarcely seen as friends. The Queen had always held a grudge against them over the Crimean War, and she had not been best pleased when the prettiest of her granddaughters, Alexandra (known as Alicky), daughter of the dead Princess Alice, had married Nicky just a matter of weeks before he became Tsar of All the Russias. She predicted tragedy, and she was right. Nicholas and Alexandra – within twenty years history would deal them a dreadful fate, as it did too to the Archduke Franz Ferdinand of Austria, now waiting to pay his respects in person to Victoria. His violent death in 1914 would be the fuse that fired the First World War, leading in turn to their violent deaths at Yekaterinburg in 1918 and a new era in Europe in which majesty had largely had its day.

But all that lay ahead, in a future that could not be guessed at. For now, there was no doubting this display of mighty princes. They stood magnificently attired, greatcoats hanging open to reveal brightly coloured uniforms and glittering decorations, swords at their sides, plumed helmets on their heads.

Outside the station the crowd was silent, raising a cheer only when Lord Roberts rode into the forecourt. The royal train was approaching, passing Battersea Park, where another crowd had been clinging to the railings for hours just to glimpse it. As it passed, hats were raised 'and a sigh went through that crowd of poor working people, a real expression of reverence and bereavement', according to the artist and playwright Laurence Housman, brother of the poet A. E. Housman.[4]

At two minutes to eleven the train pulled in and a bearer party of twelve sergeants from the Guards and the Household Cavalry stepped forward. The royal family rested for a moment in a specially built pavilion on the platform as the heavy oak coffin was lifted from the funeral car and laid on another gun carriage. A shaft of sunlight burst through the grey skies and, for a brief moment, flashed on the brasswork on the casket before the white pall was draped over it again.

Ponsonby and the other royal aides formed up alongside the gun carriage just as they had done at Osborne. Although he had no official place in the procession, Dr Reid managed to slip in just in front of the aides, to the left of the coffin. He had asked the King's permission to do so, and it had been granted – 'an exceptional privilege which I can never forget'. The King, the Kaiser and the other princes mounted horses. The princesses and the other women were escorted to their carriages. There was not a sound, until a hussar cantered out of the station and waved a white flag – the signal to be passed along to the next messenger and so on down the line that it was time to move off. In St James's Street the last of the twelve signalmen galloped to the head of the procession and the order was given. With rifles and swords reversed, the great ceremonial army began its slow march through the misty morning.

Back at Victoria, the Earl Marshal took up his position in front of the gun carriage and gave the order to move. The postillions in their scarlet vests urged the eight cream-coloured horses forward. The gun carriage swung out of the station and into the streets of London. Behind came the King on a bay charger, bending forward to calm the animal with a pat on the neck, beside him the Kaiser on a white horse, fixed and upright like an equestrian statue, and then the King of Portugal and the King of Greece. A glittering cavalry of forty princes and dukes followed. The pageant had begun.

In St James's, the *Standard* reporter watched the head of the column depart and caught the atmosphere.

They moved with a mournful slowness. The feet of the men seemed to fall on the sanded road as though they walked on velvet; their right hands were clasped on the butts, the left hand on the barrels of their reversed rifles. They advanced stiff and rigid, animated

figures of grief. Silence hung like a pall over the files, over the
breathless crowd, a silence oppressive and painful. It was a relief
when the Field Artillery with a battery of six guns came by, and the
jingle of chains, the rattle of wheels and the tramp of horses broke
the spectral stillness. There was more sound as the Lancers, the
Hussars and the Dragoons came clinking along, and then the Household Cavalry, massive and majestic. Behind them came the infantry
and then a detachment of Bluejackets [sailors], who disdained all
wrappings and strode along, brawny and strong, in straw hats and
thin blue shirts that made chilly landsmen on balconies shiver to
look at them. Next appeared the Headquarters Staff and Lord
Roberts, riding alone with an orderly behind him, alert, erect,
casting his supervising glance around, a true chief of men.

And now the beat of slow music was heard from a great orchestra,
the massed bands of the Guards, of the Royal Engineers and the
Royal Artillery. The passionate sadness of Chopin's Funeral March
fell upon our ears as it throbbed from the muffled drums and wailed
softly from the wind instruments. As its solemn harmonies died
away in the distance, the painful hush again fell on the multitude
for they knew it heralded the crowning stage of the cortege. And
presently it came into sight, and almost an audible exclamation of
surprise stole from the lips of beholders. For after the long train of
dark and warlike figures on which we had been gazing, the bier
itself was like a beautiful jeweller's work, a thing that seemed to
speak not of despair but of light, of hope, of serenity.

All along the route, the sight of the coffin provoked a great
sigh from the crowd – 'a strange deep whisper, which those
who heard it will never forget. "The Queen! The Queen!"
came from ten thousand throats and rolled in impressive
simplicity all down the line.' Seeing was believing. It was 'the
sight of sights and moment of moments', one observer said,
'the pall, cream-white bestrewn with orange and gold, the

pure beautiful drapery on which rest the cushion and the crown of English Majesty. It is the last passing by of the great lady, mother and Queen of the English race.' To other eyes the casket seemed so small – 'too small to hold the heart of an Empire'.

But, the *Standard* reporter went on, the moment was gone in an instant:

Almost before one had grasped its import, the little casket had glided by. And so we looked our last upon the Queen, and even as we did so were reminded that life rolls on remorselessly though the greatest and the best pass away. The Queen was dead but the King lived.

Behind the gun carriage came a giant trooper of the Household Cavalry flaunting aloft in the air the Royal Standard of England. Under its folds rode the King with the German Emperor on his right hand and the Duke of Connaught on his left, both courteously keeping a pace or two behind him, so as to give His Majesty due prominence as the central figure of the whole solemn display. He rode with a kingly dignity. Pale as he was, and worn, with the marks of much recent suffering and anxiety on his face, he looked like the ruler of a mighty empire, the heir of a long line of monarchs.

The silence of the crowd impressed everyone. 'Not a sound anywhere as we passed,' Reid wrote to his wife later. The Duke of Argyll found it uncanny, as though he was 'looking at vast masses through a glass that prevented sound from coming to the ears'.[5] For Princess Maud, following in a carriage with her mother, the Princess of Wales, and sisters, it was 'all terribly sad and impressive, the crowds of people . . . and not a single sound and all in black, and mauve the houses'.[6] It was so quiet that the wheels of the gun carriage crunching on the road could be easily heard.

Up through St James's and into Piccadilly the cortège

passed. The grand houses from here to Hyde Park Corner were all decked in purple. From her balcony, the eighty-seven-year-old Lady Burdett-Coutts, a partner in Coutts & Co., the royal family's bankers, and reputed to be the richest woman in England, had watched the coronation and the Diamond Jubilee processions. Mournfully she raised her veil now as the Queen passed for the last time; she seemed 'much touched'.

Nearby, a huge wreath of laurel and ivy was hanging from the sphinxes on the gates of Devonshire House. At the invitation of the Duchess, thirteen-year-old Violet Asquith, wearing the black mourning clothes she had bought with her nurse a few days earlier, was watching from a window. She looked down on a scene 'frozen in silence, lined with soldiers, thronged with patient, waiting crowds'. As the gun carriage went by and behind it 'the captains and kings of all the world', she was impressed by the Kaiser, 'magnificent in a Wagnerian helmet that gleamed with eagles'. But most of all she remembered 'the thud of the soldiers' feet, the music of Chopin's funeral march, which I had never heard before, the thud of the drums, the deep still grief of the crowds. It was as though everyone in England had lost their father and their mother. It was also, though I did not know it, the beginning of an end of an epoch.'[7]

To the *Daily Telegraph*, however, that epoch was far from over. As its reporter watched 'the stalwart yeomanry and militia measuring pace behind the crimson squadron of bandsmen, the khaki-clad file of sinewy colonials, the contingent of the Indian Army, the guns of the artillery, the dark massive column of the Guards and the frank fighting faces of the Bluejackets, stamped in every feature with the historic spirit of the Fleet', its resolve was that 'the Empire of which she was the rallying point must be strengthened and maintained'. The procession was 'the epitome of Empire' and an inspiration to ever vigilant and steadfast patriotism. 'To the spirit of that hour in which her coffin was carried through the streets, it is our task to be for ever true.'

The crowds were at their greatest in Hyde Park and up to Marble Arch. There an ingenious spectator at the back tied a mirror to his walking stick to hold up in the hope of catching the reflection of the procession as it passed. One ordinary soldier on duty in the park reckoned the crowd behind him was sixty to a hundred deep and, as more came to join them from behind, they swayed. 'Backwards and forwards they swung, moving about five yards each time with an impetus that grew dangerously regular, for everyone knows how difficult it is to steady a crowd when once it begins to swing.' As the crowd pressed forward, he and his fellow soldiers pushed them back with the sides of their rifles.

When the coffin was in sight, his troop came to attention, arms reversed and heads bowed, but as it passed he sneaked a look. He was not the only one. 'The regulations were universally disobeyed,' he thought, and he defended himself with passion and eloquence:

We ought to have stood with chin sunk on chest and eyes cast down. Who could do it when she was going by – the Queen, the Great Queen whose uniform we so long had worn, whom the British Army had pledged to serve in every climate and country of the globe; the Queen who for 13 years had Wellington as her commander-in-chief; the Queen who had already been reigning nearly 20 years when the army of our fathers suffered and conquered at Inkerman and Lucknow; the Queen for whom some of us had seen many a brave life thrown away without a single further thought than the honour of her arms.

She was going by for the last time and who could help looking at that which bore her past? How small it seemed and short! Just the contents of that small thing gone from us, and the whole tone and feeling of English life and army life will appear to be altered! But underneath all the caparisons, underneath the mere symbolism of the bay horses, the gilded harness, the outriders with their curly wigs, underneath the emblems of the embroidered pall and the crowns and the sceptre, one seemed to see for the last time the small devoted woman who for the nation's good had worked so hard and done so well – the woman whom the Army had loved as the personification of their country.[8]

At Paddington, the front of the procession made its way into the station, along the platform where the eight carriages of the royal train stood waiting, and straight out the other side to disperse. When the gun carriage arrived, it halted directly opposite the funeral car, converted from one the Queen had often used towards the end of her life because its doors had been widened to allow for her wheelchair. Now the divans and armchairs on which she had sat had been removed. The walls were draped in white satin divided into panels with broad purple stripes and set off by a large purple garland. A catafalque stood in the middle.

The King and the other mourners dismounted, their horses were led away by grooms, and they stood for a while before forming an avenue across the platform. The bearer party of sergeants, who had marched alongside the gun carriage from Victoria, stepped forward, lifted the coffin, and carried it to the carriage through the ranks of royals as Chopin's *Marche funèbre* was played.

The royal party boarded the train, the troops on the platform saluted, the colours were lowered, and at just after 1.30 p.m. the train steamed slowly out towards Windsor. 'London had looked its last upon the Queen,' said *The Times*, 'and was left with naught but its imperishable memories.'

Some in the crowd, however, had more tangible mem-entoes to take with them. The royal train at Victoria had been stripped. As soon as the procession left the station, a small section of the crowd outside hurried across the platform before the police realized what was happening. They made their way through the carriages that the royals had been in, and every piece of paper, flower and leaf was eagerly seized, including every copy of a German news-sheet – *Wolffs Telegraphisches Bureau* – which had been left in the Kaiser's carriage. As the vast crowds drifted slowly away from Piccadilly, a woman reached up and took a handful of leaves from one of Etta Close's wreaths hanging on a lamp-post. Others saw and followed her example, and within minutes nothing was left but the wooden frame and the wiring. Boys shinned up lamp-posts and threw the wreaths down to friends, who cut up the leaves into small bits and began selling them.

It was antics like this that upset some spectators. Far from being silent and respectful, Laurence Housman now thought, the crowds were 'voluble and excited'. There were too many cheers for Lord Roberts, and he disliked the 'stands and seats being bartered for, and boys shouting from the boughs of trees "Here she comes."' He thought Chopin's funeral march had been played far too quickly in order to get the procession through on time.

There were others with dissident opinions. Henry Labou-chere, an independent MP with republican views with which he had needled the Queen when she was alive, could not resist a complaint now she was dead. Despite his trenchant views on the monarchy, he had made sure he had a place in the special stand for the Lords and MPs in The Mall, but he had seen very little of the procession because of the crowds in front of it. What he had seen he had not liked. He thought a long line of soldiers four abreast 'never effective', and he hated the 'furs and feathers' of the military uniforms. 'I always wonder that a barbaric taste for these trappings should have survived to our day,' he wrote in his newspaper, *Truth*. The author Arnold Bennett, down from the Potteries on a rare visit to London, was also disenchanted. He too had seen very little of the procession over the heads in front of him. He judged the mood of the crowd differently from almost every-one else: 'The people were not, on the whole, deeply moved,' he wrote, 'whatever the journalists may say, but rather "serene and cheerful".'[9]

Serene the crowds may have been as they went home, queuing patiently to leave Hyde Park, waiting for the tea houses to open at 2 p.m. so they could at last get some refreshment, but cheerful they were not. They were still silent, and even the opening up of the pubs at 3 p.m. brought only a half-hearted response. Men talked in muffled tones and women refrained from laughter, according to one observer. The few hawkers out on the streets sold their goods without shouting their wares. An hour or so later, most of the drinkers had drifted away. 'Everything was shrouded in gloom,' the *Daily Chronicle* reported. 'Such a silent Saturday night has not been seen in London within the memory of man.'

# 12. Reunited

We laid her to rest near Papa . . .

Edward VII

The first person in Windsor to see the train carrying the Queen's coffin from London was a lookout who had been sent to the very top of the Round Tower. He spotted it as it passed through Slough and was steaming towards the viaduct that led across the flat water-meadow and over the river into the town. He signalled with a flag to officials below. Then he hauled down the red, white and blue Union Flag from the pole and replaced it with the royal standard. Inside the Tower a great bell began to toll – the first time it had sounded since being captured from the Russians at Sebastopol. The Queen who had left her home on the Thames seven weeks earlier was coming home for the last time.

She was late, though: half an hour behind schedule. She would have turned in her coffin had she known. Punctuality had been her code, lateness a sin. The Earl Marshal's timetable had had the royal train leaving Paddington at 1 p.m., but the march through London had taken longer than expected. The dismounting of the cavalcade of royal princes had eaten up more time, and in the end the train had not left until 1.32. It was ten past two before it steamed into Windsor, and the service at the chapel had been scheduled to start at 2 p.m.

Fritz Ponsonby was in the second carriage – crammed in

with twenty-five other members of the Household, including Sir James Reid and Sir Arthur Bigge – and, as the train came to a halt, he made sure he was the first out on to the platform, so that he could rush through to the station yard. He was anxious to check that his orders had been carried out and everything was ready for the procession.

He had sorted out the problems and avoided a disaster, or so he thought. The coffin was carried off the train, past the massed ranks of sailors from HMS *Excellent* forming a naval guard of honour, and placed on the Royal Horse Artillery gun carriage waiting outside. The King, the Kaiser and the army of princes were to follow on foot, and they took up their positions. Behind were the ranks of ambassadors and envoys from all over the world. Ponsonby stepped up to the King, saluted, and asked his permission to begin. The King told him to carry on, and the equerry stepped to one side and held up his hand, the signal for the band to start up and the gun carriage to set off.

But the horses had become skittish after standing still in the cold for an hour and a half. The two at the rear tried to walk on before the two in front had moved, and they reared up in the traces, kicking and plunging. For one awful moment it looked as if the coffin was about to topple to the ground. The traces snapped and, as the Life Guards at the front of the procession, the massed bands and even the Commander-in-Chief, Lord Roberts, striding out ahead, disappeared round a corner, the gun carriage stayed exactly where it was. Ponsonby went cold with horror. 'I had contemplated all sorts of things going wrong, but such a mishap had never occurred to me,' he recalled.

He sent a corporal off at the double to stop the procession, then went to examine the damage. Artillerymen were still hanging on to the bucking horses and trying to move them out of the way, while a number of officers were looking at the broken straps and wondering if they could make a quick repair. When that proved impossible, they moved rapidly into a discussion of what else could be done. Could the two front horses, whose traces were intact, haul the carriage on their own? It was thought unlikely. They would not be able to manage the steep climb up to the castle and there would be a danger of the gun carriage, coffin and all, slipping backwards out of control. It was unthinkable. Perhaps two horses could manage it if they took the quickest route to the castle, but that would mean disappointing the thousands of people waiting along the road.

Ponsonby went to the King to explain the problem. It was no easy task to have to tell the monarch that his beloved mother's funeral was stuck, brought to a halt by a technical hitch. As the equerry walked away after delivering the sorry news, Prince Louis of Battenberg whispered something in the King's ear, then caught Ponsonby's attention. 'You can always get the naval guard of honour to drag the gun carriage,' he suggested. Ponsonby seized on the idea. It was practical and it was immediate. He returned to the King and asked permission to go ahead with this plan. 'Certainly,' said the King. The Prince ordered the hundred sailors to 'Ground arms and stand by to drag the gun carriage', and as they stacked their rifles Ponsonby told the officer in charge of the Artillery team to move the horses away and let the sailors take their place.

An argument broke out, all in a whisper so that the King would not hear. The Artillery men, their honour at stake, demanded to be allowed to sort out the problem themselves. Others got involved. Ponsonby's boss, Sir Arthur Bigge, an Artillery man himself, took the side of the officers and angrily told him that, as an Infantry man, he did not know what he was talking about when it came to horses. He should stop interfering before he ruined the entire ceremony. Ponsonby would not yield. He was carrying out the King's command, and that was an end of it. Bigge went off to protest to the King, but he was brushed aside. 'Right or wrong, let Captain Ponsonby manage everything. We shall never get on if there are two people giving contradictory orders.'

Ponsonby sent the stationmaster scurrying off to find a rope to attach to the gun carriage, but all the man could come up with was a steel hawser, which would have cut the sailors' hands as they hauled on it. The Artillery men, having been pushed aside and looking on in a sulk, saw the chance of things swinging back in their favour. The horses would be needed after all, they chortled to themselves. The officer in charge of the naval guard came to the rescue. His men went foraging, grabbed the communication cord from the royal train, and fashioned the remaining traces into draw ropes. Within minutes they were in front of the gun carriage in ranks of four and ready to pull. With the King's permission, Ponsonby raised his hand and the procession began all over again.

As the gun carriage left the shelter of the railway station and emerged into the road, there was a gasp from the crowd. They had been puzzled by the delay, the starting and stopping of half the procession. Now they caught sight of the phalanx of sailors in their white shirts and blue collars. What had happened was a mystery to them, but they liked what they saw. 'It was universally felt that nothing finer could have been done. The daughter of a long line of sea kings, herself a lover of the sea, was being taken to her tomb by the men of her own Royal Navy. Men and women alike were moved to tears.'[1]

Up through the town the slow-marching sailors hauled the gun carriage, passing silent crowds who had been packing the streets since early that morning, along the High Street and into the castle grounds by the Long Walk gate. Behind the carriage came the King, looking careworn, the Emperor, walking with soldierly erectness, and King Leopold of Belgium, leaning heavily on a stick. Ordinary Seaman E. Haines, one of the naval contingent, surreptitiously sneaked his hand alongside the coffin and then up under the pall to feel the wood, 'just to be able to say I had done so', as he told his mother later.[2] He and his fellow sailors felt they had done something unforgettable, and were proud and elated when they returned to Portsmouth by train that evening, even though, in the chaos of arrangements, they had not been fed from dawn to dusk.

As the procession entered the castle walls, it was as if it had come into its natural setting. 'All around now spoke of regal dignity. The grey walls of the noble towers, the frowning battlements, the antique buildings, the solemn chapels – all made a background to the slowly moving and resplendent line of illustrious mourners. The wailing strains of the Funeral March rose and fell upon the wintry air.'[3] The carriage skirted the Round Tower and descended the slope to St George's Chapel, three men hovering at each wheel ready to throw their weight behind it if the brakes looked like slipping. The cortège came to a halt at the wide stone steps, the sides of which were lined with two thousand wreaths. On the lawn opposite, ranks of guardsmen in grey topcoats leaned on reversed rifles.

As the funeral at St George's waited to get under way, prayers for the Queen were being said throughout the country. Every church held a service, every town and city a solemn procession. Most had been timed to coincide with the Windsor service, and went ahead on schedule in ignorance of the delay there. At Brighton, the front of the Royal Pavilion was draped in mourning, as was the Queen's statue. Eight thousand people filled Gloucester Cathedral. At York Minster, the Lord Mayor and corporation in full robes joined a congregation of ten thousand – so many that the service had to be held in two parts, one in the nave and one in the choir. Thankfully there were thirty clergymen present to help out. A further two thousand mourners were meeting at the Nonconformist Centenary Chapel. In Swansea, twenty thousand gathered in the market for a sacred concert. A large choir sang Welsh funeral hymns. A spirit of tolerance unusual for the times prevailed, so that when the 'dissenters' (as a newspaper correspondent called them) at Lavenham in Suffolk sent a deputation to the Anglican rector saying they would like to join the congregation in the parish church, he instantly agreed. Many of the services were for men only, upholding a tradition that women should not go to funerals.

Church apart, the country was at a complete halt. Blinds were drawn in almost all private houses. In windows, people put up pictures of the Queen. Businesses closed everywhere – spontaneously in the main, but sometimes on the orders of the local council. Birmingham Council shut the public baths but, in the spirit of free trade, refused to issue outright instructions to shops and factories to close. This angered a local paper, the *Daily Gazette*, which attacked the council for half measures and said the city needed to learn some manners. In Leeds the tram drivers needed a similar lesson. At the last minute, they decided that, if everyone else was having the day off, so should they, even though they had previously agreed to run a limited service to ferry people to the city centre for memorial services. In Bradford, the Tory evening paper was not printing on the day of the funeral but the Liberal one decided to publish, feeling that this was a day of all days when its readers would want to be told what was going on, particularly in London and Windsor, though its paper boys were urged not to shout out their wares in the street.

The Empire shut up shop too. In India, churches, mosques and temples were overflowing for memorial services. Cape Town was wholly draped in black, and there was a ceremony at the Queen's statue, where the Loyal Women's Guild assembled to sing the hymn 'Now the labourer's task is o'er'. General Kitchener and his staff attended a memorial service at St Alban's Cathedral in Pretoria. Montreal and Toronto were draped in black.

In capitals all over Europe there were solemn services – even in Paris, where anti-British feeling was put aside for a day and the President sent a representative to the service in the embassy church. In Vienna, the Emperor himself had intended to be at the chapel in the British Embassy, a comfortable chair having been specially placed for him in the front of the pews. But he had caught a cold, the weather was bitter and windy, and his doctors would not let him out of doors. The Americans paid a unique tribute by closing the New York Stock Exchange on Saturday and President McKinley went to a memorial service in Washington. Even in China there were services. In Tien-tsin the British community paraded despite the intense cold and the great bell was tolled for one hour. In Constantinople, Ibrahim Bey, Grand Master of the Ceremonies, represented the Sultan at a service in the chapel of the British Embassy.

The world had stopped, its thoughts turning to Windsor.

James Vincent, the *Times* special correspondent, had bypassed London and gone straight from the Isle of Wight to Windsor. Now he sat in St George's Chapel, breathing in the overpowering fragrance of the flowers stacked in the choir. A wreath of roses and lilies from the President of France seemed to be giving off the strongest smell. He looked up at the embossed ceiling and around him at the long, wide nave. He knew that in the vault beneath the nave lay the remains of Henry VIII and the beheaded Charles I, for whom the Queen had had a deep admiration, always referring to him as 'the Royal Martyr'. Ahead was the screen separating off the choir, with its two towering rows of elaborately carved wooden stalls for the knights of the Garter, their banners hanging above. It was truly a majestic setting for the day's sad business.

He shivered a little as the cold of the chapel seeped through to his bones. Distinguished guests were being shown to their seats. He could see the Prime Minister and Mr Balfour and other Cabinet ministers in privy-counsellor uniforms, the Lord Mayor of London in his black-and-gold robes, the Lord Chief Justice in scarlet and ermine. There was Earl Spencer, Lord Cross, Lord Stanley, Lord Rosebery and the Duke of Devonshire. The might and majesty of Britain were on parade. Beefeaters in their red costumes stood in the aisle, resting on their pikes, and gentlemen-at-arms in their high-plumed helmets were by the door. But it was not a settled gathering. There was much shuffling around of places when some people were asked to leave their seats and move forward from the nave to the choir.

The Earl Marshal had made a disastrous mistake in his arrangements. He had issued tickets for the stalls of the Garter knights to high dignitaries, forgetting that many of them would be in the procession and be standing in the aisle throughout the service. As guests took their seats, one of his officials thought it strange that the choir was not filling up as it should have done; then he grasped what was wrong. Leaving empty places there would be too conspicuous, he decided. He hurried into the body of the chapel to invite some of those already seated there to come forward. This left gaps in the nave. The tiers of seating that Mr Nutt and his men had carefully built and the guardsmen had so energetically tested were almost empty. The Bishop of Winchester was annoyed:

Tickets had been sought for from every quarter by all kinds of people and hundreds had been told that there was no corner for them, whereas in the end the nave was not much more than half full. The officials had to spread the people out when the hour drew near to cover the seats and hide the mistake that had been made. It was rather sad.

The congregation was still and silent by two o'clock – the cortège was expected at any minute. They were unaware of delays – now approaching an hour, as the trouble with the horses had compounded the late arrival of the train from London. They waited mutely, trying not to let the chill air of the chapel get to them as the afternoon temperature dropped. Some had been in their places for hours already. The printed invitation from the Earl Marshal's office had given the start of the service as 1 p.m., and not everyone had seen the urgent notice in *The Times* changing it to 2 p.m. They stirred and sat up as the clergy and the choir entered the church in procession, led by the Archbishop of Canterbury and the Archbishop of York. This should have coincided with the arrival of the coffin, but the timetable was now hopelessly adrift. In their white surplices and richly embroidered robes, the clerics stood in the nave for forty minutes, which exhausted the ageing Bishop of Oxford, who had to be allowed to sit down. It was another 'blunder' as far as the Bishop of Winchester was concerned.

As the time slipped by, the silence in the chapel was pierced only by the distant sound of big guns firing in salute outside and the creaking of the door as an anxious official opened it up a fraction and peeked out to try to see what was happening. Soon after three o'clock the mournful sound of Chopin could be heard in the distance, and not long after the great west doors of the gloomy chapel were finally flung open and the light and the full sound of the music outside flooded in.

The heralds and the Earl Marshal were the first of the procession to sway slowly into the chapel. From the gun carriage, a bearer party of Grenadier Guards lifted the coffin on their shoulders. Some of them struggled as they marched up the steps, and, as they buckled under the weight, comrades moved in quickly to shore them up. The coffin hung precariously for several moments. It looked as if the strain was too much and they were about to let it slip. The adventure-story writer Henry Rider Haggard, who was watching from the house of one of the Windsor clergymen directly opposite, was twice certain it was going to fall. But, to his relief, the guardsmen reached the top without dropping their load. Haggard was deeply moved by the 'gorgeous' procession that followed. At close quarters he took in 'the cloaked King Edward walking immediately behind followed by a galaxy of princes; the troops with arms reversed; the boom of the solemn guns; the silent, watching multitude; the bright sun gilding the wintry scene; the wind that tossed the plumes and draperies. All these and more made a picture never to be forgotten.'[4]

Walter Parratt struck up a dirge on the organ, which, to Seaman Haines outside, now standing easy with his shipmates after their heavy labour, sounded grand but 'rather creepy'. The procession moved down the nave towards the choir, the coffin held on high and followed by the King, dressed as a field marshal of the British Army, the Kaiser in the same uniform and carrying his baton, and the Duke of Connaught. The cloaks the mourners had worn for the walk from the station had been discarded, revealing 'a feast of colour and defiant brightness'. James Vincent's eyes strayed to the younger members of the family – Prince Arthur of Connaught in the uniform of a gentleman cadet and some little princes in Highland dress. Still the line of mourners came on, until the head of the procession stopped in the choir, leaving the rest of the princes and ambassadors filling the nave all the way back to the door in 'one glittering mosaic of gold and silver and precious stones, of scarlet and grey and white and blue'.

The coffin was laid on a purple bier in front of the altar. The Lord Chamberlain and the Earl Marshal stood at the foot, the mourners at the head, as the choir sang the Ninetieth Psalm and the Archbishop of Canterbury and the Bishop of Winchester led the burial service. Standing at the altar and looking back down the length of the chapel, the Bishop marvelled at the extraordinary sight. 'The candles were all lit and the little lights glimmered like jewels in a dark casket. The stalls were nearly all occupied by diplomats and great officials in brilliant uniforms. The music was perfect and the whole effect was overwhelming.' From the organ loft Walter Parratt filled the air with Purcell and Gounod and Tchaikovsky. Sweet and solemn, the choir moved many to tears with 'How blest are they whom Thou hast chosen and taken unto Thee, O Lord'. Reid stood near the coffin, so rapt in the moment that he hardly noticed the glittering array of 'notabilities' around him.

As the light through the stained-glass windows faded and the candles shone more brightly, a herald walked to the head of the coffin to perform his last duty. His voice echoed against the stone walls as he boomed out the public words honouring the dead Queen, the final farewell. 'Thus it hath pleased Almighty God to take out of this transitory life, unto His divine mercy, the late Most High, Most Mighty and Most Excellent monarch, Victoria, by the grace of God, of the

United Kingdom of Great Britain and Ireland, Queen, Defender of the Faith, Empress of India and Sovereign of the Most Noble Order of the Garter.'

The two archbishops walked to the altar and knelt in prayer. The King motioned to the Kaiser, and they walked past the coffin and out of the chapel. As the chapel emptied and the guests walked up the hill for lunch – seventy royals in the castle dining room and six hundred guests in the hall – the coffin was carried into the smaller chapel at the rear of St George's dedicated to the memory of Prince Albert and laid in front of the altar. It would stay there until Monday morning, when it would be taken to Frogmore.

The day had been exhausting. The Bishop of Winchester was planning an early night and would be in bed by eight o'clock. Reid had skipped the official lunch after the funeral service and was having a quiet tea in his room. He was composing an emotional letter to the King expressing 'my heartfelt gratitude for being allowed to accompany the remains of the Queen on their last sad journey and to take part in the funeral throughout. Your Majesty could have granted me no greater privilege than that of being to the last near her whom, during long years of close attendance, I had come to regard with feelings not only of the truest loyalty and veneration but also of the deepest affection.' Fritz Ponsonby was in search of some rest too. He had had a 6 a.m. start at Gosport, a three-and-a-half-mile walk round London, then Windsor and all the drama of the horses and the gun carriage, and there was still the last leg of the funeral to go, which he was organizing. But as he finished a very late lunch at the stand-up buffet in the hall he was called to the King to discuss arrangements for the mausoleum.

The King came to the point. The dragging of the gun

carriage by the Navy had pleased him a great deal and he
wanted it repeated. Ponsonby tried to be diplomatic. He
pointed out how hurt the Artillery would be at this slight.
Should they not have the chance to redeem themselves? The
King sympathized. It had not been their fault, he said – just
an unfortunate accident. They were not being punished. It was
just that the sailors had added great dignity to the procession
through Windsor. The discussion went vigorously back and
forth, but Ponsonby persisted until finally the King, tired out
after the long day, gave in and told him, 'Very well, the gun
carriage will be drawn by the Artillery. But if anything goes
wrong I will never speak to you again.' Ponsonby, his career
once more on the line, would get little sleep for yet another
night.

At the suggestion of Lord Esher, he held a rehearsal late that
night for the ceremony on Monday, using a box the same size
and weight as the coffin. It was pitch-black as the gun carriage
pulled up outside the mausoleum. Lanterns made ghostly pools
of light, shining on the faces of the dozen men of the bearer
party standing on the steps. Mindful of the fact that the coffin
was so heavy it had nearly been dropped at St George's, it was
decided that one party of six would carry it up the two flights
of steps and the others would take over at the top to take it
inside the building. The transfer presented problems, and they
practised the manoeuvre over and over in the dark before they
got it right. But it saved a possible disaster.

At six the next morning Ponsonby was at the doors of
St George's to meet the officers of the Artillery detachment
with the horses and the gun carriage for a second rehearsal,
walking the whole route from the chapel to the mausoleum
to make sure the horses would not shy. All went well, but
Ponsonby secretly had ropes and hooks hidden in the cloisters
for the next day in case something again went wrong. He told

the captain of the Queen's Company that if the horses kicked over the traces again his guardsmen were to stow their rifles and prepare to pull. 'I felt that as far as it was humanly possible to ensure that no mishap would occur again, every precaution was being taken.'

He still had work to do. The King had changed his mind about the procession to the mausoleum being a purely private family event. The public were to be allowed into Windsor Great Park to watch it pass. A limited number of spectators would also be let into the private grounds of the castle to see the start of the procession from St George's Chapel. Tickets were in great demand, but Ponsonby charitably managed to find one for a distinguished-looking officer, dressed in khaki and wearing a row of medals, who sought him out with a special plea to be there to see his Queen's last journey.

That Sunday the Bishop of Winchester stayed in bed until ten o'clock before getting up for morning service at eleven in St George's. The Bishop of Oxford gave the sermon, but he was unwell – still suffering the effects of standing around in the cold the previous day – and could barely be heard. In the afternoon, Davidson joined the King, Lord Esher and Fritz Ponsonby at the mausoleum to check the final arrangements. The tomb had been opened, revealing Prince Albert's velvet-covered coffin, which was about three-quarters the size of 'the needlessly huge coffin containing the little queen', according to Davidson. Hers was so big because, on her instructions, it had been made to match the great elmwood coffins of previous monarchs. This, however, meant that several inches had to be cut from the inside of the sarcophagus to allow her to be lowered in beside Albert. A wooden platform had been built around the tomb, covered in purple cloth with the letters VRI in gold. The Prince's effigy lay at one side. All was ready.

That evening, the royal family stood round the Queen's

coffin in the Memorial Chapel for a private service. A little harmonium had been brought in for Walter Parratt to play, and, as Davidson had suggested, Madame Albani sang – though she put a little too much effort into the two anthems and her voice was overpowering in the small space.

On a cold and bleak Monday afternoon they walked the Long Walk, the tree-lined avenue that runs from the rear entrance of the castle through Windsor Great Park. Mist was swirling over the parkland, and a bitter wind knifed through the elms. The Queen's Company led the way, rifles reversed. The gun carriage followed, down lines of Grenadier Guards and tens of thousands of onlookers, mainly from the town, who had come to watch the final journey. In the hazy light, they looked like ghosts. Guns boomed out from fifteen-pounders in the park, and the bell in the Round Tower tolled. Pipers played laments and the band of Lifeguards and Grenadiers slow funeral marches.

The King walked behind with the Kaiser, the King of Belgium and the King of Portugal. A small group of princes followed, and behind them the princesses, still in their identical mourning dresses, led by the Princess of Wales, who seemed overwhelmed with grief as she struggled along leaning heavily on a stick. By her side, with slow, firm steps, marched a lad in a sailor suit, fair curly hair squashed under his cap, a solemn look on his face. It was her grandson, the six-year-old Prince Edward of York, destined to be a king himself, though not for long. Thirty-five years later his abdication to marry a divorced woman, after just eleven months as Edward VIII, would bring down scandal upon the monarchy that Victoria had spent her reign endowing with such high moral standards, his denial of his duty a rejection of everything she stood for. For now, though, the sight of 'the boy before whom stretches so great a future', holding tightly to his grandmother's hand, brought tears to the eyes of spectators.

Where the earlier processions had been grand military events, now there was a sadness and a poignancy as this small band took the Queen to lie beside her dead husband.

Towards the front, the Bishop of Winchester was walking with the Dean of Windsor. A third clergyman should have been beside them – Clement Smith, the vicar of Whippingham. He had telegraphed that he was coming to Windsor, and the King had given him a place in the procession. Unfortunately, nobody told the poor vicar he was to go to the mausoleum and, just as he had been out of the room at the moment of the Queen's death at Osborne, so he missed her burial too.

At the rear of the procession came the members of the Household, a number of the Kaiser's aides – and a stranger. A man had slipped from the crowds on the lawn opposite the entrance to St George's Chapel and mingled with the German entourage. Now, unchallenged, he walked with them towards the mausoleum.

They took the turning off the Long Walk to Frogmore, leaving behind the last of the spectators lining the road. The public had seen their last of the Queen. Now it was a private affair. One of those walking behind the coffin, the Duke of Argyll, felt 'inexpressibly sad in the solemn journey to the tomb with one whom we have loved'.

To Ponsonby's relief, the horses pulling the gun carriage behaved perfectly. At the steps of the mausoleum, the drill he had worked out in the dead of night with the bearer party also went without a hitch – 'no whispering, no hesitation, simply the slow tread of the men' as they carried in the coffin. Outside, snowdrops were pushing their way through the brown earth. Inside, white flowers lay around the walls, caught in the flickering light from the gold–and–bronze lamps that hung from the roof. Pipers broke into a lament, just as they had when the coffin left Osborne three days earlier. The choir of St George's Chapel walked in front of the coffin singing 'Yea, though I walk through the valley' to music by Sir Arthur Sullivan. The royal party followed, and the iron gate was shut behind them as they grouped themselves around the sarcophagus.

Ponsonby was with the members of the Household standing in the transept when a voice whispered in his ear, 'Who is that old bird with a beard?' He turned and saw that the speaker was a stranger, the officer in khaki he had given a ticket to yesterday, his arm pointing at the King of Belgium. 'Hush!' Ponsonby hissed, and grabbed the man, pushed him towards the gates, and threw him out.

After prayers and anthems, the Bishop of Winchester committed the body to the ground and the coffin was lowered slowly into the tomb. 'Earth to earth,' intoned the Bishop, and Lord Edward Clinton, Master of the Queen's Household, stepped forward to throw earth on it. The service ended with an anthem specially composed by Parratt with words the poet Tennyson had written for the death of the Queen's grandson, Prince Albert Victor, the Duke of Clarence:

> The face of death is towards the sun of life.
> His shadow darkens earth. His truer name
> Is 'Onward' – no discordance in the roll
> And march of that eternal harmony,
> Whereto the world beat time, tho' faintly heard.
> Until the great hereafter, mourn in hope!

It was time for final farewells. One by one the royal family were to climb some steps and pass across a platform to look into the grave where the coffins of Queen Victoria and Prince

Albert now lay side by side. The King led the way, but instead of just walking by he knelt down. His Queen, Alexandra, came forward and did the same, but little Prince Edward, who was holding her hand, was frightened and pulled back. The King reached round to hold the boy and gently pulled him to his knees. It was a touching sight as the three of them made their obeisance in front of the open grave. 'We laid her to rest near Papa,' the King wrote to his sister Vicky in Germany. It was 'the most touching ceremony for us her children'.[5]

The rest of the family walked by the open grave, followed by members of the Household. Reid, his service to the Queen over at last, stooped to take a handful of flowers. 'The last act of the drama is over,' he wrote later. 'All went well.'

Outside the mausoleum, the officer in khaki was waiting. Ponsonby strode up to him and confronted him for his impertinence in pushing his way into a private family occasion. He demanded his name and regiment so he could report him. The man gave his details, saluted, and marched away.

The royal family left the mausoleum and climbed into carriages waiting to take them back up to the castle. In the courtyard there, Ponsonby spotted the khaki officer again. Undaunted by the reprimand he had received, he had ridden back in a carriage with the Kaiser's entourage and was now among the kings, princes and princesses who were standing around talking at the entrance to the royal quarters. They were clearly baffled by who he was, even slightly alarmed by this stranger's presence, and relieved when Ponsonby firmly took him by the arm and led him away to be dealt with by the police. It turned out that he had been invalided out of the Army after a bad bout of sunstroke in South Africa and was mentally unbalanced.

Somehow, though, the presence of this unknown soldier at the very end seemed fitting. His extreme loyalty and devotion to the point of smuggling himself into her funeral were precisely what the Queen had inspired in those who served her. In return, she had loved her soldiers. Their suffering in South Africa had been her suffering too – few doubted it had hastened her death. All along the route from Osborne House to this final resting place had been veteran soldiers and sailors who, during campaigns in India, Africa and the Crimea, had watched their comrades in arms die for her and had sworn they would do the same if they had to. The officer in khaki had simply achieved what each and every one of them would have wished for himself – to be at her side.

Moreover, since she was 'Mother, friend and Queen' to her people, since she had made them all her family, how could it be anything other than right and proper for one of her subjects to be there among her real family as they laid her to rest, to be one of them, one of her very own? And if he was a little mad, touched by the sun, then so were the millions who mourned her with such unrestrained words and tears in those last days of Queen Victoria. They had been touched by her glory, and they knew the country, the Crown, the Empire would never be quite the same again.

Back at the mausoleum, Lord Esher supervised the workmen who placed the stone over the tomb and sealed it. He picked up a laurel wreath and some lilies and held them in his hand as he watched. Outside, snow was beginning to fall. It was a time to reflect. 'So ends the reign of the Queen,' he wrote later as he recalled that moment. 'And now I feel for the first time that the new regime, so full of anxieties for England, has begun.'[6]

# Epilogue

Do you think that could be Grandmama's spirit?

An unnamed princess

Queen Victoria would never be forgotten – or so every tribute, every obituary, every speech by loyal Britons earnestly prophesied. 'Her name shall live for ever and our children's children shall call her blessed,' said the *Morning Post*. They were emotional words, forged in the heat of the moment. The moment passed.

For a fortnight the world had stood still. Now it moved on. It had to. As the *Westminster Gazette* put it:

In a funeral at sea the ship is slowed down when the body is committed to the deep but once that has taken place there can be no waiting – the order is Full Steam Ahead. It is so with national affairs. Everything has been slowed down to do honour to our Queen, but the ship of state cannot tarry long. Full steam ahead is today's order – just because it can be nothing else.

People looked sadly to the past, inquisitively if nervously to the future. Thomas Hardy's sentiments were typical. He was unsettled by the Queen's death but was also anxious to be rid of his pennies and halfpennies with her head on them – 'my money looks all old fashioned pending the new coinage', he wrote to a friend.[1]

As the newspapers ended their blanket coverage of the Queen's death, they turned their attention again to South Africa, where a small English post to the south-west of Johannesburg had been overwhelmed by the enemy before help could arrive. But their thoughts were still on the past. 'Thus we said goodbye to one who has filled a large part in our lives,' the *Daily Chronicle* signed off. 'It seemed as though we had bidden farewell to an era, the greatness of which we can scarcely gauge.'

Those who thought themselves entitled to 'gauge' were already at work, and within two months an article appeared in the *Quarterly Review* daring to be critical of the old Queen and suggesting that the reaction to her death sailed close to 'idolatry'. 'The time has come to begin to abandon the note of indiscriminate praise and to put even this revered personage into the crucible of criticism.' The complaints were mild enough – she was rather ordinary in her cultural tastes, a little too tyrannical with those around her, loving 'the exercise of power for its own sake'.[2] But it was the fact that they had been voiced at all that was significant. And so soon.

The last years of Victoria's reign had not been free of criticism but now, with her gone, everything was a target for those who wanted to carp – even the manner of her departure. How poorly the British had paid their last respects to her, complained the controversial Lady Colin Campbell in her newspaper column.

In what other capital in Europe would such an occasion have been marked by skimpy bits of purple cloth of all kinds of excruciating shades from dirty beetroot to sulky blue? Where were the garlands of laurel and victorious palms that should have marked the last route of Victoria the Victorious, the flags of an Empire such as the world has never seen? When one thinks what Paris did for the funeral of

Victor Hugo, one is ashamed to think of the childish attempt at decoration made by London.[3]

The Kaiser went home after the friendliest of official lunches with the King at Marlborough House and cheers from a hugely enthusiastic crowd at Charing Cross. He had been in England for three weeks. It took less than that time back in Berlin for the anti–British faction in government there to win him back to their side. Rows over South Africa and then China quickly curdled all the goodwill he had milked from his grandmother's death.

The war in South Africa had another sixteen months to run and, though it ended in victory, it could by no means be called a triumph. Twenty-two thousand British soldiers had died by then. More significantly, the glad, confident belief in an empire united and strong under British rule was shot to ribbons.

For Fritz Ponsonby and Sir James Reid there would be influential jobs in the new King's court, but it would be a court in which the tone changed almost beyond recognition. Everything was lighter and brighter. At fifty-nine, the King was not a young man, but compared with his mother's last decades he had youth and vitality. He was determined to fling out the old, and he went through Buckingham Palace clearing the collected rubbish of half a century. 'Get this morgue cleaned up,' he ordered, and pictures of long-forgotten German relatives were burned, plaster statuettes of John Brown smashed into smithereens. He demanded new drains, new plumbing, a complete overhaul. At Windsor, he put an end to the frugal squares of cut-up newspaper in the lavatories.

Tradition and prohibition had ruled the life of Victoria and those around her. Like the mess at Buckingham Palace,

Edward swept much of that away too. He kept his mistresses and his racehorses (though he could not be seen on the racetrack during the period of official mourning and had to let his string of thirteen run under someone else's colours for much of 1901). Smoke from cigarettes and cigars – previously forbidden by the Queen or pushed into corners and side rooms – filled the royal salons. The King puffed away at his first Havana of the day before breakfast, and got through another dozen before bedtime. He loved motor cars, which his mother had hated, and, his foot hard down, was thrilled at being the first man in the country to top 60 m.p.h., reaching out with glee to pump on the four-tone air horn he had fixed to the side.

Dining at the royal table was now fun and funny rather than the ordeal it had been under Victoria. Those who had experienced both felt that, where once they had been among Trappist monks, now they were at a children's tea party. Evenings with the King were convivial – in the drawing room after dinner there would be chatter, not the respectful silence that Victoria had insisted on, broken only by her conversation with whichever individual she had summoned to sit by her side.

Not everyone approved of the changes. Henry James called the King 'Edward the Caresser' and a 'vulgarian', and he predicted a reign of 'frivolity and vulgarity'.[4] The Countess of Airlie thought the reaction from the austerity and rigid moral code of Queen Victoria's court went too far in the opposite direction. 'Every kind of extravagance became the fashion. Money was the passport to society. Almost anyone who had enough of it could procure, sooner or later, an invitation to the splendid court balls at Windsor and the evening receptions at Buckingham Palace.'[5] Lord Esher thought the King in-decisive and forgetful. He would agree to something, then deny all knowledge of it only a few days later. The smack of firmness had gone. 'It may be my imagination,' Esher noted, 'but the sanctity of the throne has disappeared. The king is kind and debonnaire and not undignified – but too human!' The decade of Edward VII had an unreality to it, a sense that things were changing – though in what precise direction no one seemed quite clear. For all the surface gaiety of that period, the essential Edwardian mood was a feeling of nostalgia for what had gone and apprehension about what was to come.

The King fancied himself as a diplomat on the international stage, a clever negotiator, a peacemaker. Trading on his geniality, he sought to continue his mother's role as the head of a family of nations, but, though he was wily enough, he could never command the respect she had. The Kaiser snubbed him, deceived him, courted him when it suited, otherwise ignored him. The German fleet of battleships grew, and Britain found itself drawn into the vortex of European politics that would eventually end in catastrophic warfare and terrible bloodshed. When Archduke Franz Ferdinand of Austria was assassinated at Sarajevo in 1914, those with a memory for detail would remember a less brutal time when he had ridden in that glittering cavalry of princes that followed behind Victoria's coffin, oblivious of the fate that awaited him, Europe and the world. Very soon, in the mud of Flanders, what was left of the great Victorian epoch would finally sink for ever.

A year after the Queen was buried at Frogmore, the royal family made a pilgrimage to the mausoleum for a memorial service. Victoria and Albert lay side by side in effigy, their reunion celebrated in music by another special anthem written by the Eton master Arthur Benson:

She hath her heart's desire!
She hath her joy,
Joy that no time can tire,
Nor care destroy.

Now in the world of light –
So near, so far –
Above her burns the bright
And morning star.

Here by the stroke of Love
Her love was rent.
Now are they one above
In deep content.

As the choir sang, a sparrow was seen to be trapped inside the building and flying backwards and forwards frantically under the dome, trying to escape. One of the younger princesses in the line round the sarcophagus let her imagination take flight too and whispered to her cousin standing next to her, 'Do you think that could be Grandmama's spirit?' The question was whispered down the line, until it reached Queen Alexandra. 'No,' she replied, 'or it would not have made a mess on Beatrice's bonnet!'[6]

# Appendix

My best and truest friend . . .

Queen Victoria on John Brown

The fact that Queen Victoria was buried wearing a wedding ring given to her by John Brown, albeit his mother's, has never been disclosed before. This does not, however, mean that they had secretly married – a claim that was common gossip in the middle of her reign and which has never totally gone away.

It was in 1866, eighteen months after he had been asked to extend his duties at Balmoral to the other royal homes at Osborne and Windsor and, in effect, become the servant constantly by her side, that such rumours began. The name 'Mrs Brown' was first whispered behind gloved hands in smart London drawing rooms. Then the more daring magazines turned the relationship into satire. The foreign press, unrestrained then as now by fears of libel or lese-majesty when discussing the British royal family, went further: a marriage had taken place. It was not true.

The Queen's behaviour, however, made it open season for the gossip-mongers. This was the low point in her popularity as, still mourning Albert five years after his death, she shut herself away from her subjects. She was an absentee monarch who chose not to be seen in public. It was hardly surprising if some let their imaginations run free over what was really going on behind closed doors in the Highlands.

It is impossible to prove that an event did *not* take place, particularly one also alleged to be a secret. But there is no trace at all – not the slightest hint – of a marriage. Fritz Ponsonby talked to a number of people in the Household who might have been in on such a secret, including a duchess who was said to have been at the ceremony. 'They all laughed at the idea,' he says in his memoirs.

Moreover, everything we know about Victoria argues against such a marriage. To her, Albert was irreplaceable. But, if he were to be replaced, to do so with a man of Brown's position in life was simply unthinkable. The Queen's view of people who married beneath their station is well known. She strongly disapproved when the Hon. Susan Baring, one of her ladies-in-waiting, agreed to marry the lower-born Dr Reid. She thought it 'a great *mésalliance* – how she could accept him I cannot understand!' If the Queen had not been old and infirm and in constant need of the doctor's services, she would have fired him for his impertinence, she said, though she eventually relented and gave the couple her reluctant blessing.

If marrying down went against the grain, *re*marrying down was unforgivable. When her son-in-law Louis, the Grand Duke of Hesse, widower of her dead daughter Princess Alice, secretly married his long-term mistress, a beautiful Polish lady of high accomplishments but lowly origins, the furious Queen interfered ruthlessly – to the point of making sure the marriage was annulled. She did so even though his five children (and her grandchildren) thought remarriage was just the thing for their father, who was only forty-seven and had been a widower for six years. She did so even though the couple had a son, thereby rendered illegitimate. That was how strongly she felt.

We can take it, then, that Victoria was never John Brown's wife. But was she his mistress? Did she take this man – whose craggy looks and strong arms clearly pleased her – not just into her house but into her bed? A sex-obsessed time like ours would like to think so. Catching Queen Victoria, that symbol of puritan moralizing, blinkered to the facts of life, actually indulging in extramarital sex would be delicious in its irony – if it were true. But the evidence is against it.

It is true (and surprising to many) that she was a passionate woman. She had a fulfilling sex life with Albert. On her wedding night she did not sleep much – or so she confessed to her diary – and his words of love to her were 'bliss beyond belief'. Seventeen years later, when the birth of Princess Beatrice, her ninth child, led her doctor to warn her against getting pregnant again, she asked plaintively, 'Can I have no more fun in bed?'[1] There was a lustiness about her that belies the image that has come down to us.

With Albert's death, she would have buried those feelings in the depths of her grief. There are two compelling reasons for this conclusion. First, she believed it was God's will that Albert had died (and he had always pressed on her the need to submit herself to that divine providence). It followed that it was God's will that she should bear the consequence of his death – a celibate widowhood – however much she hated sleeping alone, and however much she missed his presence. Second, she was utterly loyal to her dead husband and his memory. She missed his companionship, his wisdom, the way he dealt with the children, the way he handled her ministers. Certainly she missed his presence in her bed too, but there is no indication that this particular longing topped the long, long list of things she missed about him.

Moreover, Albert remained a reality right to the end of her life. She *knew*, she never doubted (well, perhaps for just a second or two – a 'sudden qualm', as she told Bishop Davidson), that she would see him again. They would be reunited, and she should have to answer to him (as well as to God) on the other side. How, in the hereafter, could she possibly explain away an earthly affair with another man? And not just any man, but Albert's own ghillie, the servant he himself had chosen to look after her. That thought alone – of Albert the Good, hurt and betrayed, questioning what she had done, for the rest of eternity – would have been enough to stop her carrying on with Brown, even if the idea ever crossed her mind.

What, then, was her relationship with John Brown? She spoke of him always as a friend – 'my best and truest friend' she often called him. She trusted him; she liked having him around. Most of the people she met shrank from her. He did not shrink. He handled her not just in the sense of ordering her day-to-day life, but physically too. She liked his arms around her. She liked the comfort of being picked up by him and settled into her carriage or her chair, a rug wrapped tightly round her. 'Comfort' is a word she often used about him. That was what he was to her.

Some were sure the comfort went further. Courtiers and servants noticed little incidents and gossiped about them to their families. He was seen coming out of her bedroom – a place where, until her final illness, even her grown-up daughters rarely went, if ever. He treated her, touched her sometimes, with a familiarity that suggested a greater intimacy. But whether any of this amounted to an affair – a relationship involving sexual contact and penetration – is another matter. We will never know for sure – only those directly involved ever could – but it seems extremely unlikely.

Apart from the dread of having to account for herself in the hereafter, two things would have deterred the Queen: the fear of conception and the fear of discovery. At the height of the 'Mrs Brown' allegations she was in her late forties. Pregnancy would then have been highly unlikely, but not impossible.

She had conceived easily enough before – nine children in
seventeen years. It could *just* happen again. It is a risk she
would not have taken. As for discovery, there was little that
happened in the royal palaces that went unnoticed. There
was always someone around, someone watching. Before she
embarked on an intimate relationship with Brown, the Queen
would have had to be certain she could do so without being
detected. A second's thought would have led her to the
conclusion that getting away without being found out would
be next to impossible.

Moreover, if she had something to hide about her relationship, it was odd that she went to such great lengths to fight
Brown's corner. She went into battle against anyone in her
entourage who tried to curb his position and privileges, even
though by doing so she drew even more attention to him. She
insisted that Brown should have a place in her carriage; after
his death, she could see no reason why she should not write
and publish a memoir of his life. These were not the actions
of a woman with a guilty secret. It was others who were
uncomfortable about John Brown, others who saw smoke and
assumed there was fire. She saw her relationship with her
servant as wholesome and above board. If it was really something else, then she was a deceiver (or self-deceiver) of amazing
proportions.

It is the actions of others, not the Queen or Brown, that
have fuelled people's suspicions. Edward VII destroyed as
many mementoes of Brown as he could lay his hands on,
including correspondence. Then a bundle of three hundred
letters from the Queen to Alexander Profeit, her estate manager at Balmoral, surfaced a few years after her death and their
content about Brown was apparently so sensational that the
royal family were blackmailed. Sir James Reid conducted the
negotiations with a member of Profeit's family and retrieved

the letters on behalf of the King. He must have looked them over before handing them to his sovereign, because he noted that many of them were 'most compromising'. We must take Reid's judgement at face value – he was a trustworthy witness throughout the story of the Queen's death – but, since the letters themselves have disappeared (it is presumed the King burned them), it still amounts to innuendo, not evidence. I find it hard to imagine what the Queen would have had to say to her estate manager about her relationship with Brown that could have compromised her. It seems unlikely that she would have revealed her feelings to someone with whom her dealings would primarily be about the business of Balmoral rather than love affairs. Brown's work and conduct – his drinking, for example – might indeed have been a well-trodden subject between them. Profeit did not like Brown, and they often clashed. But what matter could their correspondence have trespassed on to tarnish a Queen's reputation?

The mystery remains – and probably, with so much evidence destroyed, always will. So does the fascination. This is because the relationship between Queen Victoria and John Brown satisfies three of today's popular preoccupations: sex, the royal family, and conspiracy/cover-up theories.

The wedding ring we now know that the Queen received from John Brown is an important and intriguing new piece of information. It shows just how close he was to her heart, and she to his. We can imagine the scene. His mother had given him her wedding ring in 1875. He had worn it himself for a while, then handed it over to the only other woman he loved – the Queen. She accepted it. Whether she wore it in his lifetime is not made clear, but when he died suddenly in 1883 she put it on and, as her written instructions about the contents of her coffin declare, wore it constantly from then on. Clearly she valued it enough to order that it should remain on her finger in death, alongside rings from her husband, from her mother and from her children. He was as dear to her as they were.

But the fact that she could mention it only in her most secret instructions – those that not even her family (*particularly her family*) were allowed to see – also tells us something. She knew the animosity it would provoke. She knew how easily her wishes, just like her devotion to Brown and his to her, would be misunderstood.

# Sources and Notes

## Preface

1. *South Wales Daily News*, 23 January 1901.
2. *Daily Express*, 2 January 1900.
3. Quoted in Samuel Hynes, *Edwardian Occasions* (Routledge & Kegan Paul, 1972).

## 1. *The Eyes Grow Dim*

The sources for this chapter, as for much of the book, are the first-hand accounts of those who were actually present at the events described. Sir Frederick Ponsonby's *Recollections of Three Reigns* (Eyre & Spottiswoode, 1951) was published long after his death in 1935 from a manuscript he had been working on for the last three years of his life. It is fascinating for its detail about life at the Queen's court and for the modest and self-deprecating way in which he portrays his own role. His storytelling was masterful, particularly since, on his own admission, much of it was from memory. In forty years as a courtier, he had kept not a single note or diary. Fortunately his wife had hung on to all his letters to her, and they were his inspiration to, as he wrote, 'fill in the gaps'.

By contrast, Sir James Reid, the Queen's personal doctor, kept everything – meticulous diaries, letters, scrapbooks – with the result that the wife of his grandson was able to compile an intimate account of the court and the Queen that is second to none. *Ask Sir James* by Michaela Reid (Hodder & Stoughton, 1987) is a treasure trove – a historical document without which my own account could not have been written.

Nor could I have got very far without the Queen's own words to call on in *The Letters of Queen Victoria: A Selection from Her Correspondence and Journal*, ed. George Earle Buckle (Murray, 1932). She too kept everything – or rather her daughters did, and, though they may have weeded out rather more than historians would wish, the volumes that remain are fascinating. Her journal, kept until almost a week before she died, tells us how she was feeling: the letters she received indicate what others felt about her. The letters she wrote to her eldest daughter are to be found in Agatha Ramm (ed.), *Beloved and Darling Child: Last Letters between Queen Victoria and Her Eldest Daughter 1886–1901* (Sutton, 1990). Quotations from all these and other papers lodged in the Royal Archives are published with the gracious permission of Her Majesty Queen Elizabeth II.

Several of the Queen's ladies-in-waiting wrote about their time attending her – though, regrettably, not those closest to her in the last days and weeks. The nearest in time was Marie Mallet, whose poignant observations of the declining strength of the Queen are chronicled in her son Victor Mallet's book *Life With Queen Victoria* (Murray, 1968). Another observer, though less frequent, was the Revd Cosmo Lang, later Archbishop of Canterbury. His diaries are reprinted in John Gilbert Lockhart's *Cosmo Gordon Lang* (Hodder & Stoughton, 1949), and are quoted by courtesy of Lambeth Palace.

1. Victoria's reference to the 'new century' is confusing. When did the twentieth century actually begin? A similar semantic/ mathematical debate to the one we have recently experienced over the proper starting date of the new millennium took place a century ago. Then, most plumped for the pedantic resolution – 1900 was the *last* year of the old century and 1901 the first of the new. Certainly most of the newspapers kept to this convention. But it was clearly hard for people not to see the

change from an 18 to a 19 as a symbolic moment of transition – even for a queen.

2. Said to Randall Davidson, Bishop of Winchester, as the Queen lay dying. (See the introduction to the notes on Chapter 5.)

3. Elizabeth Longford, *Victoria R.I.* (Weidenfeld & Nicolson, 1964).

4. Quoted in Longford, *Victoria R.I.*

5. 'Mother' was a widely used sobriquet for her. Some papers referred to her as the Queen-Mother (note the hyphen). Her obituaries were to use the word constantly. When the royal standard flew over Buckingham Palace, the policeman outside would tell inquirers, 'Mother's home.'

6. There had been twenty morning papers throughout Britain at the start of her reign. By the end there were more than 100. At the start of her reign they cost 5d. By the end – with the abolition of stamp duty in 1855, the introduction of cheaper, faster printing, and a fall in the cost of paper – most were a penny or a halfpenny, though *The Times* cost 3d. 'The increase of railways, the introduction of the telegraph and the spread of education have made the press a power in the land,' declared the *Newspaper Press Directory* of 1901. Proving this with actual circulation figures is next to impossible. Accurate, believable, figures were non-existent. There was only claim and counter-claim – and no audit bureau as there is today. As Lucy Brown tells in her hugely informative *Victorian News and Newspapers* (Oxford University Press, 1985), when the *Leeds Daily News* claimed in 1894 that its circulation of 75,578 had been certified by an independent accountant, the rival *Leeds Express* offered to pay £500 to charity if it was proved. To get some indication of how confident the *Express* was in its challenge, consider that £500 then is equivalent to £35,000–£40,000 today – not a sum to be trifled with on an idle bet.

But that there was a huge newspaper readership in 1901 compared with the start of Victoria's reign is indisputable. In

1848 the biggest-selling paper was *The Times*. Its circulation?
Thirty thousand. By the end of the century the *Daily Mail* was
claiming leadership, with something between 750,000 and a
million sold. The market had boomed everywhere. The bigger
provincial morning papers were selling 30,000 to 40,000 copies
a day, provincial evening papers sometimes two or three times
as many. The *London Evening News* was up to 800,000. What
does this all add up to? At the start of the nineteenth century,
little more than one in a hundred people read a newspaper
regularly. By its end, a quarter of the population were probably
buying one every day.

7. Lady Frances Balfour, *Ne Obliviscaris* (Hodder & Stoughton,
   1930).

8. William Henry Davenport Adams, *Notable Women of Our Own
   Times* (Ward Lock, 1883).

9. Louisa, Countess of Antrim, *Recollections* (King's Stone Press,
   1937).

10. Article in *Quarterly Review*, April 1901.


## 2. *Trials and Anxieties*

The Bishop of Winchester's thoughts on Victoria's religious beliefs
are detailed in George Kennedy Bell's *Randall Davidson* (Oxford
University Press, 1935).

1. These claims were common in the spiritualist literature of the
   day. William Rossetti, brother of the pre-Raphaelite painter
   Dante Gabriel Rossetti, noted the allegation in his diary in
   1870 after a long conversation with a spiritualist. But Elizabeth
   Longford scrutinized them closely for her *Victoria R.I.*, and
   found no convincing evidence that they were true.

2. Quoted in a letter to the *Pall Mall Gazette*, 4 February 1901,
   from the Venerable Basil Wilberforce, Archdeacon of Westminster.

3. The *Spectator*, 26 January 1901.
4. Letter in the Royal Archives reproduced in *Letters of Queen Victoria*, ed. Buckle.
5. 'They seemed so touched, and many had tears in their eyes' – from the Queen's journal, 22 March 1900.
6. Quoted in a footnote in *Letters of Queen Victoria*, ed. Buckle.
7. Reprinted from Elizabeth Longford (ed.), *Darling Loosy: Letters to Princess Louise* (Weidenfeld & Nicolson, 1991).

## 3. *Whispers and Denials*

The picture of British life at this time is built up from copious reports in national newspapers. Details of events at Osborne are based largely on Reid's account and the Queen's journal. For the precision of the facts about Osborne House I am grateful to Edward Sibbick, its unofficial archivist. Having been a carpenter there all his working life, he became the guardian of its history on his retirement. Being guided round by him was a privilege. He loves the place almost as much as Victoria did – and a good deal more than the Prince of Wales clearly did. As King, he got shot of it as quickly as he could, shifting Princess Beatrice and her family from their rooms at the top of the house to a cottage in the grounds and handing the house over to the nation. It remains, however, an extraordinary place to visit, preserved largely as it was the day Queen Victoria left it in her coffin.

1. Asa Briggs, *Victorian Things* (Folio Society, 1998).
2. Told to the Bishop of Winchester and recorded in his private memoir, lodged in Lambeth Palace library.
3. Ibid.
4. Baron Hermann von Eckardstein, *Ten Years at the Court of St James', 1895–1905*, trans. and ed. Professor George Young (Thornton Butterworth, 1921).

## 4. *The News Breaks*

1. Daisy, Princess of Pless, *From My Private Diary*, ed. Major Desmond Chapman-Huston (Murray, 1931).
2. Quoted in Hannah Pakula, *An Uncommon Woman: The Empress Frederick* (Weidenfeld & Nicolson, 1995).
3. Reported in Eckardstein, *Ten Years at the Court of St James'*.
4. Quoted in *The Shy Princess*, a biography of Princess Beatrice by David Duff (Evans Brothers, 1958).

## 5. *Clinging On*

In this chapter, Reid's recollection of events at Osborne is supplemented by the experiences of Randall Davidson, Bishop of Winchester. Davidson gave graphic accounts of what was happening in the house in letters home to his wife. Later he wrote an 8,000-word memoir of all he had seen and heard from the moment he was told the Queen was ill through to the final burial at Frogmore. It is full of anecdote and opinion, but is often self-serving. He loved being an intimate of the highest in the land, and he clearly felt that this was a moment in history in which he had a central part to play. Taken alongside Reid's account, it is equally clear that here were two professional gentlemen who were not best pleased to be working alongside each other, and theirs is another of the personal tensions that add to the drama of the Queen's dying. The Bishop's account was never published but is lodged in Lambeth Palace library. I am most grateful for having had the opportunity to read it.

Another eyewitness has much to add here, though not about bedside matters. Baron von Eckardstein was the number two at the German Embassy, though, with the actual ambassador being ill, he was to all intents Berlin's principal diplomat in London. His memoirs tell us about what was going on between the Prince of Wales and the Kaiser and between Britain and Germany as a whole.

All anecdotes about how the country reacted to the Queen's illness come from contemporary newspapers.

1. Quoted in Longford, *Victoria R.I.*
2. Viscount Esher, *Journals and Letters* (Nicholson & Watson, 1938).
3. Eckardstein, *Ten Years at the Court of St James'*. The Kaiser reported his conversations with the Prince of Wales.

## 6. *Sunset*

The doctor and the priest – Reid and Davidson – were witnesses to the deathbed scene. This account is based primarily on theirs. The description of the journalists at the gates of Osborne House comes from their own detailed reports in their newspapers. I am grateful to the archivist of *The Times* for information about James Vincent, the paper's special correspondent.

1. Margot Asquith, *Autobiography* (Eyre & Spottiswoode, 1962).
2. Balfour, *Ne Obliviscaris*.
3. Princess Marie Louise, *My Memories of Six Reigns* (Evans Brothers, 1956).
4. Quoted in Longford, *Victoria R.I.* Annie Macdonald was one of the Queen's favourite servants.
5. Described in M. E. Sara, *The Life and Times of HRH Princess Beatrice* (Stanley Paul, 1945).

## 7. *A World in Shock*

The newspapers of a hundred years ago were stuffed full of the minutiae of people's lives. Unlike today, news was pretty well anything that somebody somewhere wanted printed. Every organization sent a report of its meetings to the local paper. Every local correspondent sent a report from his area to the regional paper or to the nationals. Take the *Aberdeen Journal* as an example. The day after the Queen's death it printed reports from seventy towns and villages in its area, in alphabetical order, from Aberchirder to Whitehouse, all pretty well saying the same thing – 'The news has been received with profound sorrow in . . . The bell in the Old Kirk was tolled.' Reporters wrote down what they saw, even if it wasn't sensational. The *Daily Telegraph* printed lists of wreaths – from the Empress Eugenie's and President McKinley's down to the one from 'the sons of the late Canon and Mrs Prothero'. The need to inform was deemed more important than the wish to excite. As a result, the papers can make dull and repetitive reading, but as historical records they are a goldmine.

My researches began with me staring at microfiches in the British Library's newspaper section in Colindale, north London, but then I found an even richer seam. In 1901 some hapless soul in the royal household was given an Everest of a task – to acquire every newspaper reporting the illness and death of Queen Victoria, cut out the articles, however long (and some, such as the full obituaries, went on for dozens of broadsheet pages), and paste them into cuttings books. These are now leather-bound and occupy several shelves at the Royal Archives in Windsor Castle. To find your source material handily packaged and in one place is a dream come true. I sat for days on end ploughing through these volumes, looking up from my desk in the Round Tower only to marvel that just outside the window was where my story had actually begun and ended.

1. First-person report, signed W.F.W., in the *Pall Mall Gazette*, 23 January 1901.
2. Esher, *Journals and Letters*.


## 8. *Secret Last Wishes*

1. Lady Violet Bonham-Carter, *Winston Churchill as I Knew Him* (Weidenfeld & Nicolson, 1995).
2. *Daily Telegraph*, 23 January 1901.
3. Ibid., 24 January 1901.

4. Quoted in Randolph Churchill, *Winston Churchill. Vol. 1: Youth* (Heinemann, 1966). Reproduced with permission of Curtis Brown Ltd, London, on behalf of the Estate of Sir Winston S. Churchill. © Winston S. Churchill.
5. The descriptions of the Accession Council and the swearing-in ceremonies in Parliament are from newspaper reports and the memoirs of Lord Esher and of Lord Halsbury.

## 9. *In Memoriam*

Local newspapers, a flourishing sector at the turn of the century, were also caught up in the frenzy of reporting and reaction. They are an important source for what was happening across the country.
1. *Daily News*, 28 January 1901.
2. In the end, it was generally agreed that the Duke had done a decent job.
3. The hunt for the Queen's effigy is told by Lord Esher in his *Journals and Letters*.
4. The *Standard*, 26 January 1901.
5. The Kaiser then told Eckardstein: see his *Ten Years at the Court of St James'*.
6. Horace Mann, quoted in Asa Briggs, *Victorian Cities* (Folio Society, 1996).
7. Reported in Eckardstein, *Ten Years at the Court of St James'*.

## 10. *Crossing the Bar*

Details of the rows over funeral arrangements come from the accounts of Ponsonby and Davidson.
1. *The Times*, 30 January 1901. It does not name the City firm.
2. Hardie's presence on the boat was logged by the *Standard* – as was that of seven Irish Nationalist MPs.
3. *The Times*, 2 February 1901.

## 11. *The People's Farewell*

Newspaper reports are the source for the bulk of this chapter.

1. Quoted in Ronald Pearsall, *Conan Doyle* (Weidenfeld & Nicolson, 1977).
2. *Morning Post*, 2 February 1901.
3. Letter dated 2 February 1901 to Frances Blogg, who was to become Chesterton's wife that year, quoted in Michael Ffinch, *G. K. Chesterton* (Weidenfeld & Nicolson, 1986).
4. Laurence Housman, *The Unexpected Years* (Jonathan Cape, 1937).
5. Duke of Argyll, *VRI: Her Life and Empire* (Eyre & Spottiswoode, 1901).
6. Royal Archives, G5/CC45/229.
7. Bonham-Carter, *Winston Churchill as I Knew Him*.
8. *Daily Chronicle*, 4 February 1901, anonymous first-hand report headed 'From the ranks'.
9. Frank Swinnerton (ed.), *The Journals of Arnold Bennett* (Penguin, 1971).

## 12. *Reunited*

The events at Windsor are reconstructed from Ponsonby's memoirs, the Bishop of Winchester's memoirs and newspaper reports.

1. The *Standard*, 4 February 1901.
2. Letter lodged in the Royal Archives, RA VIC/ADD J/1624.
3. *The Times*, 4 February 1901.
4. Sir H. Rider Haggard, *The Days of My Life, Vol. 2* (Longman, 1926).
5. Royal Archives, RA VIC/ADD A4/198.
6. Esher, *Journals and Letters*.

## Epilogue

1. Letter to Florence Henniker, 15 February 1901, in *The Collected Letters of Thomas Hardy, Vol. 2*, ed. R. L. Purdy and M. Millgate (Clarendon, 1980).
2. Edmund Gosse in *Quarterly Review*, April 1901.
3. The *World*, 6 February 1901.
4. Letter to Clara Benedict in *The Letters of Henry James, Vol. 4*, ed. Leon Edel (Harvard University Press, 1984).
5. Mabel, Countess of Airlie, *Thatched With Gold* (Hutchinson, 1962).
6. Story recounted in Louisa, Countess of Antrim, *Recollections*.

## Appendix

1. Giles St Aubyn, *Queen Victoria* (Sinclair-Stevenson, 1991).

# Bibliography

*Newspapers and magazines*

Contemporary accounts in:
*Daily Chronicle, Daily Express, Daily Graphic, Daily Mail, Daily News, Daily Telegraph, The Echo, Evening News* (London), *The Financial News, The Globe, Morning Advertiser, Morning Post, The Observer, Pall Mall Gazette, St James's Gazette, The Sketch, The Standard, The Star, The Sun, The Times, Westminster Gazette, The World*

*British Medical Journal, The Economist, Farmer and Stockbreeder, Illustrated London News, Local Government Chronicle, Quarterly Review, The Queen, Railway Times, The Saturday Review, The Spectator, Truth*

*Aberdeen Evening Express, Aberdeen Free Press, Aberdeen Journal, Birmingham Daily Gazette, Birmingham Daily Mail, Birmingham Daily Post, Brighton Gazette, Bristol Mercury, Bristol Times and Mirror, Cork Examiner, Daily News* (Portsmouth), *Daily Record* (Glasgow), *Edinburgh Evening News, Freeman's Journal, Glasgow Evening News, Hull Daily News, Irish Daily Independent, Leeds Mercury, Liverpool Courier, Liverpool Mercury, Manchester Courier, Manchester Guardian, Newcastle Daily Chronicle, Northern Whig* (Belfast), *Nottingham Daily Guardian, Nottingham Evening News, Nottingham Evening Post, Southern Daily Mail, South Wales Daily News, Western Daily Press, Western Morning News, Yorkshire Evening Post, Yorkshire Herald*

## Books

Airlie, Mabel, Countess of, *Thatched With Gold* (Hutchinson, 1962)

Antrim, Louisa, Countess of, *Recollections* (King's Stone Press, 1937)

Argyll, Duke of, *VRI: Her Life and Empire* (Eyre & Spottiswoode, 1901)

Asquith, Margot, *Autobiography* (Eyre & Spottiswoode, 1962)

Balfour, Lady Frances, *Ne Obliviscaris* (Hodder & Stoughton, 1930)

Bell, George Kennedy, *Randall Davidson* (Oxford University Press, 1935)

Briggs, Asa, *Victorian Things* (Folio Society, 1998)

Brown, Lucy, *Victorian News and Newspapers* (Oxford University Press, 1985)

Clarke, Peter, *Hope and Glory, Britain 1900–1990* (Allen Lane, 1996)

Coulter, John, *London of 100 Years Ago* (Sutton, 1999)

Duff, David, *The Shy Princess* (Evans Brothers, 1958)

Eckardstein, Baron Hermann von, *Ten Years at the Court of St James',  1895–1905*, trans. and ed. Professor George Young (Thornton Butterworth, 1921)

Engel, Matthew, *Tickle the Public: 100 years of the popular press* (Gollancz, 1996)

Esher, Viscount, *Journals and Letters* (Nicholson & Watson, 1938)

Gilbert, Martin, *History of the Twentieth Century, Vol. 1* (HarperCollins, 1997)

Hibbert, Christopher, *Edward VII: A Portrait* (Allen Lane, 1976)

Homans, Margaret, and Munich, Adrienne, *Remaking Queen Victoria* (Cambridge University Press, 1997)

Hough, Richard, *Edward and Alexandra* (Hodder & Stoughton, 1992)

Houghton, Walter, *The Victorian Frame of Mind* (Yale University Press, 1957)

Hynes, Samuel, *Edwardian Occasions* (Routledge & Kegan Paul, 1972)

Koss, Stephen, *The Rise and Fall of the Political Press in Britain* (Hamish Hamilton, 1981)

Lockhart, John Gilbert, *Cosmo Gordon Lang* (Hodder & Stoughton, 1949)

Longford, Elizabeth, *Victoria R.I.* (Weidenfeld & Nicolson, 1964)

—— (ed.), *Louisa, Lady in Waiting: The Personal Diaries and Albums of Louisa, Lady in Waiting to Queen Victoria and Queen Alexandra* (Cape, 1979)

—— (ed.), *Darling Loosy: Letters to Princess Louise* (Weidenfeld & Nicolson, 1991)

Mallet, Victor, *Life with Queen Victoria* (Murray, 1968)

Marie Louise, Princess, *My Memories of Six Reigns* (Evans Brothers, 1956)

Nevill, Barry St John, *Life at the Court of Queen Victoria* (Sutton, 1997)

Newsome, David, *The Victorian World Picture* (Murray, 1997)

Packard, Jerrold M., *Farewell in Splendor: The Passing of Queen Victoria and her Age* (Dutton, 1995)

Pakenham, Thomas, *The Scramble for Africa* (Weidenfeld & Nicolson, 1991)

Pakula, Hannah, *An Uncommon Woman: The Empress Frederick* (Weidenfeld & Nicolson, 1995)

Pless, Daisy, Princess of, *From My Private Diary*, ed. Major Desmond Chapman-Huston (Murray, 1931)

Ponsonby, Sir Frederick, *Recollections of Three Reigns* (Eyre & Spottiswoode, 1951)

Pretorius, Fransjohan, *The Anglo Boer War* (Don Nelson, 1985)

*Private Life of the Queen. By One of Her Majesty's Servants* (Arthur Pearson, 1897; reprinted by Gresham, 1979)

Ramm, Agatha (ed.), *Beloved and Darling Child: Last Letters between Queen Victoria and Her Eldest Daughter 1886–1901* (Sutton, 1990)

Reid, Michaela, *Ask Sir James* (Hodder & Stoughton, 1987)

Robbins, Keith, *The Eclipse of a Great Power, Britain 1870–1992* (Longman, 1994)

St Aubyn, Giles, *Queen Victoria* (Sinclair-Stevenson, 1991)

Sara, M. E., *The Life and Times of HRH Princess Beatrice* (Stanley Paul, 1945)

Smith, G. B., *Life of Queen Victoria* (Routledge, 1901)

Strachey, Lytton, *Queen Victoria* (Chatto & Windus, 1921)

Tuchman, Barbara, *The Proud Tower* (Macmillan, 1980)

Victoria, Queen, *The Letters of Queen Victoria: A Selection from Her Correspondence and Journal, 1896–1901*, ed. George Earle Buckle (Murray, 1932)

# Index

Throughout this index, with the exception of the three main entries under her name, Victoria has been abbreviated to V.